Student Companion to

Ernest
HEMINGWAY

Recent Titles in
Student Companions to Classic Writers

Student Companion to

Ernest
HEMINGWAY

Lisa Tyler

Student Companions to Classic Writers

Greenwood Press
Westport, Connecticut • London

Library of Congress Cataloging-in-Publication Data

Tyler, Lisa, 1964–
    Student companion to Ernest Hemingway / Lisa Tyler.
      p. cm.—(Student companions to classic writers, ISSN 1522–7979)
    Includes bibliographical references (p.) and index.
    ISBN 0–313–31056–4 (alk. paper)
    1. Hemingway, Ernest, 1899–1961—Criticism and interpretation—Handbooks,
manuals, etc. 2. Hemingway, Ernest, 1899–1961—Examinations—Study guides.
I. Title. II. Series.
PS3515.E37Z893   2001
813'.52—dc21   2001023326

British Library Cataloguing in Publication Data is available.

Library of Congress Catalog Card Number: 2001023326
ISBN: 0–313–31056–4
ISSN: 1522–7979

First published in 2001

Greenwood Press, 88 Post Road West, Westport, CT 06881
An imprint of Greenwood Publishing Group, Inc.
www.greenwood.com

Printed in the United States of America

The paper used in this book complies with the
Permanent Paper Standard issued by the National
Information Standards Organization (Z39.48–1984).

10 9 8 7 6 5 4 3 2

For my husband, James Tyler,
who convinced me I could write this book,
and for my daughter, Rose,
who was my favorite distraction

Contents

Series Foreword

This series has been designed to meet the needs of students and general readers for accessible literary criticism on the American and world writers most frequently studied and read in the secondary school, community college, and four-year college classrooms. Unlike other works of literary criticism that are written for the specialist and graduate student, or that feature a variety of reprinted scholarly essays on sometimes obscure aspects of the writer's work, the Student Companions to Classic Writers series is carefully crafted to examine each writer's major works fully and in a systematic way, at the level of the non-specialist and general reader. The objective is to enable the reader to gain a deeper understanding of the work and to apply critical thinking skills to the act of reading. The proven format for the volumes in this series was developed by an advisory board of teachers and librarians for a successful series published by Greenwood Press, Critical Companions to Popular Contemporary Writers. Responding to their request for easy-to-use and yet challenging literary criticism for students and adult library patrons, Greenwood Press developed a systematic format that is not intimidating but helps the reader to develop the ability to analyze literature.

How does this work? Each volume in the Student Companions to Classic Writers series is written by a subject specialist, an academic who understands students' needs for basic and yet challenging examination of the writer's canon. Each volume begins with a biographical chapter, drawn from published sources, biographies, and autobiographies, that relates the writer's life to his or her work. The next chapter examines the writer's literary heritage, tracing the literary influences of other writers on that writer and explaining and discussing the literary genres into which the writer's work falls. Each of the following chapters examines one or more major works by the writer, featuring those works most frequently read and studied by high school and college students. Depending on the writer's canon, generally between four and eight major works are examined, each in individual chapters. The discussion of each work is organized into separate sections on plot development, character development, and major themes. Literary devices and style, narrative point of view, and historical setting are also discussed in turn if pertinent to the work. Each chapter concludes with an alternate critical perspective from which to read the works, such as a psychological or feminist criticism. The critical theory is defined briefly in easy, comprehensible language for the student. Looking at the literature from the point of view of a particular critical approach will help the reader to understand and apply critical theory to the act of reading and analyzing literature.

Of particular value in each volume is the bibliography, which includes a complete bibliography of the writer's works, a selected bibliography of biographical and critical works suitable for students, and lists of reviews of each work examined in the companion, all of which will be helpful to readers, teachers, and librarians who would like to consult additional sources.

As a source of literary criticism for the student or for the general reader, this series will help the reader to gain understanding of the writer's work and skill in critical reading.

Acknowledgments

Ernest Lockridge of Ohio State University deserves mention first for sparking my critical interest in Hemingway's writings. I am grateful to Susan Beegel, the esteemed editor of the *Hemingway Review*, for referring Greenwood Press to me and for suggesting on the Hemingway list serve the value of an ecofeminist approach to *The Old Man and the Sea*. I owe thanks to Barbara Rader, who recruited me for this project; Lynn Malloy, for her efforts to improve this book; and Nicole Cournoyer, for her attention to detail: She has saved me from many of my own mistakes. Laura Wright and Jim Tyler generously helped me proofread the galleys. Finally, I am grateful to Marian Sautter Beery for her love, Jim Tyler for his encouragement, and Rose Tyler for her good cheer during the writing of this book.

1

The Life of Ernest Hemingway

Ernest Hemingway is one of the most famous American authors of the twentieth century. His name is internationally recognized, even by many people who have never read any of his books. His familiar image has been used to sell cars, clothes, and furniture. He is famous in part for how he lived—spending time in exotic and glamorous settings (including Paris, Pamplona, Key West, Havana, Sun Valley), witnessing frontline combat in several wars, traveling to East Africa to hunt dangerous game, fishing in the Gulf Stream, and of course running with the bulls in the fiesta of San Fermin in Pamplona, Spain. Wealthy and glamorous, he befriended film stars like Marlene Dietrich, Ava Gardner, Gary Cooper, and Ingrid Bergman. As his youngest son, Gregory, wrote in his memoir, *Papa,*

He had always had everything. Handsome as a movie star in his youth, with an attraction for women you wouldn't believe unless you saw it; extremely sensitive, blessed with a constitution, energy, and resiliency that allowed him to abuse his body and recover from trauma, both physical and emotional, that destroyed lesser men; supremely imaginative and yet possessed of tremendous common sense, perhaps the rarest combination of qualities; and luck, almost always good, the genetic good luck to have all of the above, and the luck to survive a major war wound with the knowledge of what the edge of nothingness is like. (4–5)

As his son's tribute suggests, Hemingway is also famous for the pain he experienced—including his World War I wounding, alcoholism, three divorces, mental illness, self-destructiveness, and eventual suicide. But he is best known for the quality of his writing.

CHILDHOOD

Ernest Hemingway was born July 21, 1899, in Oak Park, Illinois, now a suburb of Chicago. The Oak Park of Hemingway's childhood was affluent, Protestant, and deeply Republican, as well as sometimes prudish, narrow-minded, racist, and anti-Semitic. His parents were Clarence Hemingway, an obstetrician, and Grace Hall Hemingway, who had trained as an opera singer before choosing to marry and start a family. Ernest was the second of six children and the first son. He had an older sister, Marcelline, and three younger sisters—Ursula, Madelaine, and Carol—as well as a younger brother, Leicester. His mother gave music lessons and at times earned more than her husband; the family hired servants to handle much of the housework.

The family spent its summers at Bear Lake (later Walloon Lake) in the upper peninsula of Michigan, which at that time was rural, heavily forested, and still populated by the remnants of the Ojibway Indian tribe. The family stayed in a cottage called Windemere, and eventually Grace had a separate cottage built across the lake for her to retreat to when she wanted to get away from her family.

Hemingway's mother encouraged his creativity and knowledge of the arts, although he later came to prefer literature and the visual arts to the performing arts that she enjoyed. His father taught him hunting, fishing, and camping skills and fostered what became a lifelong love of nature and the outdoors. Ernest may also have inherited from his father a genetic predisposition to manic depression, for his father often had dark moods and spent occasional vacations away from his family in an effort to restore his mental health.

Hemingway's mother twinned him with his older sister Marcelline, dressing both children in dresses until Ernest went to kindergarten (Lynn 42). At the time, it was common for young boys to wear dresses until they reached the age of two and a half, but few parents kept boys in dresses until age four or five (Lynn 39). In Michigan, both children wore overalls and other boyish clothes but sported long, girlish hairstyles (Lynn 38). Ernest and Marcelline had similar haircuts as well, and in her family scrapbooks Grace described them as twins, even though they were 18 months apart in age. Grace even had Marcelline repeat kindergarten so that she and Ernest could begin first grade together.

There is a great deal of speculation about what effect this forced "twinning" had on Ernest's sense of himself and his sexuality. Scholar Carl Eby suggests that Ernest's childhood experiences left him confused and anxious about his gender identity and that he later drew on fetishes—certain physical objects like hair, fur, silk, ivory, suntanned skin, and cats—to relieve that anxiety in both his private life and his work. Certainly Ernest's experiences of twinning seem to have influenced the posthumously published novel *The Garden of Eden*, in which characters talk about transforming from one gender to another.

Hemingway was not particularly athletic or popular with girls in high school. He rarely dated in high school, and his mother insisted he take his sister Marcelline to the junior prom. He wrote for the school newspaper, the *Trapeze*, and became its editor in his senior year. He also began writing short stories for *Tabula*, his high school's literary magazine. Those early short stories seem to have been influenced by the stories of Rudyard Kipling, O. Henry, and Jack London (Meyers 19–20). Some of that fiction still exists, including "The Judgement of Manitou," "A Matter of Colour," and "Sepi Jingan."

His high school courses were fairly demanding by today's standards. A list of the works he was assigned to read in high school appears in the book *Hemingway's Reading* by Michael Reynolds (39–43). Ernest's parents wanted him to go to college; his father, in particular, had hoped that his son would follow in his footsteps by attending Oberlin College in Ohio and then going to medical school to become a doctor. At one time Hemingway apparently intended to major in journalism at the University of Illinois, but he eventually decided to take a job his Uncle Tyler Hemingway helped him land at the Kansas City *Star* in the fall of 1917.

In the winter of 1917, the Red Cross asked for American volunteers to drive ambulances on the Italian front. Unable to join the American armed forces because of a bad eye, Ernest Hemingway volunteered to serve with the Red Cross. He later lied about his service, claiming to have fought for the Italian army. He spent only about three weeks as a Red Cross ambulance driver in Italy before he was wounded in the leg by shrapnel on July 8, 1918, while passing out chocolate and cigarettes to Italian troops along the Piave River. He sustained multiple shrapnel wounds in his right leg and at one time feared he would have to have the leg amputated.

Recuperating from his wounds in a hospital in Milan, Italy, Hemingway fell in love with Agnes von Kurowsky, a well-educated American nurse who was eight years older than the young man who fell in love with her. Hemingway later drew on and embellished this romance in *A Farewell to Arms*. Jim Gamble, a captain who befriended Hemingway during their service with the Red Cross, offered to pay for Hemingway to travel with him for a year. Agnes, uncomfortable with this idea, urged Hemingway to go home and get a job, telling him they could not get married until he could earn his living. He returned home, and soon afterward, Agnes wrote him to announce her engagement to an Italian. The forgettable 1997 film *In Love and War*, starring Sandra Bullock and Chris O'Donnell, was loosely based on this relationship as it was depicted in the book *Hemingway in Love and War: The Lost Diary of Agnes von Kurowsky*, which, in addition to Agnes's diary and her and Ernest's letters to each other, also contained essays written by fellow Red Cross veteran Henry Villard and Hemingway scholar James Nagel.

In November 1919, not long after his return from the war, Hemingway began working with Bill Smith on a series of sketches that they called "Cross Roads." Hemingway briefly took a job as a paid companion to Ralph Connable, a young man whose father headed the Woolworth chain of stores in Canada, but soon Ernest began writing features for the *Toronto Star*.

The summer of 1920 in Michigan, when Hemingway turned 21 years old, he finally compelled his mother to throw him out of the nest. Ernest unwisely stayed out most of the night with some friends, including two girls who were only 13; the understandably anxious mother of one of the girls confronted Grace Hemingway, and when Ernest arrived at home, a furious Grace kicked him out of the house. He went to Chicago and roomed with Bill Horne, a friend from the Red Cross, while he looked for a job.

Hemingway met Elizabeth Hadley Richardson while she was visiting Chicago that fall of 1920. Her father had committed suicide when she was only 14, and her mother had just died, leaving Hadley with a sizable trust fund. Eight years older than Hemingway, Hadley had attended Bryn Mawr for a year before leaving college. When she returned to her home in St. Louis, she and Hemingway began a correspondence.

Hemingway took an editorial position on the *Co-Operative Commonwealth*, a weekly magazine published by the Co-Operative Society of America, a group that encouraged farmers to unite to demand better prices for what they sold. He continued to write short stories in his spare time, although they were consistently rejected by the magazines to which he submitted them. In January of 1921 the aspiring writer met Sherwood Anderson, the author of *Winesburg, Ohio* and a writer Hemingway respected. Anderson mentored the young Hemingway, suggesting books for him to read, giving him feedback on his writing, advising him on how to become a professional author, and urging him to go to Paris.

Hemingway married Hadley in a modest ceremony September 3, 1921, at Horton Bay, Michigan, and honeymooned in his family's cottage, Windemere. During his honeymoon, the president of the Co-Operative Society of America went bankrupt, leaving thousands of people with worthless certificates purchased from the company, and several of the company officers were indicted for fraud. Hemingway continued to write for the magazine until it finally went under in October.

At Anderson's urging, the couple decided to go to Paris. To smooth their way, Anderson wrote letters of introduction to several of his American friends in Paris, including lesbian modernist Gertrude Stein and the poet and editor Ezra Pound. Before they left, Hemingway secured an agreement from the *Toronto Star* to publish human interest features he sent them from Paris. The Hemingways arrived in Paris in December 1921.

THE 1920s: PARIS

In Paris, the Hemingways associated with other American expatriate writers, including Pound; Stein and her partner, Alice B. Toklas; and F. Scott Fitzgerald and his wife, Zelda. Hemingway had read Fitzgerald's early novel *This Side of Paradise* while he was still in Chicago. Fitzgerald read some of Hemingway's earliest work, offered editing advice, and later encouraged his own editor, Maxwell Perkins of Scribner's, to consider publishing Hemingway's work. Hemingway repaid him by mocking him briefly in "The Snows of Kilimanjaro" and at greater length in *A Moveable Feast*, his memoir about Paris during the 1920s.

Hemingway borrowed books from Sylvia Beach, whose legendary Paris bookstore and lending library, Shakespeare & Co., is where he also met and befriended James Joyce, the expatriate Irish author of *The Dubliners* and *Ulysses*. Hemingway later helped edit *transatlantic review*, a literary magazine, for Ford Madox Ford, the British author of the brilliant modernist novel *The Good Soldier*. During the 1920s Hemingway traveled throughout Europe, including Italy, Switzerland, and Turkey, sometimes for fun and sometimes in his role as a reporter for both the *Toronto Star* and (under the byline John Hadley) Hearst's International News Service, an American wire service. A trip to Constantinople gave him the material on which he later drew in writing "On the Quai at Smyrna."

Throughout their marriage, Hadley was unusually supportive of her husband's writing career, even though his earnings were so modest that they lived primarily on the income from her trust fund. She consistently and willingly subordinated her needs to his and participated with enthusiasm in the lifestyle he chose.

In December 1922, Hemingway wrote Hadley asking her to join him in Lausanne, Switzerland, where he was covering an international conference for the *Toronto Star*, and he requested that she bring his manuscripts. When she arrived, she was crying too hard to talk to him, and it took some coaxing before she admitted what had happened. She had packed all the manuscripts in a suitcase. While the porter put them in her compartment, she left to buy bottled water and something to read. When she entered the compartment, the manuscripts were gone. Hemingway could not believe she had lost all of his stories, including the carbon copies, and immediately took the night train to Paris to check. Of all the work he had completed, only "My Old Man" and "Up in Michigan," which he had submitted to *Cosmopolitan*, remained. He was devastated by the loss, which permanently damaged his relationship with Hadley, and recalled it bitterly in *A Moveable Feast*.

Hemingway gradually began to publish his poetry in small but important European literary magazines like *The Double Dealer*, *Poetry*, and *Querschnitt* during the 1920s. Six of his vignettes—brief, intense sketches he called "unwritten stories"—were published under the title "In Our Time" in the Spring 1923 issue of the *Little Review* (Reynolds, *Paris* 369). That year Robert McAlmon also published Hemingway's first book, *Three Stories and Ten Poems*. The three stories were "Up in Michigan," "Out of Season," and "My Old Man." The book, which was dedicated to Hadley, sold only a handful of copies, although Hemingway told others it had sold out.

As a young man in his early twenties, Hemingway was good-looking, energetic, and, according to those who knew him, great fun. "He was then the kind of man to whom men, women, children and dogs were attracted," his first wife, Hadley, later recalled. "It was something" (Milford 117). Yet he had rarely dated in high school, was inexperienced with the opposite sex, and was very likely a virgin until his marriage.

A terrific listener, Hemingway paid close attention to what people told him and frequently asked probing questions in an effort to learn more. He combined great literary ambitions with a secret, intense fear that he could not live up to his dreams. It has become a truism that he covered up his intense sensitivity with a tough, macho exterior. "He was so complicated; so many sides to him you could hardly make a sketch of him in a geometry book," his wife Hadley told an interviewer years later (qtd. in Brian 52).

Hadley became pregnant in January of 1923, and that summer the Hemingways traveled to Spain, where they attended the fiesta of San Fermin, a week-long festival of music, dancing, and wine, in addition to the running of the bulls and the *corrida*, or bullfighting. Hemingway was fascinated and called the bullfight not a sport but a tragedy in which the bull was doomed to die. He wrote five vignettes about the *corrida* and later drew on these experiences more extensively in *The Sun Also Rises* and *Death in the Afternoon*.

Hemingway and Hadley returned to Toronto in August 1923. While Hemingway was in Europe, his boss had been promoted. Ernest quickly came to resent his new supervisor, who, he complained, made him work long hours and sent him to report stories Ernest regarded as trivial. Hadley gave birth to Hemingway's first child, a seven-pound son named John Hadley Nicanor Hemingway, on October 10, 1923 (Baker, *Life* 117). His parents nicknamed him Bumby and later Jack. Ernest was out of town covering a story when Hadley went into labor, so he rushed back to visit her in the hospital. When his boss complained that Hemingway should have filed his story before going to the hospital, Hemingway became furious and decided to quit the paper. He immediately joined the staff of the *Toronto Star Weekly* and in January 1924 returned to Paris. Gertrude Stein and her partner, Alice B. Toklas, were godmothers to the Hemingways' baby.

Once back in Paris, Hemingway began to write seriously and completed eight stories in three months (Reynolds, *Paris* 167). His work was gradually gaining attention. His short story "My Old Man" was included in the anthology *The Best Short Stories of 1923*, edited by Edward J. O'Brien; unfortunately the book was dedicated "To Ernest Hemenway" (Hanneman 91). In Paris in the spring of 1924, Bill Bird published *in our time*, a 30-page collection of 18 of Hemingway's vignettes, as one book in a series called *The Inquest*. The American poet Ezra Pound had selected the manuscripts to be included in the series (Hanneman 6–7).

Boni & Liveright published the short story collection *In Our Time* in October 1925. Hemingway then sent them his next manuscript, as his contract legally obligated him to do. It was *Torrents of Spring*, a parody of the novel *Dark Laughter* by Sherwood Anderson. Because Boni & Liveright was also Sherwood Anderson's publisher, the company refused to publish the second book, freeing Hemingway to send both *Torrents of Spring* and his next book to F. Scott Fitzgerald's publisher, Charles Scribner's Sons. "The Killers," his first short story published in an American magazine, appeared in *Scribner's Magazine* in March 1927. Scribner's remained Hemingway's publisher for the rest of his life and continues to publish his work to this day.

In Paris, Hemingway and Hadley became friends with Pauline Pfeiffer, a 30-year-old fashion reporter for Paris *Vogue*. She and her younger sister, Jinny (short for Virginia), were living in Paris on their trust funds. Pauline first befriended Hadley and spent most of her time with the Hemingways. But she soon began an affair with Ernest, and when Hadley confronted Ernest about it, he insisted he couldn't help himself and then blamed Hadley for breaking up their marriage by bringing it up. Hadley, deeply hurt but believing the affair would never last, moved to a new apartment and agreed to give Ernest a divorce if he would not see Pauline for 100 days. A little over a month later, in October 1926, Hadley wrote to Ernest that she was convinced the marriage was over and told him she would grant him the divorce he wanted. In the same month, October 1926, *The Sun Also Rises* was published. Its dedication reads, "This book is for Hadley and for John Hadley Nicanor," and Hemingway signed all of the profits from the book over to his first wife.

To marry Pauline, who was Catholic, Hemingway testified that he was baptized at the front during the war. His attitude toward religion has long been a highly controversial subject. Although he has sometimes been dismissed as purely a "nominal" Catholic who converted only to make his marriage to Pauline possible, Hemingway prayed, attended Mass, donated to the church, and otherwise indicated that his faith was important to him (Stoneback, "In the Nominal"). He once told his friend A.E. Hotchner that he wished he were a better Catholic (142). Moreover, he chose several of his titles from religious sources, including popular prayers and the Bible. Religion plays a significant (if ambiguous) role in many of his stories and novels, including most notably "Today Is Friday," "Now I Lay Me," "God Rest You Merry, Gentlemen," "A Clean, Well-Lighted Place," "The Gambler, the Nun, and the Radio," *For Whom the Bell Tolls*, and *The Old Man and the Sea*.

Ernest and Pauline were married twice, both in a civil ceremony and in the Catholic Church. Pauline became pregnant quickly, and Hemingway soon afterward published a second collection of short stories, *Men without Women*. The newlyweds traveled extensively, going to the south of France for their honeymoon; several cities in Spain; Berlin for a brief pleasure trip; Gstaad, Switzerland, to meet Pauline's sister Jinny; Key West, Florida; Piggott, Arkansas, to visit the Pfeiffer family, and finally Kansas City for Pauline's delivery. Ernest's second son, Patrick, was born by caesarean section on June 28, 1928. Hemingway began work on *A Farewell to Arms* in Paris; continued writing the novel in Key West, Piggott, and Kansas City; and traveled with a friend to Wyoming, where he finished the first draft in August 1928.

That fall, he also traveled to Oak Park to visit his family. Less than two months later, when Ernest was taking his and Hadley's son, Bumby, by train from New York to Key West, he was handed a telegram informing him of his father's death. He left his son in the conductor's care to finish the trip and returned to Oak Park, where he learned that his always moody and sometimes depressive father, distraught over financial problems and diabetes, had shot himself. Hemingway was deeply wounded by the manner of his father's death, and suicide later became a more prominent theme in his writings. Ernest later (and probably unfairly) blamed his father's suicide on his mother and criticized her for what he saw as her cruelty, egotism, and hypocrisy for the rest of his life. There is little evidence to support his harsh judgments about her, and it is probable that in condemning her he was initiating a pattern he was later to repeat (with Gertrude Stein, Sherwood Anderson, and F. Scott Fitzgerald, for example) of maligning people whom he owed a debt of gratitude.

THE 1930S: FAME

In 1929, Hemingway used part of his profits from *A Farewell to Arms*, as well as money borrowed from Pauline's wealthy uncle, Gus Pfeiffer, to establish a trust fund that would provide income for his mother for the rest of her life. In March 1930 he began planning his next book, a study of bullfighting, which eventually became *Death in the Afternoon*.

About many things—the rearing, fighting, and demise of bulls, a history of bullfighters, an explanation of their art, a guidebook to Spain, a discussion of writers and their craft, of critics and their shortcomings, a book full of landscapes with and without figures, a philosophy of life in the lap of death, a Spanish food and wine digest—it is a discursive book of huge risks which no publisher would have encouraged had the author not been Ernest Hemingway. (Reynolds, *1930s* 41)

In April 1931, the Hemingways bought a house in Key West, Florida. On November 12, 1931, their son Gregory Hemingway was born after a difficult labor and ultimately another caesarean section, and Pauline was told that further pregnancies would endanger her life. Because she was Catholic, she was reluctant to use birth control, and Hemingway later blamed the end of his marriage with Pauline on the effects that dilemma had on their sex life.

In 1933 Hemingway began work on a short story, set in Havana, about Harry Morgan, a fishing guide who also smuggles rum into Prohibition-era America. The story, along with two others about Harry Morgan, eventually evolved into the novel *To Have and Have Not,* "a brutal, depression-era story about money" (Reynolds, *1930s* 146). Published in 1937, the book sold 38,000 copies in its first five months and prompted *Time* to feature Hemingway on its cover (Reynolds, *1930s* 280–81).

For two and a half years, Hemingway contributed essays to the newly established and extremely successful *Esquire* magazine. (Many of those essays were later reprinted in *By-Line: Ernest Hemingway*, edited by William White.) The Hemingways went to Africa on a safari funded by Pauline's Uncle Gus in late 1933 and early 1934. The trip inspired the nonfiction work *Green Hills of Africa* and two of Hemingway's best short stories, "Snows of Kilimanjaro" and "The Short Happy Life of Francis Macomber." In 1934, Hemingway used the proceeds from his *Esquire* "letters" to order a fishing boat, which he named the *Pilar.*

In 1936, the North Atlantic News Alliance (NANA), which supplied articles to 60 major newspapers, offered to send Hemingway to Spain to report on the civil war, and Hemingway readily accepted. Joris Ivens, a Dutch communist filmmaker, asked Hemingway to help him in making a documentary about the war, and the two endangered their lives more than once filming combat scenes. Hemingway wrote the narration for the film, which, unlike the newsreels, was sympathetic to the Republican cause. Titled *The Spanish Earth*, the film was originally to be narrated by actor Orson Welles, but Hemingway narrated the final version.

In Spain, Hemingway began a love affair with Martha Gellhorn, a 28-year-old professional journalist who had written for *The New Republic* and Paris *Vogue*, as well as having published a novel and a collection of short stories. Her second short story collection, *The Heart of Another*, was published in October 1941 by Scribner's. She was friends with Eleanor Roosevelt and was occasionally mentioned in the First Lady's newspaper column. A fearless war correspondent, Gellhorn was in Prague in 1938 when Hitler took over Czechoslovakia, and in December 1939 she covered the Russian bombing of Finland for *Collier's* magazine. She even went ashore on D-Day to report on the Allied invasion of France. Hemingway, who watched the invasion from a ship offshore, bitterly resented her success.

In October 1937 he began writing a play later titled *The Fifth Column*, which he published in the 1938 volume *The Fifth Column and the First Forty-Nine Short Stories*. The character of Dorothy Bridges in the play was an unkind caricature of Martha Gellhorn. Hemingway began writing *For Whom the Bell Tolls* in February 1939 in Havana.

THE 1940s: WAR

Although still technically married to his second wife, Pauline, Hemingway lived with Martha Gellhorn for 18 months in Finca Vigía, a house that they rented together in Cuba. The couple also traveled together to Sun Valley, a newly established ski resort near Ketchum, Idaho. Being Catholic, Pauline was reluctant to agree to a divorce but eventually gave in. Despite misgivings and a last-minute sense of entrapment, Gellhorn married Hemingway in November of 1940 in a ceremony performed in Cheyenne, Wyoming, by a justice of the peace (Reynolds, *Final* 35). The following January the two writers left for Asia to cover the war between China and Japan, Martha for *Collier's* magazine and Ernest for a newspaper called *PM*. Gellhorn later wrote about the experience in her book *Travels with Myself and Another*. By the end of the year, both writers were working on new projects: Gellhorn on a novel, later titled *Liana*, and Hemingway on short stories and an introduction to *Men at War*, a collection of fiction and nonfiction he edited.

Hemingway used his fishing boat, *Pilar*, to scout for German submarines in the Gulf of Mexico and gathered intelligence on Cubans who had supported the fascist government in Spain and might be willing to aid the Nazis. He nicknamed the covert operation the "Crook Factory." Although there is some evidence that the U.S. government took Hemingway's contributions seriously, Gellhorn found his activities ridiculous and told him so.

The relationship between Hemingway and Gellhorn deteriorated rapidly. Gellhorn left for England in the fall of 1943 to cover the war for *Collier's*. Feeling abandoned, Hemingway sent her a telegram asking her whether she wanted to be a war correspondent or his wife (Reynolds, *Final* 90). Hemingway offered himself to *Collier's* as its front-line correspondent; when the magazine hired him, Gellhorn blamed him for taking away her job; however, Hemingway biographer Michael Reynolds points out that at the time, Gellhorn, as a woman, would not have been able to cover the front lines anyway. Women correspondents were limited to hospital areas and could face court-martial if they tried to defy the rule (Reynolds, *Final* 92).

In London, Hemingway met journalist Mary Welsh, who wrote for both *Time* and *Life*. Although both of them were married at the time, he told her soon after they met that he wanted to marry her. They quickly became lovers.

During the summer of 1944, Hemingway covered the Normandy invasion, flew with British Royal Air Force pilots, and allegedly fought with the French Resistance. He took extraordinary risks and seemed indifferent to the possibility of injury or death. He was brought before a military hearing on charges that he had participated in the fighting as an armed combatant, but thanks to what he later said were lies in his own sworn testimony, it was determined that there was no reason to court-martial him.

Hemingway returned to Cuba in 1945 and invited Mary Welsh to spend the summer there with him. Welsh both enjoyed her stay at the Finca Vigía and resented Hemingway's dominance. Despite her mixed feelings, she gave up her career completely and married him the next year in a Cuban civil ceremony on March 13, 1946. Hoping to give Hemingway the daughter he had always wanted, Mary became pregnant, but in August she nearly bled to death when the ectopic pregnancy ruptured a fallopian tube, causing massive internal bleeding. Only Hemingway's quick thinking enabled the physician to stop the bleeding and save her life.

Hemingway soon began working on a new novel, "The Sea." Portions of the 1600-page manuscript eventually evolved into *Islands in the Stream* and *The Old Man and the Sea* (Reynolds, *Final* 137). In 1948, Hemingway visited Venice for the first time, and there he met and fell in love with 18-year-old Adriana Ivancich. She called him "Papa," as many of his friends came to call him, and he called her "Daughter"—an endearment he eventually extended to many of the women he knew. Adriana, who apparently admired the writer but did not return his feelings, was the inspiration for the character of Renata in Hemingway's novel *Across the River and Into the Trees*.

THE 1950S: DETERIORATION

Across the River and Into the Trees, with a cover illustration by Adriana Ivancich, was first published in several parts in *Cosmopolitan* magazine from

February to June of 1950. The novel spent 21 weeks on the bestseller list of the *New York Times Book Review*, seven of them in first place (Hanneman 61–62). The novel's protagonist, Colonel Richard Cantwell, is a battered 51-year-old veteran of two world wars. Dying of heart disease, he falls in love with Renata, a beautiful, 18-year-old Italian aristocrat, and spends his last days with her in Venice, obsessively recalling the loss of half of his regiment. The critics panned *Across the River and Into the Trees*, and even Hemingway's wife Mary, to whom the novel was dedicated, called it "his poorest book" (103).

In 1953 Ernest and Mary went on the safari he later described in his posthumously published fictionalized memoir, *True at First Light*. The safari ended badly, with two separate plane crashes. The second was particularly hard on Hemingway, who had to butt the door open with his head in order to escape from the burning aircraft. The experience left him with injuries to his kidneys, liver, shoulder, spinal cord, and intestines; impaired vision and hearing; and a concussion, his fourth in ten years. Newspapers all over the world had prematurely reported Hemingway dead, and he spent the days after the crash gleefully reading his own obituaries.

During the 1950s, Hemingway's health began to decline. He suffered from dangerously high blood pressure and struggled to keep his weight under control. His behavior became increasingly erratic and outrageous. He adopted the unusual habit of speaking a pidgin English in which he dropped all articles (words like "a," "an," and "the") and sounded like a bad imitation of a stereotypical Hollywood Indian. Lillian Ross recorded his newly adopted conversational style in an embarrassing profile published in the *New Yorker*, "a piece of work which was unintentionally devastating because it showed him *exactly* as he was at that time," his youngest son Gregory observed many years later (94).

Later in life, Hemingway could be boastful, patronizing, and pugnacious. He exaggerated and sometimes even lied outright about his war experiences. Although Hemingway made friends quickly throughout most of his life, the friendships often ended abruptly and acrimoniously. Yet he remained on good terms with his first wife and corresponded with her regularly until he died. According to his fourth wife, Mary, he became verbally abusive, calling her names and behaving childishly. She wrote Charles Scribner in 1950 that Hemingway's personality seemed to be disintegrating (Reynolds, *Final* 231). "He could be a handful, for all his wives and for everyone," Hemingway's son Jack once admitted (Kert 199)—yet Jack Hemingway himself once complained that Carlos Baker's biography did not do his father justice. " 'He may have been an SOB to some people,' Jack says, 'but he was not an SOB to me' " (Oliver, *A to Z* 141).

In 1954 Hemingway was awarded the Nobel Prize for Literature, an honor he found enormously gratifying. Because of his poor health, however, he did not travel to Sweden to attend the ceremony but instead wrote a short piece to be read at the event.

In 1958, because of increasing political tensions in Cuba, Ernest and Mary spent the winter in Ketchum, Idaho. Hemingway spent the summer of 1959 in Spain, attending bullfights so that he could update *Death in the Afternoon*—a goal he never achieved. Instead, he agreed to write an essay on bullfighting for *Life* magazine, and the article's enormous length meant that it was published in three parts in *Life* during 1960. A fuller version was posthumously published as the book *Dangerous Summer* in 1985.

THE 1960s: THE HEMINGWAY LEGACY

In November of 1960, Hemingway was hospitalized at the Mayo Clinic in Rochester, Minnesota, for psychological problems that included nightmares, insomnia, paranoia (he was convinced the FBI was after him), and depression. His hospitalization was kept secret for much of his nearly eight-week stay because of the stigma then attached to mental illness.

He was diagnosed with what was then called manic-depressive illness but is now known as bipolar mood disorder. People with this illness have very extreme mood swings, from great energy, confidence, and euphoria during the manic phase of the illness to apathy, fear, melancholy, and often suicidal tendencies during the depressive phase. Evidence now suggests that the illness has a genetic component, and it seems likely that bipolar disorder runs in the Hemingway family, since in addition to his father, one of his sisters, Ursula, and his brother, Leicester, as well as his granddaughter also committed suicide. Two of his sons, Gregory and Patrick, and Gregory's daughter Lorian have all received electroshock treatments for mental illness (Jamison 230, Hays 60). Also, Hemingway's granddaughter, the actress Margaux Hemingway, committed suicide by taking an overdose of sleeping pills in 1996.

Hemingway was also given a series of ten electroshock treatments. Traditionally, electroshock has sometimes been effective in relieving depression. He seemed temporarily better after his hospital stay and tried to work on the book that later became *A Moveable Feast*. However, one side effect of electroshock treatment is memory loss, and some Hemingway scholars today speculate that losing his memory, even temporarily, would have been devastating to a writer who drew so extensively on his memory to create his fiction. Hemingway's inability to write after his electroshock treatment may ultimately have deepened his depression. The April news reports of the disastrous Bay of Pigs invasion, in which the CIA unsuccessfully attempted to overthrow Fidel Castro's communist government in Cuba, almost certainly worsened Hemingway's condition: "[H]e was certain he would never see the Finca, his library, the *Pilar*, or his paintings. The manuscripts for what would become *Islands in the Stream* and *True at First Light*, the African novel, were, he thought, lost to him" (Reynolds, *Final* 354).

Hemingway was twice discovered alone with a shotgun, and on the way to the hospital, where he was readmitted in April 1961 because of his suicidal behavior, he tried to walk into the whirling propeller of a plane on the airport runway. To his wife's dismay, he was nevertheless released again at the end of June. On July 2, 1961, he shot himself with a double-barreled shotgun in the foyer of his home in Ketchum, Idaho. Initial news reports indicated that his death was an accident, perhaps in part to spare the feelings of his wife and children.

After his death, Mary was able to retrieve some of his manuscripts from the Finca Vigía, although the house itself was confiscated by the Cuban government, along with Hemingway's fishing boat. Most of Hemingway's original manuscripts and letters were later placed in the care of the John Fitzgerald Kennedy Presidential Library and Museum in Boston, where they remain today. Princeton, the Harry Ransom Center at the University of Texas at Austin, the University of Virginia, and the Museo Hemingway at the Finca Vigía, Hemingway's former home in Cuba, also have smaller but important collections of Hemingway-related materials. Edited versions of several of the unpublished manuscripts given to the Kennedy Library have been published posthumously, including *A Moveable Feast, Islands in the Stream, The Garden of Eden*, and *True at First Light*. All four became bestsellers.

Mary Welsh Hemingway agreed to cooperate with Carlos Baker, who had corresponded with Ernest during his lifetime, on a biography of Hemingway. She granted him access to private letters, original manuscripts, and other documents and asked Hemingway's friends to cooperate with Baker's requests for interviews and information. Mary herself later wrote a book about their lives together, *How It Was*, published in 1976. Later Hemingway biographers include Kenneth S. Lynn, Jeffrey Meyers, James Mellow, and most recently Michael Reynolds, whose five-volume biography has won critical acclaim. In 1980 the International Hemingway Society was founded to foster the study and appreciation of Hemingway's writings. It sponsors a conference on Hemingway's writings every two years and every fall and spring publishes *The Hemingway Review*, a scholarly journal.

Ernest Hemingway's major works have never gone out of print. As he once told the writer Malcolm Cowley about writing well, "It's enough for you to do it once for a few men to remember you. But if you do it year after year, then many people remember you and they tell it to their children, and their children and grandchildren remember and, if it concerns books, they can read them. And if it's good enough, it will last as long as there are human beings" (Cowley, "Portrait" 101).

Literary Heritage

HEMINGWAY'S JOURNALISM

Ernest Hemingway's work as a journalist at the *Kansas City Star* from October 1917 to April 1918 helped forge his distinctive writing style, particularly his reliance on short, declarative sentences. Michael Reynolds suggests that Hemingway's experience as a journalist had both positive and negative effects on his writing:

The newspaper game taught him the necessity for exact and believable facts, a lesson reinforced by [American poet Ezra] Pound. It taught him to avoid passive voice, long sentences, and polysyllabic words. But it also taught him the reporter's passive role of being witness to the event without participating in it. . . . In Hemingway's early fiction, the reporter's stance produced oddly passive characters to whom things happened but who seldom took action on their own. (*Paris*, 97)

Hemingway himself told an interviewer that on the *Star* he learned how to write simple declarative sentences, a skill that would be helpful to any young writer (Plimpton 116). The paper's style sheet gave reporters 110 straightforward rules to follow to improve their writing, and many of them are reflected in Hemingway's work. The first paragraph stated, "Use short sentences. Use short first paragraphs. Use vigorous English. Be positive, not negative" (qtd. in Fenton 31). Other guidelines included the recommendation that slang is effective only if it's new and a caution against using adjectives (Fenton 32–33).

"Those were the best rules I ever learned for the business of writing," Hemingway said in 1940. "I've never forgotten them. No man with any talent, who feels and writes truly about the thing he is trying to say, can fail to write well if he abides with them" ("Back to His First Field" 21).

Hemingway's writing owes its terseness in part to his extensive experience with "cablese." As a foreign correspondent in Europe for the Toronto *Star*, Hemingway often sent his stories in by telegrams, for which the newspaper was charged by the word. To keep costs down, he had to convey his messages by cable in as few words as possible, creating a dense, information-packed style jokingly termed "cablese."

LITERARY INFLUENCES ON HEMINGWAY'S STYLE

Besides influencing his writing style, Hemingway's early experience as a journalist exposed him to experiences that later became subject matter for his fiction. But Hemingway also benefited from the counsel of older, more experienced writers. Sherwood Anderson and Gertrude Stein became two of the earliest and most important literary influences on Hemingway's writing style. Anderson was a well-known and respected novelist when Hemingway met him in Chicago in the fall of 1920 and soon afterward followed his sage advice to go to Paris. Anderson was also the author of *Winesburg, Ohio*, a 1919 work which like Hemingway's *In Our Time* is a collection of interrelated short stories. Because of its setting in the horse-racing world, its colloquial language, and its focus on the father-son relationship, Hemingway's short story "My Old Man" is generally recognized as the work most closely resembling Anderson's work, specifically his short story "I Want to Know Why." In a backhanded acknowledgment of his debt to Anderson, Hemingway later wrote the brief novel *Torrents of Spring* to parody what he saw as Anderson's comically bad writing later in his career.

Gertrude Stein influenced Hemingway to experiment with automatic writing and free association to stimulate his writing, techniques similar to the freewriting taught today in composition classes. When he first brought her some poems and the beginning of a novel to read, she responded bluntly, as she reports in *The Autobiography of Alice B. Toklas*: "There is a great deal of description in this, she said, and not particularly good description. Begin over again and concentrate, she said" (Stein 262). After reading a draft of "Big Two-Hearted River," she told Hemingway, "remarks are not literature" (Stein 270) and wisely advised him to cut the introductory material (published after his death as "On Writing") from the beginning of the story. She also strongly encouraged him to give up his job as a reporter for the sake of his art.

His contemporary F. Scott Fitzgerald recommended Hemingway's work to the attention of Maxwell Perkins, Fitzgerald's own editor at Scribner's. He wrote a favorable review of *In Our Time* for *Bookman* and counseled Hemingway to cut the first two chapters of *The Sun Also Rises*. He also advised him to cut a joke from the short story "Fifty Grand." Hemingway complied, although he still regretted the decision years later. The two corresponded off and on for years. Although Hemingway was less than kind in his characterization of Fitzgerald in *A Moveable Feast*, he respected Fitzgerald's work, and *The Great Gatsby* made a lasting impression on him.

Other contemporaries who influenced Hemingway's writing included Ezra Pound, whom he once called "the man who taught me to distrust adjectives" (*AMF* 134); T.S. Eliot, from whom he claimed to have learned the art of allusion (*DIA* 139); D.H. Lawrence, who shared his mysticism about the spirituality of heterosexual love, and whom in *True at First Light* he specifically mentioned regretting never having met; and James Joyce, whom he did meet, and whose work he consistently admired and praised. Perhaps because Hemingway spent his twenties in Paris at a time when it was the vibrant center of the art world, he developed a passionate love for art, especially the works of Modernist artists such as Picasso, Miro, and Cezanne. He also claimed other kinds of artists as influences, including Bach, Mozart, and the sculptor Rodin.

Hemingway read extensively all his life. Although he was not college-educated, he was extraordinarily well read, particularly in nineteenth- and twentieth-century European literature. He read newspapers everywhere he went, packed boxes of books to take with him even on his African safaris, and frequently drew up lists of literature he recommended to would-be writers. Even in his later years, when his health was failing, he subscribed to more than a dozen magazines and read 200 to 300 books a year (Reynolds, *Final* 202–03).

In interviews and in his *Esquire* articles he mentioned many authors and other artists whose work had influenced his, including French authors Gustav Flaubert, Stendhal, Guy de Maupassant, and Marcel Proust; Russians Fyodor Dostoyevsky, Ivan Turgenev, Leo Tolstoy, and Anton Chekhov; the German writer Thomas Mann; British authors Andrew Marvell, Henry Fielding, W.H. Hudson, Emily Brontë, Rudyard Kipling, Henry James, and Shakespeare; and the medieval Italian poet Dante. Two other important influences on his work include the King James Version of the Bible and the *Oxford Book of English Verse*, two works that gave him some of his best titles.

"All modern literature comes from one book by Mark Twain called *Huckleberry Finn*," Hemingway writes in *Green Hills of Africa* (22). Hemingway himself may have owed his use of vernacular American English to Twain. From Stephen Crane's *The Red Badge of Courage*, he learned how to write about war in an honest, naturalistic way rather than in the overblown, sentimental Victorian style. He also learned from Crane's well-researched historical Civil War novel (published in 1895) that it was possible for an author to describe with convincing accuracy a battle he had never seen—a feat of which Hemingway later proved himself capable in *A Farewell to Arms*. Crane, who was not born until 1871, well after the American Civil War ended in 1865, nevertheless wrote so perceptively about war that Hemingway included the whole text of *The Red Badge of Courage* in *Men at War: The Best War Stories of All Time*, an anthology he edited.

Rudyard Kipling, now best known for his children's books, *Just So Stories* and *The Jungle Book*, was also an important influence on Hemingway's work. Although Kipling is sometimes dismissed by contemporary readers as an apologist for British imperialism in India, the Nobel Prize-winning poet and novelist was highly respected during Hemingway's youth, and the themes of his work—action and adventure, brutality and human responses to it, and the difficulty of becoming a man—turn up in Hemingway's work as well. Hemingway praised Kipling's work in his private letters, mentioned it favorably in *Green Hills of Africa* and his magazine articles, and included a Kipling story in the collection *Men at War*.

Hemingway also drew inspiration from his boyhood reading of Captain Frederick Marryat, a British naval officer and author of adventure stories and children's literature. Literary critic Mark Spilka suggests that what Hemingway found so compelling in Marryat's writings were depictions of boys rebelling against conventional parents, the representation of the man of action with masculine values, themes of vengeance and reprisal, and the emphasis on the "stiff upper lip" a gentleman was expected to maintain. From American novelist Jack London, author of the 1903 book *The Call of the Wild*, Hemingway took a naturalistic outlook, rugged subject matter, and a tough, macho attitude towards suffering.

Hemingway was also interested in Theodore Roosevelt's commitment to wilderness preservation and his advocacy of a vigorous masculinity typified by soldiering and hunting. Hemingway was drawn to Africa in part as a result of reading Roosevelt's account of his own safari. Hemingway himself acknowledged that he learned from popular short story writer O. Henry, author of the famous Christmas tale "Gift of the Magi," how to end his stories with what Hemingway called a "wow"—a tactic Hemingway later prided himself on having eventually *un*learned (*DIA* 182).

WRITING PROCESS

In his articles, nonfiction, and interviews, Hemingway described his development as an artist in unusual and extensive detail. In his early twenties, as he recalled decades later in *A Moveable Feast*, Hemingway often wrote at Paris cafés. In the 1950s Hemingway told George Plimpton of the *Paris Review* that he stood while he wrote. He typically wrote his first drafts in handwriting. He tried to write daily, generally beginning early in the morning and working until early afternoon, and kept track of his progress by counting the words written each day. He tried to stop each afternoon while he knew what would happen next in the story, so that when he returned to the work the next day, he would have an idea already in mind of what to write. In the meantime, he consciously tried to avoid thinking about his work because he believed that putting it out of his mind both enabled his subconscious to work and made him a better observer of what went on around him. Before he began drafting, he would reread and edit what he had written the previous day, marking up the pages with handwritten corrections. He made further changes when the drafts were typed and sometimes continued to tinker with the work even after it was typeset and he received the galleys to proofread before publication.

Once his work was published, Hemingway paid close attention to his publisher's marketing efforts, writing frequently to his editor, Maxwell Perkins, to criticize a book's cover art or to complain about the way his books were advertised. Although money was never his chief concern, he was nevertheless demoralized when his early work was repeatedly rejected, especially when the editors reviewing his short stories persisted in calling them anecdotes or sketches rather than stories. He later paid close attention to his books' sales figures and was always aware of what his work was worth in economic terms.

Hemingway avoided talking about his writing before it was published because he believed that talking would rob him of the need to write and ruin his enthusiasm for the project. In *A Moveable Feast* he recalls reading parts of *A Sun Also Rises* aloud to friends, and it's clear he came to despise himself for what he later perceived as a deplorable lack of professionalism. He writes with scorn of the pleasure he took in his audience's favorable reactions, and it is apparent that he believed he should have been writing for his own satisfaction as an artist rather than pandering to an audience whose tastes he later came to distrust.

In his first drafts, Hemingway tended to overwrite—that is, to give too much extraneous background information, to repeat himself, to pontificate. He often revised by cutting, sometimes extensively. On Fitzgerald's recommendation, Hemingway cut 15 pages (more than a chapter) from the beginning of *The Sun Also Rises* manuscript; when Gertrude Stein acerbically observed that "remarks are not literature," he cut nine pages from "Big Two-Hearted River" (Stein 270). He worked especially hard on the endings to his stories and once told an interviewer he had revised the last page of *A Farewell to Arms* 39 times before he was happy with it (Plimpton 113)—a claim that his manuscripts substantiate.

Hemingway hated to be interrupted while he was working and later in life frequently complained about the telephone calls and visits from fans that came with fame. He expected his wives to manage the household and his children while he worked and deeply resented his third wife, Martha, because she rejected this traditional wifely role, believing her writing was as important as his.

Hemingway saw his talent as a moral responsibility and wrote often in his work about artists who perverted, squandered, or abused their talent—for example, in *To Have and Have Not*, "The Snows of Kilimanjaro," and *A Moveable Feast*. He believed that "a writer should be of as great probity and honesty as a priest of God" ("Introduction" xiii). As he explained in his conclusion to *Death in the Afternoon*, "The great thing is to last and get your work done and see and hear and learn and understand; and write when there is something that you know; and not before; and not too damned much after" (278).

In the short story "Fathers and Sons," the story's autobiographical protagonist, Nicholas Adams, thinks to himself, "If he wrote it he could get rid of it. He had gotten rid of many things by writing about them" (*SS* 491). There is some evidence that Hemingway, Nick's creator, felt the same way. He once told F. Scott Fitzgerald that whenever he was hurt he should use his pain in his work. According to a memoir by one Hemingway associate, the movie star Ava Gardner once asked Hemingway if he had ever had a psychoanalyst. "Sure I have. Portable Corona number three," he responded, referring to his typewriter. "That's been my analyst" (Hotchner 152). He sometimes used his writing to exorcise painful emotions. Both in interviews and in his written response upon receiving the Nobel Prize, Hemingway emphasized the writer's loneliness and isolation. Yet decades earlier, he had once written, of Nick Adams' writing, and probably of his own as well, "It was really more fun than anything. He had never realized that before. It wasn't conscience. It was simply that it was the greatest pleasure" (*NAS* 238).

GENRES

Ernest Hemingway wrote published and unpublished works in an astonishingly broad range of genres. His published work includes newspaper articles, poetry, short stories, novels, a parody, a play, magazine articles, a memoir, and book-length nonfiction. He also corresponded extensively with his friends, relatives, and ex-wives, writing letters when he could not write fiction. Biographer Carlos Baker conservatively estimated that Hemingway wrote some six or seven thousand letters during his lifetime, and after discussion with scholars, Stephen Plotkin, the former curator of the Hemingway Collection at the John F. Kennedy Presidential Library, believes that the actual number could be as high as twice that many. Hemingway also wrote a documentary film script, edited a book of writings on war, contributed introductions to the books of other writers, and once wrote a beautifully moving eulogy at the request of a friend's widow.

Although his novels *The Sun Also Rises* and *A Farewell to Arms* regularly appear on lists of the best works of American literature, Hemingway's short stories are on the whole regarded even more highly than his novels, and it would be difficult to find an anthology of twentieth-century short stories that does not include one of his works. His poetry is less highly regarded, and it is generally acknowledged that he wrote his best poetry in the lyrical prose of his novels and short stories.

Despite his obvious productivity as a writer, however, Hemingway suffered increasingly throughout his life from severe bouts of writer's block. In his worst moments of artistic doubt, deepened by his depression, Hemingway sometimes nearly despaired that he would ever write again. Writing was rarely easy for him. "The hardest thing in the world to do is to write straight honest prose on human beings. First you have to know the subject; then you have to know how to write. Both take a lifetime to learn . . ." he wrote in one of his columns for *Esquire* magazine in 1934 (*By-Line* 159).

In *A Moveable Feast*, Hemingway, although plagued by self-doubt, tells himself, "Do not worry. You have always written before and you will write now. All you have to do is write one true sentence. Write the truest sentence that you know" (12). David Bourne offers himself a similar reminder in the posthumously published novel *The Garden of Eden*, telling himself, "it is all very well for you to write simply and the simpler the better. But do not start to think so damned simply. Know how complicated it is and then state it simply" (37). That emphasis on one true sentence—that apparent simplicity, so difficult to achieve—characterized his best and most memorable work.

HEMINGWAY'S LITERARY INNOVATIONS

The strength of Hemingway's writing is his style, which is so distinctive that it has inspired the ultimate backhanded tribute: an annual Bad Hemingway Contest, in which entrants vie to write the funniest parody of Hemingway's work. Before Hemingway, much popular American fiction was written in a sweetly sentimental late-Victorian prose that seemed stale and laughable after the horror and disillusionment of World War I. Frances Hodgson Burnett's 1886 classic *Little Lord Fauntleroy* is typical of this flowery style. By contrast, the characteristics of Hemingway's style include short declarative sentences, a preference for simple, often one-syllable words, and an emphasis on the concrete rather than the abstract.

In *Death in the Afternoon*, Hemingway explained the importance of the concrete: "I was trying to write then and I found the greatest difficulty, aside from knowing truly what you really felt, rather than what you were supposed to feel, and had been taught to feel, was to put down what really happened in action; what the actual things were which produced the emotion that you experienced" (2). Hemingway wrote something very similar in a letter to his father from Paris in March 1925, explaining passionately that he was trying not to depict life but to make an experience come alive for the reader (*Selected Letters* 153). In 1942, in his introduction to *Men at War*, he wrote, "A writer's job is to tell the truth. His standard of fidelity to the truth should be so high that his invention, out of his experience, should produce a truer account than anything factual can be" (xiv).

Apart from his style and his emphasis on the concrete detail, perhaps Hemingway's most noteworthy contribution to literature is his theory of omission, which he practiced even in his earliest work: "I always try to write on the principle of the iceberg. There is seven-eighths of it underwater for every part that shows. Anything you know you can eliminate and it only strengthens your iceberg. It is the part that doesn't show. If a writer omits something because he does not know it then there is a hole in the story" (qtd. in Plimpton 125). "I sometimes think my style is suggestive rather than direct," he wrote in an article not published until after his death. "The reader must often use his imagination or lose the most subtle part of my thought" (qtd. in Wagner-Martin, *Six Decades* 275). In *A Moveable Feast* Hemingway recalls that in writing the short story "Out of Season" (published in *In Our Time*), he had described an actual fishing trip that went wrong because of a drunken guide, but had left out the real-life aftermath, the guide's suicide after he was fired as a result of Ernest's complaints: "This was omitted on my new theory that you could omit anything if you knew that you omitted and the omitted part would strengthen the story and make people feel something more than they understood" (75). The chief disadvantage of this theory is that it opens the door to all sorts of rather frightening misreadings by people who insist that they know what Hemingway "left out."

One of Hemingway's most famous omissions occurs in "Hills Like White Elephants," where neither of the characters ever names the action—a proposed abortion—about which they are arguing. Part of what he omits in many of his writings is the emotion. At the end of *A Farewell to Arms*, Frederic Henry expresses so little of the grief he feels that some imperceptive critics have erroneously called him emotionally stunted.

MODERNISM

Hemingway's writings are associated with the literary movement called modernism. A decided break with the Victorian and Edwardian periods that preceded it, modernism is generally associated with literary works produced between 1914, the beginning of World War I, and 1939, the beginning of World War II. As Virginia Woolf writes in her essay on character, "Mr. Bennett and Mrs. Brown, . . . in or about December, 1910, human character changed" (320).

In some ways, modernism was a response to the changes created by startling new theories about human life and behavior. According to the theory of evolution proposed by the British naturalist Charles Darwin (1809–1882), human beings, rather than being the center of a divinely created universe, were little better than animals at the mercy of their own biology. Russian economist Karl Marx (1818–1883) theorized that economic forces controlled human beings and determined their actions and even their beliefs. With his theories of the unconscious, Sigmund Freud (1856–1939), the Austrian father of psychoanalysis, argued that human beings were not even in full control of their own minds. If those theories weren't enough to discourage faith in humanity, the carnage of World War I destroyed any lingering doubts.

As scholar Paul Fussell has shown in *The Great War and Modern Memory*, the young men England sent off to fight in World War I envisioned a picturesque war involving heroism and chivalry. Instead they found themselves mired in mud-filled trenches, fighting desperately for weeks to gain a foot of ground. Bitter and disillusioned, the surviving members of the younger generation came to blame the older generation—and specifically their fathers—for what was perceived as the pointless sacrifice of so many young lives.

Modernist writers responded to the culture's destruction of faith in humanity by dropping the notions of heroism espoused by their parents and turning instead to a sometimes savage irony. A classic example occurs at the end of the first chapter of *A Farewell to Arms*: "At the start of the winter came the permanent rain and with the rain came the cholera. But it was checked and in the end only seven thousand died of it in the army" (4). Modernist writing is also characterized by aesthetic innovation and radical experimentation, including the stream-of-consciousness novels of James Joyce, Virginia Woolf, and William Faulkner; the new, nonrhyming verse forms of h.d. and Ezra Pound; and the fragmentation of Hemingway's *In Our Time*, John Dos Passos' *U.S.A.* trilogy of novels, and T.S. Eliot's poem "The Waste Land."

In part as a result of World War I, gender roles began to change dramatically in Western culture during the 1920s. Thanks to tireless campaigning by countless suffragists, American women became eligible to vote when the 19th Amendment to the United States Constitution was ratified on August 26, 1920. Women began to wear shorter skirts and cut their hair short, an action F. Scott Fitzgerald memorialized in the short story "Bernice Bobs Her Hair." Thus was born the "flapper," also sometimes referred to as the "New Woman." Unlike her predecessors, the New Woman smoked, drank, and used birth control. She might go to college, although few women went on to work, and she enjoyed an unprecedented new sexual freedom. These changes made many men uneasy and uncomfortable, and those feelings are reflected in the literature written by male modernist writers. In Hemingway's 1926 novel *The Sun Also Rises*, for example, Jake Barnes' sexual incapacity and oddly feminized role with respect to Lady Brett Ashley (he is passive, chaste, and long-suffering) perhaps reflect Hemingway's masculine anxiety about the New Woman and her effect on his own gender role.

Also significant in the rise of modernism is the corresponding development of new technologies in the early twentieth century, including the radio, the airplane, and the relatively inexpensive automobile produced by Henry Ford's newly invented assembly-line process. These technologies made the kind of global travel we associate with Hemingway easier, which helps explain why so many Modernist writers—Sherwood Anderson, Gertrude Stein, James Joyce, Ezra Pound, Djuna Barnes, and T.S. Eliot, for example—became expatriates. Inventions first created decades earlier also became more readily available to the general public, including the camera, the typewriter, the phonograph, the telegraph, and the telephone. Yet technology also created increasing alienation and culminated in the machine guns and poison gas of World War I. Partly in response to the dehumanizing and alienating effects new technology could have on human civilization, writers like D.H. Lawrence, T.S. Eliot, and W.B. Yeats espoused a return to primitivism or drew on mythic traditions. For example, Lawrence called for a return to what he called the dark blood knowledge of human sexuality, Eliot evoked ancient Greek myths in his poetry, and Yeats encouraged interest in the traditional Celtic folklore of his native Ireland. Especially influential were works like Sir James Frazer's *The Golden Bough* and Jessie Weston's *From Ritual to Romance*, which traced the influence of ancient fertility cults upon early Christianity.

Many modernist writers chose to become expatriates in part because Paris offered them a much more stimulating intellectual climate than America did. They could also associate with other writers and artists in a freer social environment in which unorthodox behavior—including eccentricities, irregular work schedules, homosexuality, alcoholism, and creativity—was tolerated and sometimes even encouraged rather than condemned. Vital in the establishment of modernism were small communities of writers who encouraged each other, provided free editorial help and advice, and promoted and sometimes published each other's work, communities such as the Bloomsbury Group in London or the loosely associated Parisian expatriates of whom Hemingway was a part. So-called "little magazines," literary magazines such as *transition* and *The Dial* that often operated on shoestring budgets, published modernist fiction and poetry when no other magazines were interested in such difficult, experimental writings.

THEMES

Modernist writings were often difficult to publish because of their content as well as their style. Modernist writers wrote with relative openness about homosexuality, abortion, and prostitution—topics that the American public saw as immoral and disgusting. World War I and the younger generation's revulsion at its cost in human lives comprise an important theme of many modernist works, including Wilfred Owen's poetry, Hemingway's *In Our Time* and *A Farewell to Arms*, and Virginia Woolf's *Jacob's Room* and *Mrs. Dalloway*. Hemingway's work is also typical of modernism in its fragmentation (*In Our Time*), its irony, and its characters' rejection of religious belief (for example, Brett in *The Sun Also Rises*, Catherine in *A Farewell to Arms* and the waiter in "A Clean, Well-Lighted Place").

But the chief theme of Hemingway's writing concerns how best to cope with suffering and defeat, how to live with dignity in a world that is racked with violence and loss. Hemingway described this theme in a succinct and memorable phrase that his friend Gerald Murphy recalled him first using on a ski trip they took together with John Dos Passos in March 1926. Murphy, a novice skier, was in over his head on the slopes but did not want to let his friends down, even though Hemingway was a much more experienced skier. Murphy later wrote of Hemingway, "[W]hen we got to the bottom, about a half an hour later, he asked me if I'd been scared. I said yes, I guess I had. He said then that he knew what courage was, it was grace under pressure. It was childish of me, but I felt absolutely elated" (qtd. in Donnelly and Billings 22). Hemingway often included the expression in his letters and mentioned it to Dorothy Parker, who cited it in her 1929 *Vanity Fair* profile of Hemingway. President John F. Kennedy borrowed the phrase "grace under pressure" in his 1956 essay collection, *Profiles in Courage*, and it has remained a hallmark of Hemingway's work for decades.

Also a hallmark of Hemingway's work is its persistently elegiac quality, which is neatly captured in an online joke. In a twist on the old riddle, "Why did the chicken cross the road?," answers are given in the style of various writers. The response in the Hemingway style is: "To die. In the rain." As a writer, Hemingway has a nostalgic preoccupation with loss, sometimes even to the extent of painfully anticipating the loss before it occurs, as for example when he is homesick for Africa even before he leaves it: "All I wanted to do now was get back to Africa. We had not left it, yet, but when I would wake in the night I would lie, listening, homesick for it already" (*GHOA* 72). Most of his novels end bleakly, often with a death. As the narrator of *Death in the Afternoon* points out to his listener, "Madame, all stories, if continued far enough, end in death, and he is no true-story teller who would keep that from you" (122).

On the brighter side, Hemingway's richly evocative descriptions of places—particularly Paris and Pamplona—are a strength of his writing, one on which he prided himself: "For we have been there in the books and out of the books—and where we go, if we are any good, there you can go as we have been" (*GHOA* 109). His detailed descriptions of European cities—their cafés, hotels, cathedrals, works of art, public squares, and religious festivals, and the natural beauty of the surrounding countryside—are so vividly compelling that some readers have used his books as travel guides, prompting Hemingway aficionados to create coffee-table books like *Hemingway's Paris* and *Hemingway's Spain*, complete with color photographs of locations mentioned in his novels. His writings on food have inspired the creation of a seven-page glossary defining the dishes mentioned in *A Moveable Feast* alone, various articles on food and eating in Hemingway's writings, and even a cookbook of recipes for the dishes featured in various Hemingway works.

He repeatedly emphasized that writing should be based on personal experience: "You throw it all away and invent from what you know. I should have said that sooner. That's all there is to writing. That, a perfect ear (call it selective absolute pitch), the devotion to your work and respect for it that a priest of God has for his, and then have the guts of a burglar, no conscience except to writing, and you're in, gentlemen. It's easy" ("Art" 134).

PERCEPTIONS OF HEMINGWAY'S WORK

Hemingway's books were unevenly received by both reviewers and the public. Both *In Our Time* and *The Sun Also Rises* were very successful, although as Hemingway scholar Susan F. Beegel observes, neither could compete with a blockbuster like Margaret Mitchell's 1936 novel, *Gone with the Wind*. His short story collections were well received, but *To Have and Have Not* was published to mixed reviews. His nonfiction works, *Death in the Afternoon* and *Green Hills of Africa*, sold less well and were largely panned by the critics. His reputation revived first with the 1940 publication of *For Whom the Bell Tolls* and again, after the disappointing *Across the River and Into the Trees*, with *The Old Man and the Sea* in 1952. However, both of these initially acclaimed works have declined in reputation somewhat since their first enthusiastic reception. Many of his novels and short stories have been made into films, and his works are regularly taught in high school and college classrooms around the world. His posthumous works, although heavily edited, have sold well, and although *Islands in the Stream* and *True at First Light* are inferior to his best work, their publication seems to have done little harm to his reputation. Because of its sensational subject matter concerning sexual transformation, *The Garden of Eden* has provoked perhaps the most interest, although *A Moveable Feast* is arguably the best of the posthumously published works.

Because in his fiction Hemingway employed the language people used in everyday conversation, he had trouble with censorship of his language all his life. The first story in *In Our Time*, "Up in Michigan," had to be replaced because its sexual content might have caused the publisher a legal battle on obscenity charges. The first paragraph of the short story "Mr. and Mrs. Elliot" was revised to remove the repetitive and potentially offensive references to how the couple "tried very hard to have a baby" (Reynolds, *Paris* 292). When *Scribner's Magazine* published *A Farewell to Arms*, it replaced some of Hemingway's language with blanks, but the magazine was still banned in Boston because of moral objections to the sexual content of the story. "Condom" was cut from *Green Hills of Africa* when it was published in *Scribner's Magazine* (Reynolds, *1930s* 205–6). To twenty-first-century readers the censorship seems oddly focused, however. As Michael Reynolds points out with respect to the publication of "White Man, Black Man, Alphabet Man," one of the stories that later made up *To Have and Have Not*, "*Esquire*, not allowed to say that a person was 'kicked in the ass,' had no trouble printing this story's numerous references to Wesley as 'the nigger' " (*1930s* 217).

Contemporary readers of the last three decades have objected to certain elements in Hemingway's work that they deem immoral or at least troubling. Feminist literary critics such as Judith Fetterley and Millicent Bell have complained of what they perceive as Hemingway's hostility toward women. Toni Morrison, the African-American novelist who, like Hemingway, has won both the Pulitzer and the Nobel Prize, has criticized the way in which Hemingway has constructed an Africanist presence in his writings, specifically in *To Have and Have Not* and *The Garden of Eden*. Scholar Debra Moddelmog has pointed out the obliviousness of Harry's protagonist to his own privilege in "The Snows of Kilimanjaro." Hemingway's attitudes toward homosexuality can also be disturbing. When Jake Barnes wants to punch one of the gays who enter the dance club with Brett, it is difficult to tell whether Hemingway sympathizes or disapproves. Finally, environmentalists and animal rights supporters have objected to the hunting, fishing, and bullfighting scenes in Hemingway's work on the grounds that they glorify cruelty to animals and the destruction of species.

Some of these charges have arisen in part because most of the critics who have studied Hemingway's work have been white heterosexual men of European descent, and they have emphasized the presence in Hemingway's work of the elements that most interested them: "When potential readers reject Hemingway as indifferent to minorities and hostile to women, they are often responding not to Hemingway's fiction, but to the indifference and hostility of some of his early critics, and a negative image of the author those influential first admirers unintentionally projected" (Beegel, "Conclusion" 277).

Hemingway's attitudes are more complicated than has generally been appreciated. In his work he often couples ugly expressions of sexism, racism, or anti-Semitism, on one hand, with an imaginative and sympathetic depiction of the effects of such cruelty on the other. That schizophrenic tension between Hemingway's own worst impulses and his empathy for another's suffering explains why he is his best and most ethical self in his work as an artist.

One of Hemingway's oldest published short stories, for example, "Up in Michigan," describes a date rape from the point of view of the female victim, a young waitress named Liz Coates. The fact that he originally wanted this story to appear as the first story in *In Our Time* suggests that he believed that the trauma of rape paralleled the trauma of combat. Many of the other women characters in his writings are more complex than earlier critics would have readers believe. For example, the heroic Catherine of *A Farewell to Arms* understands what Frederic never learns until after her death, and Pilar of *For Whom the Bell Tolls* is one of the strongest characters, male or female, in any of Hemingway's works.

Lesbian critic Debra Moddelmog has observed that critics have overlooked or dismissed as inferior such intriguing stories as "The Mother of a Queen," "The Sea Change," "The Simple Enquiry," and *The Garden of Eden* because of their own discomfort with Hemingway's depictions of gay and lesbian characters and homosexual themes. Environmentalist critics have noted that Hemingway sometimes expresses eco-friendly sentiments as, for example, in *Green Hills of Africa* when he describes the damage caused by human exploitation of the earth (284). More than once Hemingway writes from the point of view of the hunted animal or the bull in the ring, an approach that suggests that Hemingway possessed a more nuanced view of these activities than is generally acknowledged. For example, in "The Short Happy Life of Francis Macomber," he describes the lion's shooting from the lion's point of view, and in Chapter X of *In Our Time* he presents the suffering of the horse in the bullring in horrifying detail. He closes "On the Quai at Smyrna" with the cruelty of the Greeks toward the mules they had used as pack animals, and his sympathy for the abused animals is clear.

Nevertheless, it's too facile to simply dismiss these charges of sexism, homophobia, anti-Semitism, racism, and cruelty to animals as biased and unfounded.

Hemingway once scolded his wife for using the term "nigger" and was less overtly anti-Semitic than many of his contemporaries, including T.S. Eliot and Ezra Pound. But it would be foolish to argue that Hemingway was free of the prejudices endemic in twentieth-century Europe and America (any more than we, his readers, are free of the prejudices of our own twenty-first century society). It is perhaps more useful to ask if knowing that he sometimes demonstrates disturbing prejudices and disappoints modern-day expectations makes his art unworthy of appreciation or renders readers unable to appreciate it. By that standard, Hemingway's work continues to maintain its place in the literary canon.

It has been suggested that true art lends itself to interpretation and reinterpretation. By that standard as well, Hemingway's writings belong in the canon. Critics have examined Hemingway's work for its biographical parallels, applied psychoanalytic techniques to explicate its meaning, dissected the various literary and artistic influences that contributed to the final product, and criticized it from feminist, lesbian, ecocritical, and postmodern perspectives. Philip Young, one of the first scholars to publish a book-length study on Hemingway's fiction, established an important tradition in interpreting Hemingway's work. Young developed the notion that most of Hemingway's writings featured what he called a "code hero" and a "Hemingway hero." The Hemingway hero, often the story's protagonist, has much to learn about how to live in the world, while the code hero, who has the wisdom to know how to live properly, is—because of his adherence to an unspoken code of behavior—a mentor and example to the usually younger Hemingway hero. In *The Old Man and the Sea*, for example, Manolin is the Hemingway hero learning how to live from Santiago, the code hero. In *A Farewell to Arms*, Frederic is the Hemingway hero who is learning the Hemingway code from Catherine. Hemingway scholars Earl Rovit and Gerry Brenner further developed this notion, labeling these characters the tutor and the tyro.

Young defined the Hemingway code as "made of the controls of honor and courage which in a life of tension and pain make a man a man and distinguish him from the people who follow random impulses, let down their hair, and are generally messy, perhaps cowardly" (63). Unfortunately, the sexism inherent in his definition made it harder to see Hemingway's women characters—such as Catherine, or Liz Coates of "Up in Michigan"—as exemplars of the code. Some of Hemingway's protagonists—Jake Barnes of *The Sun Also Rises*, for example—behave in ways that seem inconsistent with the code as Young defined it. Furthermore, Young's influence was so pervasive that it sometimes obscured other possible readings of Hemingway's work and caused works that did not fit readily into this framework (e.g., stories like "A Canary for One" or "The Sea Change") to suffer unjust neglect. The concept of the "code hero," although historically important in Hemingway studies, is no longer as influential as it once was.

Young also argued in 1952 that Hemingway's 1918 war wound had so traumatized him that he returned to it again and again in his writings—for example, by giving Frederic Henry a similar injury, depicting Nick Adams as traumatized by the war, having Colonel Cantwell of *Across the River and Into the Trees* return (as Hemingway did) to the site of his own wounding, and focusing so relentlessly on death in so many stories and novels. As early as 1952, Young presciently suggested that Hemingway concentrated on shooting animals to avoid shooting himself.

Aware of Young's "wound theory," Hemingway resisted and opposed Young's work, granting permission for Young to quote his writings only begrudgingly. He was similarly uncomfortable with the work of other early scholars of his writings, such as Carlos Baker and Charles Fenton. Hemingway despised critics and scholars of his work, calling them "the lice who crawl on literature" (*GHOA* 109). He hated to discuss the symbolism in his own writings, arguing facetiously that the professional explainers of literature needed work and that he would hate to deprive them of a living. He believed his work should stand by itself. As he once advised an interviewer, "Read anything I write for the pleasure of reading. Whatever else you find will be the measure of what you brought to the reading" (Plimpton 120).

HEMINGWAY'S INFLUENCE ON OTHER WRITERS

Asked upon Hemingway's centennial about his influence on other writers, novelist Russell Banks commented, "If you want to write in American vernacular English—and most of us do—then you have to turn to Hemingway. It was his invention" (qtd. in Paul 116). Hemingway's influence is particularly associated with minimalism, an American literary movement that began in the 1970s. Best represented by writers like Raymond Carver and Ann Beattie, minimalism is characterized by ordinary subject matter, an effaced authorial presence, a passive and affectless protagonist, very little plot in the traditional sense, the use of the historical present tense, and a spare, emotionally restrained writing style.

Hemingway's terse, impassive prose in works like "The Killers" and *To Have and Have Not* inspired later crime writers such as Raymond Chandler, Dashiell Hammett, and other authors of hard-boiled detective novels. The famous American novelist Norman Mailer, with his direct prose and sometimes intensely masculine subject matter, is generally considered one of American literature's chief inheritors of the Hemingway tradition.

"Abstract words such as glory, honor, courage, or hallow were obscene beside the concrete names of villages, the numbers of roads, the names of rivers, the numbers of regiments and the dates," Frederic Henry thinks to himself in one of the most famous passages from *A Farewell to Arms* (185). In his emphasis on the concrete, especially in wartime settings, Hemingway influenced writers like Heinrich Böll, the German author whose writings about Germany during and after World War II garnered him the 1972 Nobel Prize, and Tim O'Brien, the American author whose Vietnam war novel *Going After Cacciato* received the National Book Award in 1979. O'Brien's brilliant short story "The Things They Carried," in which he lists and describes in heartbreakingly specific detail the various personal items the American soldiers carried with them into the war in Vietnam, is particularly indebted to Hemingway.

"He was a genius, that uneasy word, not so much in what he wrote (speaking like an uncertain critic) as in how he wrote; he liberated our written language," Martha Gellhorn, Hemingway's third wife, wrote of Hemingway in a 1981 article for the *Paris Review* (301). "All writers, after him, owe Hemingway a debt for their freedom whether the debt is acknowledged or not."

3

In Our Time
(1925)

First published in 1925, *In Our Time* originally included 14 short stories (15 if the two parts of "Big Two-Hearted River" are counted separately) and 16 italicized "chapters"—brief, vivid sketches, which Hemingway called "unwritten stories" (qtd. in Reynolds, *Final* 308). All of the chapters (but not the stories) were originally published in *in our time*, a limited-edition book published in Paris in 1924. The ironic title of the collection comes from a line in the Anglican Church's *Book of Common Prayer*: "Give us peace in our time, O Lord."

Like *Dubliners* by James Joyce and *Winesburg, Ohio* by Sherwood Anderson, *In Our Time* is a collection of interrelated short stories. D.H. Lawrence once called it a "fragmentary novel" (93). In a letter to the distinguished literary critic Edmund Wilson, Hemingway claimed that despite its fragmentary nature, the book possessed a certain unity and compared the effect created by the alternating short stories and vignettes to the experience of looking at a coast with the naked eye and then examining it with binoculars.

Nick Adams, the protagonist in 12 of the short stories and one of the chapters, is a semi-autobiographical character who appears in many short stories Hemingway wrote throughout much of his career. These stories have been gathered and published, along with several previously unpublished works about Nick, in a 1972 collection titled *The Nick Adams Stories*, edited by Philip Young. But while Nick Adams bears a certain resemblance to Hemingway, it is dangerous to confuse the two. In "On Writing," material Hemingway cut from "Big Two-Hearted River," he wrote, "Everything good he'd ever written he'd made up" and added a page later, "Nick in the stories was never himself" (*NAS* 237–38).

Hemingway's original plan for *In Our Time* included a short story called "Up in Michigan" about an apparent date rape told from the woman's point of view. The story demonstrates that Hemingway could imaginatively enter into the feelings of a traumatized woman and would have shown that the violence that Nick Adams confronts is not restricted by gender. Regrettably, Hemingway's publisher deemed the story's sexual content unpublishable and asked him to provide another work in its place. Hemingway wrote another Nick Adams story, "The Battler," to complete the collection (Reynolds, *Paris* 280), and "Up in Michigan" was not published in the United States until 1938.

In the second American edition of *In Our Time*, which was published in 1930, Hemingway added an "Introduction by the Author," which he retitled "On the Quai at Smyrna" when it was published in the 1938 volume *The Fifth Column and the First Forty-Nine Stories* (Hanneman 9). He based the chapter on a news story he covered, the evacuation of refugees from Smyrna after the 1922 Turkish invasion of Asia Minor, then held by the Greeks (Reynolds, *Paris* 77). The sketch neatly captures both the horror of the wartime scene he describes and the equally disturbing attitudes of those who witness such terrible events calmly.

Other stories and chapters (sometimes referred to as "interchapters" or "vignettes") were inspired by his childhood summers in Michigan, his reporting days at the *Kansas City Star*, his own wartime experiences, and the war stories of his friend the 23-year-old Irish World War I veteran, Captain Eric Edward Dorman-Smith of the Fifth Northumberland Fusiliers, whose clipped British tones and habit of understatement Hemingway adopted for the unidentified narrator of Chapter IV. Nicknamed "Chink," Dorman-Smith was the "young British officer" who, in order to console the ignorant 19-year- old Hemingway ("Introduction" xii), gave him a quotation from Shakespeare's *Henry IV Part II* (III.ii.234–37), which Hemingway used years later in "The Short Happy Life of Francis Macomber": "By my troth, I care not: a man can die but once; we owe God a death . . . and let it go which way it will, he that dies this year is quit for the next."

Many of the chapters of *In Our Time* focus on violent events—the stylized violence of the bullfights, the state-sanctioned violence of biased police and the executions of criminals, the self-inflicted violence of a throat cutting, and the medically necessary violence of a forced caesarean without anesthesia, as well as many wartime incidents. Those that aren't overtly violent often feature psychological violence, such as tense marital arguments, Nick's reluctant and coerced acceptance of his wife's pregnancy, and a soldier's wrenching return to home after the war. Critics have often accused Hemingway of an excessive preoccupation with violence, particularly in *In Our Time*, but Jackson J. Benson skillfully defended Hemingway against that charge, arguing that the author is preoccupied not with violence for its own sake, but with the emotional responses of human beings confronted with violence.

Hemingway's use of juxtaposition in *In Our Time* suggests the technique of collage employed by cubist artists such as Pablo Picasso and Georges Braque. Through his placement of the stories and chapters, he allows each part of *In Our Time* to comment upon the next. The sensibility of Dr. Adams, for example, who treats the Indian woman as insensitively as if she were an animal and resorts to pumping a shotgun when he is angry with his wife, is akin to the sensibility that caused the carnage of World War I. The image in Chapter II of the pregnant woman trying to give birth during an evacuation and the fear the narrator describes echo the Indian woman's terrible labor in "Indian Camp" and Nick's terror at what he witnesses.

Another literary technique for which Hemingway became famous is compression. In the chapters and in many of his short stories, Hemingway writes very lean prose, managing to convey vivid images and intense emotion in extraordinarily few words. Most of the chapters, despite their powerful impact, are only a paragraph long. The spareness of his writing was shocking to readers used to the expansiveness of the Victorians, who typically published 800-page novels in three-volume sets. Even compared to his fellow Modernists—F. Scott Fitzgerald, William Faulkner, Virginia Woolf, and James Joyce—Hemingway's work was distinctive in this respect.

The three stories discussed in this chapter have all received extensive critical attention, are often anthologized, and are regularly taught in high school and college classes. "Indian Camp," "Soldier's Home," and "Big Two-Hearted River" are not only three of Hemingway's best short stories, but three of the best short stories in the English language.

"INDIAN CAMP"

SETTING AND PLOT DEVELOPMENT

First published in the April 1924 issue of the *transatlantic review*, "Indian Camp" is generally recognized as one of Hemingway's best and most interesting short stories. Although its setting is never specified, the story evidently takes place in Michigan's north woods, where the Hemingways spent their summers when Ernest was growing up. The heavily forested area was then still sparsely populated by Native Americans of the Ojibway tribe.

As the story opens, a young Nick Adams arrives at the Indian camp with both his Uncle George and his father, Dr. Adams. The doctor has come to treat an Indian woman who has been laboring unsuccessfully for three days because her baby is in a breech position. Dr. Adams promptly performs an emergency caesarean section without either anesthesia or the proper medical instruments. Deliberately disregarding the screams of his patient, he delivers the baby successfully and congratulates himself gleefully upon his triumph—only to discover abruptly that the Indian father, trapped in the bunk above by a wounded foot, has slit his throat. Nick, who found the caesarean disturbing to watch, asks his father many questions about the Indian father's suicide and silently decides, at the end of the story, that he himself will never die.

CHARACTER DEVELOPMENT

Dr. Adams is coolly professional to the point of callousness. His jubilant pride in his own work immediately after the operation becomes particularly ironic when he realizes that his indifference to his patient's screams blinded him to the acute emotional suffering of her husband in the upper bunk, suffering that directly led to the man's suicide. By choosing to operate without respecting the emotions and human dignity of his patient and her husband, he has violated the prime directive of the Hippocratic oath, to first do no harm.

Equally important to the story is the father's cruelty in compelling his son to participate in a bloody, exquisitely painful operation the boy is much too young to see. Well before the suicide, the evidently overwhelmed young boy elects to stop watching the operation. The father's reference to his son as an "interne" indicates his egotistical motivation in compelling his son to witness the messy and painful surgery: He wants to remake his son into his own image.

Although Nick's age is never given in the story, in "Three Shots," a discarded beginning published after Hemingway's death in the collection *The Nick Adams Stories*, Hemingway describes him as so young that the boy is afraid of the dark on a camping trip with his father and uncle. Dr. Adams expects too much of his sensitive young son, as the son's difficult and probing questions about what he has witnessed make clear.

Even within the story, there is evidence that not everyone agrees with Dr. Adams in his callous treatment of his patient. Through his sarcastic comment and his eventual disappearance from the story, Nick's Uncle George seems to comment critically upon the doctor's conduct. When the Indian woman bites George as he holds her down, George utters a racial slur that suggests the prejudiced attitude he and the doctor share towards the people they are ostensibly trying to help. George's apparently impromptu gift of cigars upon their arrival at the Indian camp has prompted much speculation about whether he, rather than the Indian brave, is the baby boy's father. But there is little evidence in the story to support such an offbeat hypothesis, and it seems likely that his attitude should be read as paternalistic rather than literally paternal.

THEMES

"Indian Camp," which Hemingway himself rightly rated as one of the best in the collection, dramatizes what is apparently the young Nick Adams' first confrontation with profound personal suffering. In this initiation story an emotionally innocent young boy comes face to face with the suffering and death caused by his father's willed moral blindness—much as, later in the collection, Nick as a young man joins his fellow soldiers in confronting the suffering and death caused by what the British referred to collectively as the "Old Men," the fathers of society. Forced by his father to confront too much too early in life, the traumatized Nick rebels emotionally by retreating into the self-protective fantasy that he will never die. He is, suggests Rose Marie Burwell, damaged by his experience, and his abrupt conviction of his own immortality at the story's end is his way of rather desperately whistling in the dark—or rather "in the early morning light" (Burwell xii).

Anger at fathers is a theme that runs throughout the stories in this collection—perhaps because Hemingway, like many of his generation, felt they betrayed their sons into participating in World War I. The father in "Indian Camp" exposes his young son to too much, too soon, and his son is damaged as a result of the father's arrogant insensitivity. In later stories and chapters, fathers (and father figures) are preoccupied with self-interest rather than the welfare of their literal and metaphorical sons: Consider the bullfighter in Chapter XIII whose solicitousness for Luis, a hard-drinking fellow matador, is revealed as concern that he will have to fight Luis's bulls if Luis is too drunk to perform. In "The Battler," Ad Francis, who calls Nick "kid," is initially friendly but turns murderous before the story is over. Also relevant to this view of *In Our Time* are the younger priest of Chapter 15, who with his colleague urges Sam Cardinella to be a man but skips back abruptly when Cardinella is hanged, and the king (the ultimate patriarch) of the final vignette, whose chief priority is protecting himself. No wonder Nick is apprehensive about his impending fatherhood in "Cross-Country Snow." His paternal role models hardly inspire confidence.

As critics Amy Lovell Strong and Thomas Strychacz have pointed out, this story also evokes broader issues of race and gender in America in its depiction of the interaction between the know-it-all white male doctor and the incoherent, nameless Native American woman whose labor has gone horribly wrong. The white men arrive by boat, implicitly invoking the arrival of the European explorers and colonists in the New World (Strychacz, "*In Our Time*" 61–63). Insensitive and unwilling to listen, the white man, who prides himself on his superior knowledge, does what he thinks is best and in the process causes unbearable suffering. The parallels to the European conquest of the North American continent are obvious.

"SOLDIER'S HOME"

Composed in April 1924, "Soldier's Home" was first published in 1925 in *Contact Collection of Contemporary Writers*, an anthology including works by now-prominent Modernist writers such as Ezra Pound, Djuna Barnes, h.d., Ford Madox Ford, and Gertrude Stein (Smith, *Reader's Guide* 69). The short story's title has two meanings. "Soldier's Home" can be read as a contraction for "soldier is home," but it can also refer to a home where wounded and ill soldiers recover from injuries and illnesses incurred during war. Both meanings are relevant to the story, since Krebs is both newly arrived at home and convalescing from psychic wounds caused by combat.

SETTING AND PLOT DEVELOPMENT

Harold Krebs doesn't quite know what to do with himself upon his return home to his family in Oklahoma after serving in World War I. He returns in the summer of 1919, long after the war ended in November 1918, and his neighbors are no longer interested in his war stories. He learns he must exaggerate his experiences in order to make them interesting and then becomes disgusted by his own dishonesty. Emotionally numb, he drifts aimlessly through life, trying to avoid the people around him as much as possible. He spends his days reading and studying maps, trying desperately to understand the war in which he has just participated. Encounters with his sister and his mother finally propel him to decide to go first to his sister's indoor baseball game and then to Kansas City to find work. "Soldier's Home" is a semi-autobiographical story: Hemingway, too, experienced difficulty in deciding what to do with himself after the war and 'like Krebs ultimately chose to go to Kansas City, where his uncle helped him land a job in journalism.

CHARACTER DEVELOPMENT

In the field of Hemingway scholarship, the mother of Harold Krebs is (with Brett Ashley and Margot Macomber) one of the most reviled female characters in all of Hemingway's fiction. She has frequently been described as a domineering woman attempting to smother her son. In first recalling how she carried her son when he was a baby and then compelling him to kneel with her to pray, Mrs. Krebs seems to many readers pathetically unwilling to recognize her son's adulthood and emotional (if not financial) independence. Cloying in her sentimental piety, she insists on his inclusion in "God's Kingdom," even though Krebs himself has apparently rejected religious faith.

Viewed more sympathetically, however, she is a genuinely loving mother who in recalling her pregnancy and her son's infancy is trying not to infantalize Harold but to reestablish a connection with the son who she recognizes has become perilously detached and disengaged from his family and his community. In asking him to pray and insisting upon his membership in God's Kingdom, she is a little desperately trying to draw him back into the fold. She is clearly (and justifiably) frightened that his wartime experiences may have irrevocably damaged him and perhaps compromised his moral integrity.

Surely Mrs. Krebs evokes pathos rather than disgust, and Hemingway offers clear evidence within the story that Harold Krebs cares for his mother's feelings. When he tells her he no longer loves her, and that in fact he no longer loves anybody, she begins to cry. He seems genuinely sorry that he has hurt her and immediately tries to console her. At the end of the story, he acknowledges that he will have to say goodbye to her, but he plans to avoid seeing his father again altogether, which suggests that however difficult he finds his mother, his father is worse. Krebs recognizes that despite her failings, his mother honestly cares for him, but his attitude towards his father is harder to read.

His enigmatic father, who never appears in the story but speaks through Harold's mother, is apparently demanding: He cannot read the newspaper unless it's in mint condition, and he is the one who wants Krebs to land a job and go to work like the other neighborhood "boys." He has a downtown office and works in real estate, and his concern for his son is primarily materialistic. "He thinks you have lost your ambition, that you haven't got a definite aim in life," Harold's mother tells him (75). When his mother offers Krebs the use of the family car, Krebs insists that his mother compelled his father to give his permission, which suggests that she is the more generous and lenient parent.

Krebs himself is oddly detached from everyday life. Isolated by choice, he prefers studying the war to any kind of social interaction and bluntly rejects all human contact. He particularly shies away from young women, although he obviously finds them attractive; he is mentally preoccupied with them but insists to himself that he does not need them. (Some readers have cited Hemingway's repetition of the word "liked" in this part of the story as evidence of the influence of Gertrude Stein upon his early short stories, but since he used similar constructions in his juvenilia, written before he had ever even heard of Stein, this argument for her influence seems doubtful at best.) Although he resents his mother's insistence that he do something with his life, she is ultimately right in recognizing that he cannot go on as he is, remote from everyone around him.

Only his kid sister Helen loves Krebs unconditionally. Her adolescent adoration of him becomes vaguely disturbing, however, when she asks if she can be his girlfriend. She expects so little of him that it is not surprising that he prefers her company to anyone else's. But even his sister resorts to emotional blackmail to persuade him to come to her indoor baseball game, which indicates that she, too, recognizes that he cannot stay detached forever.

THEMES

The chief theme of this story is the difficult adjustment a veteran faces upon returning to civilian life. Hemingway implies, through his portrayal of Krebs, that a man who is good at war is good for very little else. Krebs is a round character who develops emotionally during the course of the story. His deceptively simple decisions at the end of the story to attend his sister's indoor baseball game and then get a job in Kansas City indicate his emotional recovery and his tentative willingness to re-engage in life.

"BIG TWO-HEARTED RIVER"

Written in 1924, "Big Two-Hearted River" was first published in the May 1925 issue of the journal *This Quarter*. At the time, Hemingway considered "Big Two-Hearted River" his best work, and it has ever since remained one of his most respected and best loved short stories.

SETTING AND PLOT DEVELOPMENT

This two-part Nick Adams story is based on a real-life fishing trip Hemingway took in 1919 with his friends Al Walker and Jock Pentecost to the upper peninsula of Michigan near the town of Seney. The river they actually fished was apparently the Fox, but he chose the name of the nearby Big Two-Hearted River for its poetry.

The story's setting is eerie: a charred landscape populated by blackened grasshoppers. All of Seney's buildings were evidently destroyed by the fire, and the burnt countryside functions as a metaphor for Nick's scarred psyche. In his 1945 introduction to *The Portable Hemingway*, critic Malcolm Cowley argued that the haunted, nightmarish quality of the work places Hemingway in the American Romantic tradition established by writers like Edgar Allan Poe, Nathaniel Hawthorne, and Herman Melville. The dream-like atmosphere of the story has prompted some critics to speculate, less than convincingly, that the story is Nick's dream or mental exercise—much like the imaginings Nick Adams describes in the opening pages of the 1933 short story "A Way You'll Never Be."

CHARACTER DEVELOPMENT

"Big Two-Hearted River" has only one character, Nick Adams. Apparently traumatized and struggling to keep his emotions under control, he draws on the familiar rituals of fishing and camping skills first learned in childhood. Nick's careful, almost obsessive attention to detail—as he makes camp, captures grasshoppers to use as bait, cooks buckwheat flapjacks, and prepares his fishing rod—suggests the intensity of his compulsive need for the restoration of order. He must exhaust himself in order to sleep and must complete simple, pleasurable tasks to keep himself calm and keep *something* at bay: "There had been this to do. Now it was done. It had been a hard trip. He was very tired. That was done. He had made his camp. He was settled. Nothing could touch him. It was a good place to camp. He was there, in the good place" (139). The passage's rhythmic phrasing suggests a litany, and the expression, "Nothing could touch him," indicates the existence of a vague threat that, by establishing his camp so methodically, Nick has somehow counteracted.

Hemingway's phrase "in the good place" evokes the concept of "the Great Good Place" from Frances Hodgson Burnett's 1911 novel *The Secret Garden*, which also celebrates the restorative power of performing simple tasks in a beautiful natural setting. Like Nick, the children in *The Secret Garden* discover the healing effects of invented rituals and thereby cure their own psychological wounds.

Although the children of Burnett's novel talk about magical spells, Nick's rituals are more prosaic, such as making coffee the way his friend Hopkins insisted it should be made. As he recalls Hopkins, Nick's thoughts wander to subjects he would rather not consider: "His mind was starting to work. He knew he could choke it because he was tired enough" (142). His overreaction to losing the big trout reveals his emotional vulnerability: "The thrill had been too much. He felt, vaguely, a little sick, as though it would be better to sit down" (150). Struggling to recover from psychic damage, he finds even the smallest of setbacks emotionally exhausting. Psychologically fragile, "He did not want to rush his sensations any" (151). His assiduous attention to how the trout "keep themselves steady" suggests his own need to learn how to keep himself steady (133).

THEMES

The chief theme of this story is the renewal and spiritual cleansing achievable through a return to nature. In the most influential interpretation of the story, Philip Young compares Nick Adams to a shell-shocked veteran attempting to control his terror by focusing on the disciplined repetition of simple, mechanical tasks. Years after he wrote the story, Hemingway once described it in a letter as a story about a soldier returning home from World War I. Although he acknowledges that the war is never mentioned in the story, he claimed (echoing his famous iceberg theory) that nevertheless the resonance of that missing information is what gave the story its meaning. In *A Moveable Feast* he recalls writing the story and again notes that the story was about the war even though he never mentioned the war in the story itself.

Hemingway biographer Kenneth Lynn has alternately suggested that what traumatized Nick was not war but family life in a conventional dysfunctional family in the conservative midwest. Writing of Hemingway's return from the war in January 1919, Hemingway's older sister Marcelline comments, "For Ernest, it must have been something like being put in a box with the cover nailed down to come home to conventional, suburban Oak Park living" (Sanford 184). Shortly before he wrote the story, Ernest and his mother had had a falling-out in which she finally threw him out of the house because at 21 years old he still refused to contribute to the running of the household in any way; he resented her for it for the rest of his life. Lynn is not alone in moving the focus of the criticism away from the traumas of combat. Increasingly in recent years, critical attention has shifted away from the role the war plays (or doesn't play) in the story to fresher approaches, such as examining the story's mythic and spiritual implications or discussing it as nature writing.

Although Hemingway never mentions any specific traumatic experience that causes Nick's tension, he does make his point obliquely: "In the swamp fishing was a tragic adventure. Nick did not want it" (155). "Tragic" is surely too melodramatic a word to apply to ordinary swamp-fishing; Hemingway's word choice here indicates that the swamp has come to symbolize for Nick all the horrors from which he has fled, whatever they may be. The story's ending—"There were plenty of days coming when he could fish the swamp" (156)—is optimistic, for it predicts that, once he has recovered further, Nick will eventually deal with whatever trauma the swamp represents for him.

LITERARY DEVICES

The story originally ended with a long, rambling coda that Hemingway fortunately cut from the manuscript after Gertrude Stein criticized it, saying "Remarks are not literature" (Stein 270). After Hemingway's death, the cut passage was published as "On Writing" in a collection entitled *The Nick Adams Stories*. Because in the coda Nick refers to himself as a writer and discusses his own writings, Moddelmog has suggested that *In Our Time* is a postmodern, self-reflexive work in which the final chapter was originally to have ended with the subtle revelation that the character Nick Adams has written the book the reader has just read.

In his role as writer of the collection, Nick considers the nineteenth-century French landscape painter Paul Cezanne at great length, admitting, "He wanted to write like Cezanne" (*NAS* 239). Hemingway shared Nick's profound respect for Cezanne's work and in his letters cited the post-impressionist artist as an influence on *In Our Time*, particularly on his depiction of the setting of "Big Two-Hearted River."

4

The Sun Also Rises
(1926)

Short story collections don't sell, but novels do. That's the advice Hemingway heard both from a publisher who rejected his work and from his friend and mentor F. Scott Fitzgerald (Reynolds, *Paris* 285). So at the age of 25, Hemingway became determined to write a novel. After one false start on a novel about Nick Adams (the central character in several of the stories in *In Our Time*), he began work in the summer of 1925 on a story he called *Fiesta* about a group of British and American expatriates living in Paris. He told the *Paris Review* that he began writing it that year on July 21, his 26th birthday, and wrote in his memoir *A Moveable Feast* that he completed the first draft of the novel in six weeks. That novel, which eventually became *The Sun Also Rises*, sold 23,000 copies by October 1927 (Baker, *Life* 182). His mother considered the novel filthy and wrote to Ernest pleading with him to put his talents to better use. In a letter to F. Scott Fitzgerald, Hemingway himself wrote that he considered the story a sad one (Bruccoli 61). *The Sun Also Rises* is widely regarded as Hemingway's best novel.

PLOT DEVELOPMENT

The Sun Also Rises consists of 19 chapters divided into three books: Chapters I-VII comprise Book I, Chapters VIII-XVIII comprise Book II, and Book III consists solely of Chapter 19. Hemingway's original beginning, which introduced Lady Brett Ashley, was cut on the advice of F. Scott Fitzgerald. Instead the novel as it was published begins with an introduction of Robert Cohn, the Jewish Princeton graduate whom the narrator, Jacob Barnes, both befriends and dislikes.

Jake Barnes is a 34-year-old American journalist from Kansas City. He lives in Paris, spends his time with a group of American expatriate friends, and works as a foreign correspondent for an American newspaper. A veteran of World War I, he has sustained a wound that clearly makes sexual intercourse impossible. Years later, Hemingway explained the genesis of Jake's injury in a letter, writing that he himself had contracted an infection of the scrotum after he was wounded in Italy and that as a result he met and sympathized with other young men who had genital injuries, including one man who had lost a penis but still had his testicles (*SL* 745). That soldier's injury evidently inspired Jake's predicament. Because of the nature of Jake's injury (which is never spelled out in the text of the novel), he still experiences sexual desires but has no way to achieve sexual fulfillment.

He is hopelessly in love with Lady Brett Ashley, an Englishwoman who is tormented by Jake's inability to consummate his desire for her. She is engaged to Mike Campbell, an American from a wealthy family. In her first appearance in the novel, she arrives at a dance club with a group of men who are stereotypically gay in their appearance and behavior. They infuriate Jake, but as Brett points out, in their company her excessive drinking is less risky than it would be in a heterosexual group. But she leaves her friends, and Jake leaves his date, a prostitute named Georgette. Afterwards, in a shared taxi ride, Brett talks to Jake about how miserable their unsatisfactory relationship makes her. She later turns up at his apartment, drunk, to commiserate about their inability to have a normal sexual relationship.

Robert Cohn, who was attracted to Brett when he first saw her at the dance club, quizzes Jake about her background and is apparently interested in her. Shortly afterwards Jake witnesses a painful scene in which Robert's mistress, Frances Clyne, bitterly complains that Robert, who had talked of marrying her, is now sending her away. Uncomfortable with how she treats Cohn, Jake goes home, where Brett soon arrives with a new friend, the wealthy Count Mippipopolous. After sending the count out for champagne, Brett tells Jake that she could not live happily with him because she could never be faithful, and that she will leave for San Sebastian, a Spanish seaside resort city, the next day. Book I ends with her farewell to Jake later that evening.

Book II opens with Jake looking forward to his friend Bill Gorton's arrival and their upcoming trip to Spain to fish and attend the fiesta at Pamplona. Robert Cohn, Brett, and her fiancé also make plans to come, although Brett confesses to Jake that she spent her time in San Sebastian having a fling with

Cohn and is worried that Cohn is coming on the trip along with her and her fiancé.

Jake, Bill, and Cohn travel to Pamplona together and await the arrival of Brett and Mike. Both Bill and Jake are repulsed when Cohn privately confesses to each of them his affair with Brett, and Jake, angry and jealous, begins to hate Cohn. Bill and Jake take a bus to the Burguete, befriend an Englishman named Wilson-Harris, and catch plenty of trout in the Irati River. After making a careless joke that he fears may have hurt Jake's feelings, Bill tells Jake how fond he is of him—and immediately deflects Jake's response by joking about homosexuality. After their idyllic fishing trip, Jake and Bill return to Pamplona, where Jake's friend, the hotelkeeper Juanito Montoya, greets him with the news of his friends' arrival. Montoya values aficionados—those who, like himself and Jake, have a passion (*aficion*, in Spanish) for the *corrida*, or bullfight. He and Jake have been friends for several years when Jake brings his Paris crowd to the hotel for the festival.

After the group go to see the bulls being unloaded in preparation for the bullfights, Mike Campbell, in a moment of drunken fury, aggressively interrogates Robert Cohn about why he persists in hanging around and staring at Brett when he's not wanted. After the ugly scene, the group reconciles to have dinner together, but the damage has been done. Uncomfortable with his friends' behavior, Jake thinks sarcastically to himself, "It seemed they were all such nice people" (146).

Two days later, the week-long fiesta of San Fermin begins. Although the fiesta is traditionally a religious festival, it is celebrated with not only a special Mass, but also bullfights, dancing, and drunken revelry. Jake's circle of friends attends the bullfights, and even the skeptical Robert is impressed by the spectacle of the event. But Brett is more impressed by the attractiveness of Pedro Romero, the 19-year-old matador.

The novel's moral center lies in Jake's decision to introduce Pedro Romero to Brett. In an earlier scene in which Montoya asks Jake for advice, it becomes clear that the hotelkeeper is trying to protect Romero from corrupting influences. Once Montoya sees that Jake has introduced the young bullfighter to Brett, Mike, and his other friends, all of whom drink excessively and behave badly, he abruptly leaves the room without even acknowledging Jake, clearly signaling his anger and disappointment. When Montoya sees Jake and Brett together later, he behaves with similar coldness, and he sends a maid with their bill rather than come near Jake himself.

Brett later asks Jake to stay with her because she has fallen in love with the bullfighter and is trembling with emotion. To his own later self-disgust, Jake becomes a procurer, finding Romero again, drawing him to the cafe table he shares with Brett, and leaving the two alone together. Robert Cohn is accurate in labeling Jake a "pimp" (190), and Jake pays for his sin by losing the friendship of Montoya, whose trust he has betrayed.

After Jake's moral failure, the relationships within the group deteriorate rapidly. Devastated by the casual way Brett treats him after their brief affair, Cohn picks fights with first Jake and then Pedro Romero. Afterward, crying, Cohn apologizes to Jake, Romero, and Brett and rents a car to leave Pamplona. Brett, Jake, and Bill witness Romero's spectacular performance in the ring despite the severe beating he sustained at Cohn's hands, and afterward a drunken Jake learns that Brett ran off with Romero. The fiesta ends, and the rest of Jake's friends return to France. Jake travels alone to San Sebastian, where Brett and Cohn spent a week together, so that he can read and swim in peace after the chaos of the fiesta. While there, he receives telegrams from Brett forwarded from Paris and Pamplona and responds, predictably, by running to Madrid to rescue her. Trembling and weeping, she insists that she will not corrupt Pedro Romero, that he is much better off without her, and that she will go back to Mike.

The novel's ending is ironic. Jake has realized that while it might be pleasant to imagine that he and Brett might have had a happy life together if it were not for his wound, he now knows better. The image of the policeman's raised baton reminds him of his own sexual incapacity, and he has come to realize that even if he were somehow capable of satisfying Brett sexually, she is no longer capable of sustaining a healthy relationship. Thus when she says, "Oh, Jake . . . we could have had such a damned good time together," he responds, "Yes. . . . Isn't it pretty to think so?" (247). "Pretty" is a word we associate with traditional femininity; Jake's ironic use of it here indicates his blunt rejection of coy sentimentality.

CHARACTER DEVELOPMENT

Jake, a newspaper journalist, describes events with a reporter's detachment and passivity. He values his work and tries to do it well. Nevertheless, it's possible to see Jake as an unreliable narrator who distorts what he sees. For example, Cohn seems less objectionable than Jake insists he is, and Brett seems less attractive than Jake finds her throughout most of the novel. Jake acknowledges his own bias, telling the reader, "Somehow I feel I have not shown Robert Cohn clearly" (45). As scholar Frederic Svoboda points out, "The potential unreliability is brought to the attention of the reader, but it is not resolved" (31).

Jake has sometimes been described as stoic, yet in the course of the novel he repeatedly breaks down in moments of understandable misery and self-pity. He is struggling to reconcile himself to his fate and has modest expectations in life. "I did not care what it was all about," he tells himself. "All I wanted to know was how to live in it. Maybe if you found out how to live in it you learned from that what it was all about" (148). When Bill asks him about Brett, Jake confesses that he has been in love with her off and on for years but claims unconvincingly to be over her.

Lady Brett Ashley, a 34-year-old alcoholic, was a V.A.D. in Jake's hospital during the war. V.A.D. refers to Voluntary Aid Detachment, volunteer nurses who helped care for wounded British soldiers in World War I. After marrying twice without love, according to Jake, she is divorcing her second husband and is engaged to Mike Campbell, an American from a wealthy family. She is beautiful and unconventional and has an attractively boyish haircut.

Presumably because she is not sexually or emotionally faithful to Mike despite their engagement, many literary scholars have pegged Brett as being exactly the kind of woman she tried to avoid becoming. When Jake tells her she likes to add men up, she ultimately concedes that he has a point, and she herself admits that if they tried to live together, she would betray him with other men. She is often described in the literary criticism as sexually promiscuous, or even a nymphomaniac, which seems extreme given that in the course of the story she has sexual relationships with, at most, three men—her fiancée, Mike Campbell; Robert Cohn; and Pedro Romero. Viewed more sympathetically, she can be seen as a self-destructive woman, traumatized by the ugly and unromantic loss of her first love to dysentery in the war: "Brett hurts no one in the novel as severely as she hurts herself. Her nymphomania, her alcoholism, her constant fits of depression, and her obsession with bathing are all symptoms of an individual engaged in a consistent pattern of self-abuse" (Whitlow 56).

The introduction that Fitzgerald prompted Hemingway to cut from the novel established that Brett's second husband had repeatedly threatened her with violence (Hemingway, "Unpublished" 80); in the published novel, Mike tells Jake that her ex-husband Lord Ashley came back from his naval service so traumatized that he refused to sleep in a bed and made her join him on the floor. He threatened to kill her and slept with a loaded gun. Still recovering from that nightmarish marriage, Brett is further damaged by her hopeless desire for Jake. When Count Mippipopolous insists that, despite her drinking, she remembers everything that happens, she cannot understand why anyone would want to.

Brett can be profoundly careless of the feelings of others. She scatters cigarette ashes on Jake's rugs, and when Romero gives her a bull's severed ear after a successful bullfight, she leaves the gift behind, stuffed in a hotel drawer. Cohn calls her a sadist when she is unmoved by the plight of the horses gored in the bullring. Certainly she uses Jake heartlessly at times, expecting him to introduce her to a man she desires, put up with her affairs, remain steadfast in his devotion to her, and faithfully run to her rescue on short notice when she finds herself at loose ends in another country. Yet she is also deeply unhappy, emotionally fragile, and ultimately generous in her treatment of the naïve young matador, if not with respect to Mike Campbell and Robert Cohn.

Cohn is from a wealthy and well-established Jewish family in New York. Formerly a middleweight boxing champion at Princeton, Cohn had learned to box to defend himself against the anti-Semitism he faced there. Cohn is divorced from his wife of five years after they have had three children together. He spent the next three years with Frances Clyne, a woman whom Jake sees as unpleasantly grasping and domineering. After using his wealth to support an arts magazine, Cohn eventually became its editor, and he enjoyed the work so thoroughly that he later began writing fiction, publishing his first novel to bad reviews. At age 34, inspired by the romantic fantasy and exoticism of W.H. Hudson's 1885 novel *The Purple Land*, he longs to go to South America and is ready to fall in love immediately with Brett. Emotional, romantic, and idealistic to the point of naiveté, Cohn is drifting aimlessly, hoping to stumble across a way to make his life meaningful.

Part of Jake's resentment of Cohn perhaps stems from how alike they are. Both men are expatriates, sportsmen, and writers. Both are hopelessly in love with Brett, but because of Jake's war wound, only Cohn is able to make love to her. Jake's hatred of Cohn might indicate his sexual and romantic jealousy. It could also reflect his despair that even if he were whole, he, like Cohn, might not be able to win the elusive Brett.

The novel's final important character is Pedro Romero, the 19-year-old bullfighter, who enters the story late. Romero is a flat rather than round character, for he does not change during the course of the novel. Born in Ronda, Romero has three years of experience fighting bulls. Jake calls him a "boy," perhaps to indicate his moral purity and innocence, and emphasizes his beauty, grace, and dignity. As Jake shows Brett by calling her attention to Romero's technique, the young matador fights the bulls with great skill and has no need to resort to trickery to impress his audience. Yet he is neither conceited nor boastful about his abilities. He is so idealized that even his name invokes honor; as Hemingway himself notes in *Death in the Afternoon*, "According to historians Pedro Romero, who was a matador in Spain at the time of the American revolution, killed five thousand six hundred bulls recibiendo" (239)—that is, in "the most difficult, dangerous, and emotional way to kill bulls" (442). Romero displays impressive courage in the ring, even after his harsh beating at the hands of Cohn.

Extraordinarily good-looking, the serious young man attracts Brett's attention immediately. He seems sexually naïve and has very traditional notions about women. Ashamed of Brett's unconventional appearance, he tries unsuccessfully to persuade her to let her hair grow long and wants to marry her in the belief that then she would necessarily remain true to him.

But Brett, as she herself acknowledges, could not remain true to anyone. Her fiancé, Mike Campbell, is aware of Brett's affairs and seems content to let her have lovers; as Brett explains, they understand each other. He is infuriated by Cohn, however, and publicly berates him in an effort to drive him away from Brett. Mike's manners deteriorate rapidly when he drinks.

Mike is from a wealthy family in Scotland and like Jake, he served in the war. He expects to inherit a fortune eventually, but at the time the events of the story take place, he is, as Brett puts it, "an undischarged bankrupt" (79). In other words, he had incurred more bills than he could pay and went bankrupt, leaving his many creditors with no payment. Mike believes that Brett enjoys taking care of people and that she was attracted to him because he needed looking after. When Brett passes out in the train to Pamplona, Mike telegraphs Jake, saying he tries to take care of Brett, but she makes the task challenging.

Count Mippipopolous, one of the many men in the novel who are attracted to Brett, unsuccessfully offers Brett $10,000 to go away with him to an expensive resort like Biarritz, Cannes, or Monte Carlo. He owns a chain of American candy stores and knows everyone in Paris. The count relishes the trappings of wealth—bouquets of roses, the best champagne, fine cigars, aged brandy, a houseful of valuable antiquities—and claims that because he has participated in seven wars and four revolutions he now enjoys life more completely. A benevolent figure, he tries discreetly to discourage Brett from drinking and rejects joking as ultimately cruel.

Frances Clyne, Robert Cohn's mistress for the past three years, is one of the sadder characters in the novel. After agreeing not to take alimony from her husband so that their divorce would go through quickly, she discovers that Cohn no longer wants to marry her. Because her mother invested money in worthless French war bonds, Frances cannot turn to her for financial support, and Robert plans to send her off to England with the equivalent in British pounds of about $500. When she protests, he raises the amount to about $1,000. Embittered, she complains to Jake about the humiliation of being compelled to visit friends who don't really welcome her visit. Nobody wants to publish what she writes. She is particularly upset that because she is slowly losing her looks, she may not be able to find someone else if Cohn leaves her and, because of her age, she might never have children. She abuses Cohn and creates a terrible scene that sickens Jake, but Hemingway himself, in giving her so much space, seems more sympathetic to her plight.

In contrast to the ugly scenes caused by Cohn's discarded mistress, Jake's friend Bill Gorton, who abhors scenes, is perpetually both cheerful and drunk. He has published a highly successful book and seems determined to enjoy his stay in Europe. Like Hemingway, he is a conventional midwesterner (he's from Chicago) and is extremely uncomfortable with Mike's financial irresponsibility. He values his friendship with Jake and tries to protect Jake's feelings. Their fishing trip together is one of the most joyous times in a story that is otherwise often bleak.

One particularly disturbing aspect of *The Sun Also Rises* is the characters' excessive reliance on alcohol to enhance their enjoyment of life and mute their unhappiness. Mike is rarely sober, Robert Cohn and Bill Gorton both show the ill effects of their drinking, and Brett frequently turns up drunk at a time when there was a serious social stigma attached to women who drank excessively in public. The American novelist John Dos Passos, in reviewing *The Sun Also Rises* for *The New Masses*, once disparaged the novel as "a cock and bull story about a lot of summer tourists getting drunk and making fools of themselves at a picturesque Iberian folk festival." Their incessant alcohol abuse perhaps reflects the scope of their discontent.

Hemingway's own pleasure in drinking was legendary, although like many alcoholics, he had developed such a high tolerance for alcohol that he rarely showed its effects. However, alcohol is probably partly responsible for his participation in several fistfights and his involvement in many accidents, including pulling a skylight down on his head, breaking his arm so badly in a serious car accident that he had to spend seven weeks in the hospital, shooting himself in both legs, and suffering multiple concussions. His drinking also contributed to his poor health later in life, and he repeatedly disregarded doctors' warnings that he needed to stop or at least cut back

Even more troubling is the bigotry of Hemingway's characters. While Bill Gorton repeatedly refers to a black prizefighter as a "nigger" (71), anti-Semitic slurs are more common in the novel than racist ones. Anti-Semitic expressions were more likely to be condoned by non-Jews before World War II, when the Holocaust demonstrated the extent to which anti-Semites could carry their hatred. Perhaps the most disturbing examples of such prejudice in *The Sun Also Rises* are Jake's casually anti-Semitic remarks, for example, that boxing improved the shape of Cohn's nose and that Cohn is stubborn because he's a Jew. Bill Gorton doesn't like the way Cohn gets "superior and Jewish" (96) and asks Jake, "Haven't you got some more Jewish friends you can bring along?" (101). Part of Jake's own intense hatred of Cohn seems to be inspired by Cohn's religious background. It's bad enough, in Jake's view, that Brett sleeps with other men, but it's even more galling when the man she sleeps with is a Jew, who presumably, in Jake's worldview, ought to be Jake's inferior.

Scribner's deleted the references to Jews in one postwar edition of the novel but eventually restored them to later editions. It's not clear whether Hemingway assumed readers would share Jake's prejudice or perceive it as a character flaw. In his private letters Hemingway himself sometimes expressed prejudice, including, for example, his remark that he did not want to have children with his third wife, Martha Gellhorn, because she was Jewish (*Final* 208). He once called his friends "kikes" in an explosion of anger (Reynolds, *Paris* 242). Screenwriter Peter Viertel recalls Hemingway making anti-Semitic remarks, too (Reynolds, *Final* 289)—but he also remembers Ernest saying that it was the characters of *The Sun Also Rises* who were anti-Semitic, not its author (Viertel 255).

It is also difficult to determine whether Hemingway shared the equally disturbing homophobia expressed by his male characters. For example, Bill tells Jake he loves him but immediately admits that he could not have said so in New York without being branded "a faggot" (116). When Brett arrives at the dancing club with a group of gay men, Jake is furious, although he acknowledges that he should be tolerant. Part of his anger perhaps stems from a combination of envy—they have what he lacks—and what he sees as the men's misuse of their sexuality—they don't use it the way he thinks they should.

THEMES

Perhaps the most important theme of *The Sun Also Rises* involves the damage done to Hemingway's generation by the institutionalized violence of World War I. Jake, who is the most obviously injured character in the novel, tells Georgette, "I got hurt in the war" (17) and later thinks to himself, "Well, it was a rotten way to be wounded and flying on a joke front like the Italian" (31). He tells Brett that "what happened to me is supposed to be funny" (26), but of course his injury is anything but funny to Jake, who is not the only one who got hurt in the war. Brett has no tangible injury but is psychically destroyed by her fiancé's death. When Count Mippipopolous shows them the marks left on his back by arrow wounds he sustained as a young man in Abyssinia, Brett turns to Jake and says, "I told you he was one of us" (60)—"us" presumably being those scarred by war. As Georgette tells Jake, "Everybody's sick. I'm sick, too" (16). She probably uses the words literally to mean that she has a venereal disease (she is, after all, a prostitute), but her words suggest that Hemingway sees much of his generation as "sick."

In part, that sickness represents a second theme of Hemingway's novel, the loss of faith in traditional values, especially religious values. Jake is a Roman Catholic, but none of his friends seems to share his beliefs. In fact, they seem to find it difficult to take his faith seriously. When Bill asks him a little disbelievingly if he is really a Catholic, Jake responds with "technically" (124). In Pamplona Jake visits the cathedral to pray, but his mind wanders so much that he thinks of himself as a "rotten Catholic" (97). "You've a hell of a biblical name, Jake," Brett tells him, referring to his given name of Jacob (22), and he later tells her he's "pretty religious" (209). Jake is preoccupied with morality and ashamed of his own vengeful feelings toward Cohn: "That must be morality; things that made you disgusted afterward. No, that must be immorality" (149).

The novel's title is taken from the Bible, specifically *Ecclesiastes* (1: 4–7), which is also the book's second epigraph:

One generation passeth away, and another generation cometh, but the earth abideth forever... The sun also ariseth, and the sun goeth down, and hasteth to the place where he arose ... The wind goeth toward the south, and turneth about unto the north; it whirleth about continually, and the wind returneth again according to his circuits ... All the rivers run into the sea; yet the sea is not full; unto the place from whence the rivers come, thither they return again.

In a letter to his editor, Hemingway explained that he meant for *The Sun Also Rises* to be tragedy and that the earth was the story's hero (*SL* 229; Bruccoli, *Only Thing* 51). What the passage seems to indicate is that the troubles of Hemingway's beleaguered generation are necessarily temporary. While many contemporary readers admired the characters and wanted to emulate their behavior, Hemingway's later comments about the novel suggest that he saw the characters as sadly damaged people rather than role models.

In pointed contrast to Jake's Catholicism, Brett is repeatedly linked to earlier, pagan faiths. For example, Cohn compares Brett to Circe, the enchantress in Homer's *Odyssey* who transforms Odysseus' men into swine. During the festival, the villagers form a circle and dance around her, as if she were a goddess of Mediterranean myth, shortly after she has her fortune told by the gypsies. She wants to accompany Jake to confession, but he dissuades her, telling her that confession is private, and "besides, it would be in a language she did not know" (151). Although Brett does not know Spanish, Jake seems to be saying that the "language" of Christianity is also foreign to her. During the festival she is prevented from entering a church because she lacks a hat and abruptly departs from a church because of nerves, acknowledging, "I'm damned bad for a religious atmosphere" (208). Spiritually lost, she calls prayer "rot," says that God never worked very well for her, and tells Jake that choosing not to hurt someone else is "sort of what we have instead of God" (245).

An important theme of the novel concerns the replacement of religious faith with earthly materialism. Jake insists that some people still have faith, yet he himself can be disturbingly preoccupied with material values: "Enjoying living was learning to get your money's worth and knowing when you had it" (148). Gertrude Stein once told Hemingway he was "ninety percent Rotarian," referring to the Rotary Clubs organized in many American communities by locally prominent businessmen (270). Like the stereotypical Rotarian to which Stein refers, Jake reduces the world around him to the barest financial transactions: "The bill always came. That was one of the swell things you could count on" (148). Jake's friend Bill echoes this cynical view of the world, although in a drunkenly nonsensical way, as they pass a taxidermist's shop in Paris: "Simple exchange of values. You give them money. They give you a stuffed dog" (72). Raised with a Protestant work ethic, both Jake and Bill are disgusted by the financial irresponsibility of Mike and Brett because to them it represents immorality.

LITERARY DEVICES

Hemingway draws on the medieval courtly love tradition in *The Sun Also Rises*. Most extensively developed in the court of Eleanor of Aquitane in the twelfth century, the courtly love tradition established a stylized code for romantic relations between aristocratic men and women in Western Europe from the eleventh to the fourteenth century. Within this tradition, a knight was expected to fall passionately in love with a lady who belonged to another man (typically through marriage) and to commit himself to her service, selflessly sacrificing his own needs in order to please her. The knight regarded himself as a mere servant to his beloved and willingly endured any trial to secure her favor.

Jake Barnes is a modern-day example of the knight who is passionately in love with a beautiful woman who is promised to another. He devotes himself to the service of his lady, who sadly fails to meet the medieval standards of chastity and religious faith and does not merit his devotion, as he belatedly comes to realize: "Lady Ashley's title betokens no moral superiority, as in the medieval tradition, but only a socioeconomic superiority, and her promiscuity undermines the courtly quality of her position at the center of a group of enamored men" (183). Hemingway, whose list of favorite authors included Italian poet Dante, was fascinated with medievalism. For example, he titled a novel he never finished *A New Slain Knight* and corresponded with Fitzgerald about writing a historical novel set in the Middle Ages. As literary critic Kim Moreland suggests with respect to Hemingway's use of medieval traditions in *The Sun Also Rises*, "In revealing the ineffectuality of knightly behavior in the modern world, Hemingway is exhibiting a nostalgia for the days when the courtly love tradition operated successfully as a system of values, when courtly ladies rewarded the adventures of worthy knights and thereby inspired them, enabling them to realize their ideal masculine identities" (190).

HISTORICAL AND SOCIAL CONTEXT

The novel's first epigraph is a quote from Gertrude Stein, and in *A Moveable Feast* Hemingway recalls at length the first time he heard it (23–31). He considered using "The Lost Generation" as the title for the novel (Baker, *Life* 155). Even today Hemingway and Fitzgerald and their friends are sometimes referred to as the Lost Generation. The term suggests that the generation that came of age during World War I (1914–1918) lost its way, perhaps because so many had literally been lost during the exceptionally bloody battles of the war. Many members of Hemingway's generation felt betrayed, lured into a bloody and pointless war by the sentimental nationalism of a callous older generation more concerned with outdated ideals and crass profit than with their own sons' lives. The Lost Generation's primary response to the war was a profound disillusionment and a loss of faith in their parents' values, which had led inevitably to the war's devastation.

The Sun Also Rises accurately reflects this disillusionment and sense of betrayal. The work is a roman á clef—a novel whose plot is based on real events and whose characters are thinly disguised versions of real people. Many of the characters are based on the friends Ernest and Hadley Hemingway made in Paris during the 1920s, and many of the events resemble those of the summer of 1925, when Hemingway went to the festival of San Fermin in Pamplona for the third time (Baker, *Life* 147). Robert Cohn, for example, is based on the Jewish-American novelist Harold Loeb, and Lady Brett Ashley closely resembles Lady Duff Twysden, a 32-year-old twice-divorced Englishwoman to whom Hemingway was attracted. Mike Campbell is based on her fiancé, Pat Guthrie, and Bill Gorton seems to be an amalgamation of Hemingway's friends Donald Ogden Stewart and Bill Smith. Pedro Romero was based on a young bullfighter named Cayetano Ordonez. In the early manuscripts of the novel, Brett is referred to as "Duff" and Jake is referred to as "Hem."

Hemingway plays with traditional gender roles in *The Sun Also Rises*. While Brett has a boyish haircut, apparently enjoys casual sex, and calls men "chaps" as if she were one of the boys, Jake is stereotypically "feminine" in his passive and long-suffering acceptance of her tendency to stray sexually. In another reversal of conventional male and female attitudes, Cohn attaches great romantic meaning to what Brett sees as a brief, inconsequential fling.

With the notable exceptions of Pedro Romero, and perhaps Bill Gorton, none of the men in the novel seems to fit the traditional male role. An extended analogy between the bulls of the *corrida* and the men of the novel highlights the disparity between these characters and social expectations. Jake explains that steers, or neutered bulls, travel with the bulls to calm them down and keep them from fighting, and it's possible that Hemingway intended readers to compare the conciliatory Jake, who is in effect neutered by his war wound, to the unfortunate steers, who are all too often injured because of their efforts to make friends with the bulls. After Jake's explanation, Mike rather cruelly calls Cohn a "steer" (141) because Cohn, who seems unable to respond gracefully to

Brett's rejection, hangs around hopelessly. Mike himself cannot fulfill the role of breadwinner and is usually too incapacitated by alcoholism to do much of anything other than joke and make ugly scenes, and Jake's wound irreparably damages his sense of his own masculinity. As Mike exclaims, "the bulls have no balls!" (176).

The bullfight invokes many of the elements traditionally associated with Hemingway's best work: the test of courage, "grace under pressure," machismo, the ability to withstand pain, and loss and death. The Spanish, or Mediterranean, tradition of the bullfight evidently evolved from an ancient ritual in which the bull was both worshipped as a god and sacrificed. Animal rights activists opposed the practice even in the 1920s, when Hemingway first became acquainted with it, because of the cruelty involved for both the bull and the horses, which were often fatally gored as their riders (or *picadors*) approached the bull to stab him with their pics and weaken him in preparation for his final confrontation with the matador. In his nonfiction Hemingway vigorously defended bullfighting but insisted that it be considered a ritual and a tragedy rather than a sport, since after all the bull has no chance and is invariably killed. The attraction of the bullfight lies purely in *how* the animal is killed. Ideally the matador (a Spanish word for "killer") must courageously risk death by coming as close as possible to the deadly horns of the bull in order to kill the animal. The matador, then, in Hemingway's view, is a performance artist who exorcises the audience's fear of mortality by first inviting death and then triumphing over it as he becomes a killer before the audience's eyes.

While Spain is associated with both the positive values of the bullfight and the fishing trip and the negative value assigned to Jake's moral lapse, Paris is linked with what Hemingway perceived as decadence—homosexuality, financial irresponsibility, and sexual carelessness, typified by Brett's behavior and Cohn's treatment of Frances. Paris had a large expatriate community in the 1920s. The city's beauty and its growing importance as a center of literary and visual arts attracted many would-be artists. Because of rampant postwar inflation, the exchange rate made it cheaper for Americans to live in Paris than in the United States. The rising American stock market in the decade before the Great Depression also made many Americans wealthy, making overseas travel affordable. Finally, France was also an attractive refuge at that time for Americans who enjoyed drinking. In America in 1920, the ratification of the 18th Amendment to the Constitution made it illegal to manufacture, sell, or transport alcoholic beverages throughout the United States. Nine months later, that same year, Congress passed the Volstead Act, better known as Prohibition, which provided for the enforcement of the amendment. France and the other countries of Europe had no such laws.

ALTERNATE READING: SOURCE STUDY

A source study is an examination of materials that the author of a work drew on in constructing that work. Although an author's intentions in creating a work are ultimately unknowable, a source study can nevertheless offer insights that help readers better understand the work. Comparing a novel's sources to the finished novel can also enhance readers' understanding of the author's artistry. One possible source for *The Sun Also Rises*—in addition to Hemingway's own experiences with his expatriate friends—is the popular 1924 novel *The Green Hat*, by the Armenian-American writer Michael Arlen.

The melodramatic plot of *The Green Hat* bears little resemblance to that of *The Sun Also Rises*. As the novel opens, the twice-widowed 29-year-old Iris Storm tries to see her alcoholic twin brother, Gerald March, and after she discovers him in a drunken stupor, sleeps with the unnamed narrator who lives in the apartment below Gerald's. Because her first husband committed suicide on their honeymoon, ostensibly "for purity" (96), society has presumed that Iris was a loose woman even at 19. The next time she tries to see her brother, the narrator discovers that Gerald, accused of molesting a woman in Hyde Park, has blown his brains out. However, the narrator tells Iris that Gerald is drunk again. He learns later that as she was driving away, she encountered Napier Harpenden, her first and only true love, and began an affair despite his recent marriage.

After asking about her in Paris several months later, the narrator unexpectedly discovers that Iris is near death in a French nursing home. He gradually discovers that she has septic poisoning after losing Napier's baby. A quick visit from Napier gives Iris hope, and after her recovery, she and Napier resume their affair. When her friends try to persuade her she is destroying a marriage, she refuses to listen and plans to run away with Napier to Rio. She finally confronts Sir Maurice Harpenden, Napier's father, who had compelled him to sacrifice their love in exchange for his future career in the foreign service. When Napier tells his father that Iris's first husband killed himself in remorse because he had exposed his wife to syphilis (then a treatable but incurable sexually transmitted disease), Iris lies to Napier, telling him his wife, Venice, is pregnant, and flees to kill herself by driving her expensive car into the tree under which she and Napier had played as children.

What links the two novels is not their plots, but the similarity between Brett and Iris. Many early reviewers of *The Sun Also Rises*—including Allen Tate of the *Nation*, Edwin Muir of *Nation and Athenaeum*, Burton Rascoe of the *New York Sun*, Schuyler Ashley of the *Kansas City Star*, and the anonymous reviewers for *Time* and the *Chicago Daily Tribune*—detected a resemblance between Lady Brett Ashley and the heroine of *The Green Hat*. Like Brett, Iris anticipated fashion: "Iris Storm was the first Englishwoman I ever saw with 'shingled' hair.

This was in 1922" (47). Both women are deemed too sexually active by the society in which they live. The narrator repeatedly calls Iris a "shameless, shameful lady" (68). Like Brett, who says that the "awful" Mike is the right sort of fellow for her, Iris despises herself: "I am the meanest of all, she who destroys her body because she must, she who hates the thing she is, she who loathes the thing she does" (51). Iris finds her own sexual behavior intolerable (88) and, like the careless Brett, seems to care little about her own welfare, as one of her friends recognizes: "She hasn't, you see, a trace of the self-preservative instinct" (94).

Just as Brett ascribes her behavior to her loss of her fiancé in the war, Iris blames her behavior on Sir Maurice for compelling Napier to give her up. Like Brett, who is linked to pre-Christian faiths and the bewitching Circe of Greek mythology, Iris describes herself as having "a pagan body" (51) and is frequently described as if she were a sorceress: " . . . if [Napier] went to sit with Iris even once more he might fall right down into the pit of dark enchantment" (202). Distinctly *unlike* Brett Ashley, however, Iris, as the daughter and sister of alcoholic men, disapproves of drinking and believes in God.

Like *The Sun Also Rises*, *The Green Hat* is laced with expressions of anti-Semitism, although here they seem more clearly consistent with the novelist's own views (34, 184, 287, etc.). The narrator seems just as upset as Jake Barnes to learn that his lady love could have slept with a Jew (87). Important scenes of *The Green Hat* take place in dance clubs, one of which even has a black drummer (163) like the one glimpsed momentarily in Hemingway's novel. In a clear anticipation of Hemingway's references to "steers," Arlen writes that a group of young men at the entrance to the Loyalty Club "looked furtively at Iris in the way that decent men will at a woman who is said to have had lovers, like cows at a bull" (125).

As that analogy suggests, the confusion of gender roles plays an important role in *The Green Hat*, just as it does in Hemingway's novel. "Never dream of a world in which men are men and women are women. You will go mad . . .," Iris warns the narrator (40). "You always choose the man's part," the narrator tells Iris (266), who is repeatedly described as boyish (46–47). He later writes, with grudging admiration, "She must meet men on their own ground always, always, and she must keep herself on their own ground without showing the effort she made" (285). A much more revolutionary character in some ways than Brett is, Iris clearly rejects patriarchy. The climax of the novel is her confrontation with Napier's domineering father, whom she shrewdly tells, "You never dream of asking a woman 'what sort of woman are you?' so long as she keeps to the laws made by men. But the first time you see a woman being a woman, you are surprised" (284). She also rejects patriarchal divisions and hierarchies, telling Hilary Townshend that she never identified with any particular social class and responding to Sir Maurice's nationalism and ambition by retorting, "To

me, a world which thinks of itself in terms of puny, squalid, bickering little na-
tions and not as one glorious field for the crusade of mankind is a world in
which to succeed is the highest indignity which can befall a good man" (287).
The narrator accurately describes her as "not caring the tremor of an eyelash for
the laws of her fathers" (227).

The novel includes occasional blanket pronouncements on the postwar
generation much like the Gertrude Stein quotation Hemingway chose as an
epigraph for his novel. The older Hilary Townshend calls the younger generation "a mess" (87), although the narrator responds, with some hostility, "All
generations are a mess" (87).

So why do we still read Hemingway's novel in the twenty-first century, but
not Arlen's? In part the answer has to do with style. Arlen wrote overwrought
prose filled with florid Victorian clichés: "Romance did not steal through the
fleshy portals of the heart, did not shiver at a Judas kiss, did not coil white trembling limbs into the puerile lusts of the mind" (46). He also tended to contort
standard English syntax, creating sentences like "thoughtful they both were"
(24). As the reviewer for the *Kansas City Star* noted: "Ernest Hemingway seems
here to have borrowed the Green Hat of Michael Arlen, knocked it out of
shape, kicked it across the room once or twice, and then gone off to a bullfight
wearing the remains pulled pugnaciously down over one eye. Personally, I prefer Green Hats worn that way; rowdiness is more palatable when it does not simultaneously affect romanticism and sentimentality" (Ashley 8). Arlen's lurid
sensationalism seems hopelessly dated compared to the spare simplicity of
Hemingway's prose.

While Iris is an antiheroine in *The Green Hat*—an unconventional figure
who rejects traditional values until she finally validates them with her conve-
niently timed suicide—no one would consider Brett the heroine of *The Sun
Also Rises*. Arlen genuinely believes that, if her first love had not been thwarted
by Sir Maurice, his heroine would have lived a conventional and happy life,
whereas Hemingway, through Jake's bitterly ironic line at the end of the novel,
finally rejects such easy sentimentality in favor of a hard-edged realism.

A Farewell to Arms
(1929)

"Nineteen twenty-nine represented, in the United States at least, the high-water mark of postwar revulsion," comments Hemingway biographer Kenneth Lynn (385). So *A Farewell to Arms*, with its soldier who rejects the war and opts instead to make a separate peace, found a ready audience. The novel was first published in serial form in six parts in *Scribner's Magazine* during the summer and fall of 1929. Despite Hemingway's strenuous objections, *Scribner's* deleted some of Hemingway's profanity, almost all of which was eventually restored to the published book. The June issue of the magazine was quickly banned in Boston because of moral objections to the story's illicit sexual relationship (Reynolds, *1930s* 11).

The book was published September 27, 1929, and the first printing of 30,000 copies had sold out by October 15 (Reynolds, *1930s* 27). By February, the book had sold more than 80,000 copies (Reynolds, *1930s* 37). A stage play based on the novel opened on Broadway in 1930, and that year Paramount Pictures bought the film rights for $80,000 (Reynolds, *1930s* 52). The book was eventually made into two movies, a 1932 film starring Gary Cooper and Helen Hayes, and a 1957 film starring Rock Hudson and Jennifer Jones. Hemingway hated the 1932 film, which altered the ending of his novel (Baker, *Life* 235).

Hemingway took the novel's title from a sixteenth-century poem by George Peele. He considered 33 possible titles for the novel, nearly half of them from *The Oxford Book of English Verse*, the same poetry anthology in which he found

Peele's poem. A list of some of the titles he considered is included as an appendix to Michael Reynolds' book, *Hemingway's First War: The Making of* A Farewell to Arms (295–97).

PLOT DEVELOPMENT

The novel's five-book structure, although apparently an afterthought, resembles the five-act structure of Shakespearean drama; indeed Hemingway himself once called the play his *Romeo and Juliet*. The novel's introduction is justifiably famous as one of the most beautifully written opening passages in literature.

A Farewell to Arms, a retrospective narrative about a relationship between an American ambulance driver for the Italian army and a British volunteer nurse, began as "A Very Short Story," one of the short stories collected in *In Our Time*. The story, a bitter recollection of the end of Hemingway's romance with Agnes von Kurowsky, was not one of his best because he was not in control of its angry tone. Hemingway loosely based the novel's major events—the wounding of its protagonist, Frederic Henry, and Frederic's relationship with Catherine Barkley—on Hemingway's own wounding and his abortive romance with Agnes. In the earliest existing draft of the novel's opening pages, the central character is named Emmett Hancock—a name with the same initials as his own. But Hemingway drew from many different experiences to create what is generally recognized as one of his finest novels:

He gives his war wound and his nurse to Frederic Henry; to his fictional nurse, he gives his second wife's pregnancy. From his first marriage with Hadley Richardson, he takes their good times at Chamby when the roads were iron-hard and they deeply in love. From maps, books, and close listening, he has made up a war he never saw, described terrain he never walked, and re-created the retreat from Caporetto so accurately that his Italian readers will later say he was present at that national embarrassment. (Reynolds, *1930s* 2)

In Book I Hemingway introduces all the major characters: Frederic, the priest, Rinaldi, Helen Ferguson (Fergy), and Catherine Barkley. Frederic, an American lieutenant in the Italian army, is an ambulance driver for troops fighting the Austrians on the Italian front. His roommate and best friend is Rinaldi, an Italian physician, who treats Frederic with the good-natured bantering of an affectionate older brother.

Rinaldi introduces Frederic to Catherine Barkley, a British volunteer nurse. When Frederic later tries to kiss her, she immediately slaps him. Catherine initially gives Frederic the impression that she is a little odd because she seems to be play-acting when they first meet (30–31). Catherine herself admits that when she first met Frederic, she was "nearly crazy" (116) and later tells him, "I was a little crazy. But I wasn't crazy in any complicated manner" (154). Devastated by the loss of her fiancé of eight years, who was "blown to bits" in the Battle of the Somme, she tries to heal herself by reenacting that relationship with Frederic.

Upon his return to the front, Frederic is wounded and one of his men, Passini, is killed when a big trench mortar shell hits their dugout while Frederic and his men are eating macaroni and cheese—a particularly prosaic and unromantic way to be wounded. In writing the passage describing Frederic's wounding (one of the most memorable passages in the book), Hemingway drew on his own experience of being wounded in the leg by shrapnel July 8, 1918, while he was distributing chocolate to troops at the front. In sharing that experience with others in letters and in conversation, Hemingway more than once described an "out-of-body experience" very similar to Frederic's peculiar sensation of his soul leaving his body (Baker, *Life* 571, Josephs, "Hemingway's Out of Body Experience" 11).

As Book II of the novel begins, the wounded Frederic is taken to the American hospital in Milan to which Catherine is also soon transferred, to Frederic's great joy: "When I saw her I was in love with her" (91). Although the house doctor prudently counsels him to wait six months, Frederic insists on having Dr. Valentini operate on his leg immediately. Frederic gradually recovers, and his relationship with Catherine evolves into a more intimate one as she works night duty so that she can spend more time with him in between caring for patients. "Maybe she would pretend that I was her boy that was killed," Frederic tells himself (37). Catherine does exactly that, only this time, haunted by the memory of what she had refused her beloved fiancé, she chooses to give herself to Frederic.

Not surprisingly, she soon afterwards becomes pregnant. When she confesses her pregnancy, Frederic responds ungraciously with an ugly statement about *his* feeling of entrapment and promptly develops jaundice, a liver disease exacerbated by his heavy alcohol intake. Miss Van Campen, the superintendent of the hospital, accuses him of drinking to bring on the illness in order to avoid returning to the front, and as a result of her suspicions, he loses his leave and is recalled to the front immediately. This book of the novel ends with a brief bittersweet interlude with Catherine in a cheap hotel across from the train station before Frederic takes the train back to the front.

The highlight of Book III is the magnificent description of the Italian retreat from the German attack at Caporetto. When two of Frederic's soldiers desert during the retreat in an incident that prefigures his own fate, he shoots at them, downing one. Taking alternate routes to avoid the interminable delays caused by the masses of people participating in the retreat, Lieutenant Henry manages to get the ambulances for which he is responsible hopelessly stuck in the mud. He and his men continue on foot but are cut off by German forces; one of the men under his command, Aymo, is killed by friendly fire when Italians apparently mistake him for a German; another deserts, presumably hoping to be taken prisoner. Italian battle police apprehend Henry and other officers to question them about why they're not with their men and summarily execute those who cannot provide satisfactory answers. Aware that his American accent will make him look suspicious, Henry jumps into the river and dodges gunshots in a dramatic scene Hemingway drew from Ambrose Bierce's classic Civil War short story "The Occurrence at Owl Creek Bridge." Betrayed by his own army, a disillusioned Frederic convinces himself he no longer has any obligation to that army and jumps a train to get back to Catherine.

In Book IV Frederic manages to reach Stresa, where Catherine has been transferred. She teasingly compares Frederic to Othello, the ex-soldier who is the title character of Shakespeare's tragedy. Without any military responsibilities, Frederic is genuinely at loose ends and doesn't seem to know what to do with himself. To pass the time, he plays billiards with 94-year-old Count Greffi, a cosmopolitan former diplomat. The count asks Frederic to pray for him and (in an echo of the priest's earlier equation of faith and love) tells Frederic that love is a religious feeling.

Warned by a sympathetic barman of his impending arrest for desertion, Frederic awakens Catherine in the middle of the night, and the two escape by rowboat across the lake to Switzerland—a journey that takes them all night. Frederic is extremely cautious, anxious that he could at any moment be spotted and apprehended by the Italian authorities. After safely arriving on Swiss soil, he and Catherine are almost punch-drunk with relief and undergo the usual red tape from Swiss government officials in a bizarre scene that Frederic afterwards compares to comic opera.

In Book V Frederic describes his idyllic life with Catherine in a Swiss chalet as her delivery draws nearer. They spend their time quietly, reading, playing cards, and taking walks through the nearby villages to Montreux. Preoccupied with her pregnancy, Catherine worries that Frederic is restless and bored, but he tells her that he wants to be only with her, a claim that sounds too good to be true. Frederic tries not to think about the people he knew, especially Rinaldi and the priest, and insists he is through with the war. Once her pains begin, Catherine's labor is long and excruciatingly painful, and when it does not progress as it should, Frederic gives his permission for the doctor to perform a caesarean section. But despite the operation, the child is born dead. When Catherine hemorrhages and dies a few hours later, a stunned Frederic is left with nothing.

Hemingway once claimed to have rewritten the ending of the novel 39 times, and there are enough endings still in existence among his collected manuscripts to substantiate this claim. Several of these variant endings are reprinted in an appendix to Bernard Oldsey's *Hemingway's Hidden Craft: The Writing of* A Farewell to Arms. Hemingway did not decide on the ending the novel has today until after the manuscript, complete with a different ending, had already been typeset for *Scribner's Magazine* (Oldsey 78).

CHARACTER DEVELOPMENT

An architecture student in his twenties, Frederic Henry seems oddly immature; Rinaldi repeatedly calls him "baby" (see, for example, pages 32, 40, 63, 64, 65, 66, 76, 77, 166, and 167) and "little puppy" (27). Catherine calls him a "silly boy" (102) or simply "darling." Perhaps in part because of his youth, Frederic's identity seems oddly undefined throughout the novel. One of the Italians in the mess hall expresses confusion about his name, which seems to be formed of two first names: Is it Frederic Henry, or Henry Frederic? After Frederic is wounded, an Englishman claims Frederic is the president's son and the son of the American ambassador in an effort to compel the medics to attend to his wounds. Because of a misunderstanding, a frightened but indignant Italian barber mistakes him for an Austrian officer. The Italians who shot Aymo mistook Henry's men for Germans, and Frederic himself is nearly executed by the Italians as either a deserter or a suspected German spy. Neither Frederic nor anyone around him seems sure of who he is.

Frederic is unable or unwilling to explain why he volunteered for the Italian army in the first place; only after he deserts does he change his mind about this rash commitment, conceding that it was a foolish decision. After Frederic's leave, he is disappointed to learn that everything has run smoothly in his absence; he is perfectly dispensable. His past is a blank, for Hemingway tells us next to nothing about Henry's childhood. Once, while drunk, Frederic mentions drawing money from his grandfather, and he later mentions a stepfather in passing. Frederic sends home only multiple-choice wartime postcards (designed to avoid problems with military censors) on which he has marked "I am well" (36) and receives from his grandfather a letter filled with news about his family, newspaper articles, and a $200 check. He tells Catherine that while he once cared for his family, their incessant quarreling exhausted their love for each other.

Frederic is often selfish, especially in his treatment of Catherine. Fergy has to ask him to give Catherine a break from the night duty because it has exhausted her. His response to Catherine's pregnancy typifies his selfishness: He is concerned with his own feelings of entrapment rather than hers. He does not seem particularly worried that he is leaving her to cope alone with an illegitimate pregnancy in a war zone, and while he is gone he thinks about her only in terms of his own loneliness for her.

Curiously naive, particularly in his views on war, Frederic believes that he will not be killed because somehow this war is dangerous only for other people. He insists that defeat is worse than the fighting, although the more pragmatic Italians argue that nothing is worse than war. Passini, another one of the drivers, is particularly vocal on the subject of the war, contending, "When people realize how bad it is, they cannot do anything to stop it because they go crazy" (50). At least a defeat would allow them all to go home, he says, whereas the war would not really end with a victory. They mean that the soldiers of the defeated side would be able to return home immediately upon the war's end, but the soldiers of the victorious army would probably be required to help maintain order in the nation they have defeated. It's also possible that they believe that a victory would encourage their leaders to launch future wars.

Despite this odd naiveté, however, Frederic is also presented as a savvy insider who speaks Italian fluently, knows where to stay in every city, plays a creditable game of billiards, knows the horse races at San Siro are fixed, and "drinks with style" (Reynolds, *Hemingway's First War* 225–30). The fact that he is also respected by older and wiser men, from Rinaldi to Count Greffi, suggests that there is more to Frederic than is immediately apparent. Frederic combines apparent intelligence with emotional immaturity—not unlike his creator, who once recalled that when he went off to war he was naïve enough at 18 to think of the American forces as the home team and the Austrians as the visiting team, as if the war were an international sporting event.

Not surprisingly, given his naïveté, Frederic is devastated by his loss at the end of the novel, and it seems clear that the narrative we have just read is his way of trying to understand and come to terms with his terrible loss. He does not seem to appreciate Catherine during the events described in the novel; only afterwards does he come to understand her character and her sacrifice. When Catherine asks him not to say or do the same things with another girl, she is steering him away from the course she took—coping with grief by reenacting her lost love. In writing this narrative of their life together, Frederic has overcome his own grief by transforming it into art.

Much like Lady Brett Ashley of *The Sun Also Rises*, Catherine Barkley is a British volunteer nurse traumatized by the wartime loss of her fiancé. They had grown up together and been engaged for eight years when he was killed in the Battle of the Somme. If she was ever religious, her faith was destroyed by the war; Catherine insists that there is no afterlife, she has no religion, and she does not believe in God. Her love for Frederic takes the place of religion, and even on her deathbed, when he asks her if she wants a priest, she responds that she wants only him. She is, however, superstitious and repeatedly tells Frederic that she is afraid of the rain because she sees herself dead in it.

The war has destroyed Catherine's faith. When Frederic vaguely expresses reservations about the finality of death, she insists that her fiancé's death was the end of their relationship, indicating she has no expectation of an afterlife (19). Interestingly, Frederic seems to have a faith she lacks: When the priest asks Frederic if he loves God, he confesses that he feels occasional fear, although not love. Ironically, however, despite Catherine's lack of faith, she gives Frederic a Saint Anthony's medal for protection, which he says he could not find after he was wounded. She also objects to his blasphemy when he shows her his raw, blistered hands after rowing to Switzerland and makes a flip allusion to Christ's wounds.

In a 1929 letter criticizing the manuscript of the novel, F. Scott Fitzgerald told Hemingway that while Hemingway was viewing the autobiographical Frederic Henry with the sophistication of hindsight, he was seeing Catherine much as he had seen Agnes during the war. Fitzgerald complained that Hemingway was overidealizing and oversimplifying his female character. Her character has been criticized for the passive, stereotypically feminine way in which she seems to let Frederic Henry control the relationship. "I'll do what you want and say what you want and then I'll be a great success, won't I?" she asks Frederic, adding later, "There isn't any me any more" (105–6). She wants him to let his hair grow so they will even look alike, and as their relationship progresses, she tells him that she wants him so much that she wants to become Frederic herself. Nevertheless, she is not the doormat she is sometimes perceived to be. Early in the relationship when Frederic treats her casually, she refuses to see him. When his umbrella-turned-sail collapses during the rough crossing to Switzerland, she laughs at him so hard she chokes. She bluntly warns him not to brag, momentarily resents feeling like a whore in their cheap hotel room, and repeatedly refuses to marry him even though he sincerely wants her to.

Because of her willingness to engage in premarital sex, Catherine would have been regarded as immoral by many readers when the book was published in 1929. Only her friend Helen Ferguson calls attention to the dangers of Catherine's unconventional behavior. When Frederic rejoins Catherine in Stresa, Catherine is happy, but the perceptive Fergy instantly recognizes that he is in trouble and cries with anger that he has gotten her beloved friend involved in it with him. Fiercely protective of her friend, Fergy orders Frederic to take good care of her, foresees Catherine's pregnancy, and foretells that they won't marry. She is so attached to Catherine that some critics have suggested that there is a homoerotic or lesbian component to their relationship, particularly given Frederic's comment to Catherine about Fergy: "I don't think she wants what we have" (257). What Catherine and Frederic have, however, is not just a heterosexual relationship but an illegitimate pregnancy in wartime Italy, and it's possible (and highly likely) that Fergy genuinely *doesn't* want that kind of complication in her life. Besides, Catherine dismisses his comment. Surely she understands Fergy better than Frederic, who seems to dislike her, probably because he doesn't want to share Catherine's attention and affection with anyone.

It is Frederic's own friend, Rinaldi, who first mentions Miss Barkley and then takes Frederic to see her. Rinaldi, who is Frederic's age and like Frederic a lieutenant in the Italian army, is a skillful surgeon who brags that his most recent operation should be written up for the British medical journal *The Lancet*. He genuinely cares for Frederic. He is the first to visit him in the hospital and is so moved by Frederic's injuries that he talks nervously throughout much of his visit. Rinaldi tells Frederic that they are brothers and best friends when Frederic returns to the front after his wounding. Exhausted after a terrible summer and fall of incessant medical work, Rinaldi enjoys only his work; he used to enjoy alcohol, but that endangers his surgical skills, and he used to take pleasure in lovemaking, but the pleasure of that is short-lived. As traumatized by the war as Catherine is, Rinaldi, too, confesses himself "a little crazy" (174).

A little jealous that Frederic will no longer be such a close friend now that he is in love with Catherine, Rinaldi calls himself the "snake of reason" whom his married friends no longer like—presumably because he thinks logically and points out the irrationality of love (170). He is further depressed by the suspicion that he has contracted syphilis, a sexually transmitted disease that at that time, before the discovery of antibiotics, could lead to madness and death. As the novel progresses, he becomes increasingly demoralized by the war.

Frederic's other friend in the novel, the priest, is clearly trying to compel Frederic to see something about the nature of the war that Frederic doesn't want to see. An unlikely spiritual advisor, the priest is young and easily embarrassed by the soldiers' frequent teasing. Even the atheistic Rinaldi tells Frederic that he approves of this priest, in a rare moment of religious tolerance, and then kids Frederic that he and the priest are a little *too* friendly (65). The priest, like Rinaldi, visits Frederic the day after he is wounded. Frederic notes the priest's tiredness, which he attributes to a disgust with the war, and compares it to the antiwar sentiments Passini expressed shortly before he was killed. The priest is dismayed and even angered that, despite the wounding, Frederic in his naïveté *still* doesn't perceive how bad the war is; the priest is grievously disappointed when Frederic returns to the front nearly as naïve as when he left.

THEMES

A Farewell to Arms has two unmistakable themes: love and war. The text is preoccupied with romantic love, sometimes to the point of silliness, as when

Frederic and Catherine experiment with mental telepathy or try unsuccessfully to fall asleep at the same moment. Catherine tells him, "There isn't any me any more. I'm you" (115), echoing Catherine Earnshaw's unforgettable declaration, in Emily Brontë's *Wuthering Heights*, "Nelly, I *am* Heathcliff—he's always, always in my mind—not as a pleasure, any more than I am always a pleasure to myself—but as my own being" (Brontë 74). The love between Frederic and Catherine recalls the Greek philosopher Plato's theory that love is the unity of two separated halves of one being.

In a letter to Hemingway, Maxwell Perkins, his editor at Scribner's, objected gently that the themes of love and war were not fully integrated in the novel and that the war disappears almost altogether in Book V. Initially committed to war, Frederic Henry turns increasingly towards Catherine's love instead, especially after the fiasco that results in his desertion from the Italian army. In one of the novel's most enigmatic passages, Frederic, recalling his friend the priest, tells himself, "He had always known what I did not know and what, when I learned it, I was always able to forget. But I did not know that then, although I learned it later" (14). What is it that Frederic does not know then but learns later? Is it about love, or war, or both? The novel is silent on that point, leaving readers free to speculate.

The most convincing explanation is that Frederic learns to understand both love *and* war. Initially naïve, convinced that the war cannot touch him personally, Frederic can sympathize with the American soldier who has deliberately discarded his truss so that his rupture will worsen and, he hopes, prevent him from having to return to the front lines. But his attitude is alien to Frederic, who praises the bravery and discipline of troops that the Italians all believe are foolhardy. While the Italians toy with the notion of ending the war by refusing to attack, Frederic insists that the war must end with a victory. The Italians under his command try to persuade him that nothing is worse than war, but he rejects that belief utterly.

He is much more equivocal in his conversation with the priest later in the novel, however, when he confesses that he no longer hopes for victory and concedes that perhaps defeat might be better. By then Frederic has watched Passini die an unimaginably painful death when his legs were destroyed by the trench mortar shell that also wounded Frederic. Afterwards, as Frederic was transported by ambulance, the man in the stretcher above his had hemorrhaged, his blood dripping down onto Frederic. Frederic is even more demoralized later, when he realizes after Aymo's abrupt death that his friend has been killed by friendly fire. After Frederic deserts rather than be killed by overzealous carabinieri, he fully realizes how much he has changed when he is not bothered by the contempt shown him by the aviators who share his train compartment on the way to Stresa. Once he would have felt compelled to fight with them to defend his masculinity, but he no longer feels that need. He has rejected war and violence. As Frederic puts it, "I had made a separate peace" (243).

He finally sees through what his society has told him about war and appreciates its true horror—a realization mocked when Count Greffi mentions the book *Mr. Britling Sees It Through*, and Frederic immediately responds that no, he doesn't see through it after all (261). Only in crafting this narrative does he come to understand how the war irrevocably damaged both himself and the people he loved the most—the priest, Rinaldi, and of course Catherine.

Through Catherine's devotion Frederic also learns to understand the philosophy of love that the priest expresses and that Hemingway implicitly endorses. "When you love you wish to do things for. You wish to sacrifice for. You wish to serve," the priest tells Frederic (72). "Ultimately, it is Catherine, not Frederic, who fulfills these criteria," offers Michael Reynolds (*Hemingway's First War* 32).

Although in the novel's opening pages the priest invites Frederic to spend his leave with the priest's family in Abruzzi and go hunting, Frederic listens to the soldiers instead and opts to go to the whorehouses of Milano. When the priest is hurt, Frederic realizes he genuinely regrets his own thoughtlessly impulsive decision, which even he cannot understand, and later, after he is wounded, he visualizes the priest's idyllic country village to help himself sleep. The odd anecdote presages Frederic's reaction to the priest's counsel: He is able to appreciate it only in hindsight.

LITERARY DEVICES

The ending of *A Farewell to Arms* is carefully foreshadowed throughout the book, creating for the reader the sense of impending and inevitable doom. "In *A Farewell to Arms*, the reader is never taken by surprise, for all the major pieces of action are economically foreshadowed" (Reynolds, *Hemingway's First War* 238). Hemingway indicates again and again that this relationship is doomed. For example, Fergy tells Frederic that he and Catherine will never marry, that couples like Frederic and Catherine fight or die rather than marry. Soon afterwards, Catherine sees herself dead in the rain. Both prophecies are accurate. When Frederic insists that Catherine is so brave that nothing can happen to her, she reminds him that the brave die, too. Another ominous note is struck when Catherine tells Frederic that the Swiss doctor mentioned that she has narrow hips. The novel's opening scene, in which soldiers carrying rifles and ammunition under their rain ponchos are compared to pregnant women, is perhaps the most disturbing and, in hindsight, the most obvious indication of what is to come.

Not surprisingly, Catherine's character has a streak of fatalism, perhaps best expressed when she bluntly tells Frederic, "life isn't hard to manage when you've nothing to lose" (137). Frederic learns this fatalism slowly and painfully and only through Catherine's death: "The world breaks every one and afterwards many are strong at the broken places. But those that will not break it kills" (249). He bitterly resents his discovery.

Immediately afterwards, Frederic puts a log on the fire and watches impassively as the ants that swarm out are burned to death. The image recalls the line from Shakespeare's *King Lear* : "As flies are to wanton boys, so we are to the gods. They kill us for their sport" (Act IV.i.36–37). The text is extraordinarily rich with such allusions. In addition to the title allusion, Hemingway drew inspiration for his novel from Stendhal's *The Red and the Black* and Stephen Crane's *The Red Badge of Courage* and alludes to "The Waste Land," the Bible, Alfred Lord Tennyson's poem "Sweet and Low" from *The Princess*, the children's prayer "Now I Lay Me Down to Sleep," Christopher Marlowe's *Jew of Malta*, and Rudyard Kipling's *Without Benefit of Clergy*, as well as folklore. Frederic quotes Shakespeare (139) and Andrew Marvell's "To His Coy Mistress"—although Catherine objects that it does not fit their situation very well since it's about a woman who would not make love with the speaker in the poem. It more aptly describes Catherine's relationship with her lost fiancé, whom she did refuse until it was too late. Lonely for Catherine, Frederic recalls the anonymous poem that begins with the line "Blow, blow ye western wind" and ends with the image of being in a lover's arms.

HISTORICAL AND SOCIAL CONTEXT

It is difficult for Americans in the twenty-first century to appreciate the devastating impact of the Great War on those who witnessed it firsthand. In his "Introduction" to the 1942 anthology he edited, *Men at War: The Best War Stories of All Time*, Hemingway himself wrote, "The last war, during the years 1915, 1916, 1917, was the most colossal, murderous, mismanaged butchery that has ever taken place on earth. Any writer who said otherwise lied" (xiii).

The armies spent much of the war in deep, mud-filled trenches, fighting savagely for days without gaining or losing a foot of ground. Technology made the war much more deadly than previous conflicts had been. Poisonous mustard gas killed many men, and those it didn't kill were left so permanently damaged that many could never resume normal lives. Several years after the war, the Geneva Protocol outlawed the use of poisonous gases in warfare. For many Europeans, the war destroyed society's confident belief in human progress.

The Battle of the Somme, in which Catherine's fiancé was killed, was exceptionally bloody even by World War I standards. It took place on the Somme

River in northwestern France and began June 24, 1916. "The Somme affair, destined to be known among the troops as the Great Fuck-up, was the largest engagement fought since the beginnings of civilization," writes Paul Fussell in *The Great War and Modern Memory*. "Out of the 110,000 who attacked, 60,000 were killed or wounded on this one day, the record so far" (12–13).

Hundreds of soldiers returned from the war suffering from shell shock, a psychological trauma that we might now call posttraumatic stress disorder. Renamed "battle fatigue" in World War II, its symptoms include nightmares, flashbacks, depression, irritability, and hypervigilance (a tendency to jump at loud noises or sudden moves, for example). The influential Hemingway critic Philip Young has suggested that Hemingway himself suffered from shell shock, but the evidence is inconclusive.

"To read any of Hemingway's fiction as biography is always dangerous, but to read *A Farewell to Arms* in this manner is to misread the book," states Hemingway biographer Michael Reynolds. He elaborates: "In writing *A Farewell to Arms*, . . . Hemingway went back to someone else's front and recreated the experience from books, maps, and firsthand sources. It is his only novel set on terrain with which he did not have personal experience; in it, his imagination, aided by military histories, has recreated the Austro-Italian front of 1915–1917 more vividly than any other writer" (*Hemingway's First War* 15–16). In *Hemingway's First War*, Reynolds documents the extraordinary accuracy of Hemingway's depiction of the retreat from Caporetto. Hemingway based his descriptions of the retreat on sources he read after the war, including newspaper accounts and military histories, and perhaps in part on the reminiscences of Nick Nerone, an Italian friend who served in the Italian army, participated in the disastrous battle against the Austrians at Caporetto, and received several medals for his service. Even Italian readers who had participated in the retreat found his description of it in *A Farewell to Arms* so accurate they could not believe Hemingway had not been there himself (Reynolds, *Hemingway's First War* 6–7). Mussolini's fascist government later banned the novel in Italy out of fear that reading about the disastrous defeat would damage the nation's morale (Oldsey 48).

ALTERNATE READING: NEW HISTORICISM

New Historicism is a critical approach that requires that readers examine a text with its original historical context very much in mind. Rather than examining a text anachronistically, from today's perspective, it asks that readers pay close attention to the world in which the work was written and first read in order to better understand the meaning of the text.

Critic Sandra Whipple Spanier has argued in two important articles that Catherine Barkley has all too often been misread because readers have forgotten the context of World War I in which the novel was set. In ordinary peacetime circumstances, for example, Catherine's extraordinary act of selflessness in sacrificing her own needs to serve Frederic's might seem masochistic or almost frighteningly self-abasing, the choice of an emotionally disturbed mind. But given the actual circumstances surrounding Catherine—her abrupt and violent loss of her fiancé of eight years, her immersion in an alien culture fighting an exceptionally bloody war, and her fatalistic conviction that the war will never end—her impassioned decision to choose love over despair is not just understandable but even heroic.

From Fitzgerald on, readers have criticized Catherine as a character. Yet based on the testimony of women whose situation was very much like Catherine's, Hemingway drew a realistic portrait of one woman's response to her horrific situation. It would be difficult to overstate the horrors faced by volunteer nurses in Europe in World War I. Mary Borden, who spent four years nursing in Belgium and France, succinctly describes in a terrifying anecdote in her book *The Forbidden Zone* what her work was like:

There was a man stretched on the table. His brain came off in my hands when I lifted the bandage from his head.

When the dresser came back I said: 'His brain came off on the bandage.'

'Where have you put it?'

'I put it in the pail under the table.'

'It's only one half of his brain,' he said, looking into the man's skull. 'The rest is here.'

I left him to finish the dressing and went about my own business. I had much to do. (151)

Borden's apparent callousness was hard earned. Like Catherine, who asks Frederic if he supposes the war will always go on and later contemplates seeing her unborn child become a lieutenant commander, Borden becomes convinced the war will last forever: "It had no beginning, it will have no end. War, the Alpha and the Omega, world without end . . ." (57).

Another V.A.D. nurse, Vera Brittain, offers an even closer real-life parallel to the fictional Catherine's experience. Brittain, who in Malta and France nursed the wounded as they arrived from the front, writes of her experiences in her memoir, *Testament of Youth*, first published in 1933. In *A Farewell to Arms*, after telling Frederic of her fiancé, Catherine mentions her "silly idea that he might come to the hospital where I was" with a "picturesque" injury (20); like Catherine, Brittain was engaged to a soldier and daydreamed that he would turn up in her hospital (Brittain 210). When he was killed in the trenches, Brittain was devastated. She once told him that if he died, she thought she would "deliberately set out to marry the first reasonable person that asked [her]" (Brittain 186) and explained her extraordinary decision to him in this way:

"You see, if one goes on obviously mourning someone, other people come along and insist on entering in and pitying and sympathising, and they force one's recollection into one's outward life and spoilt it all. But if one seems to have forgotten, the world lets one alone and thinks one is just like everyone else, but that doesn't matter. One lives one's outer life and they see that, but below it lies the memory, unspoiled and intact. By marrying the first reasonable person that asked me, I should thereby be able to keep *you*; my remembrance would live with me always and be my very own." (Brittain 186)

Brittain later spotted an advertisement in the London *Times*: "Lady, fiancé killed, will gladly marry officer totally blinded or otherwise incapacitated by the War," and Brittain's reaction alternated between understanding and dismay (Brittain 195–96). When one of her friends, Victor, was blinded and another, Geoffrey, killed in action, she recalled that ad and determined to marry Victor; before she was able to, he lapsed into delirium and suddenly died (Brittain 343, 357). When her brother, too, was killed in action, she echoed Catherine's blunt despair— " . . . he was killed and that was the end of it" (19)—rather eerily: "I knew now that death was the end and that I was quite alone" (Brittain 446). Brittain's memoir documents the uncanny psychological accuracy with which Hemingway limned his portrait of a woman driven to the brink of an emotional breakdown by the traumas of war.

Even Catherine's near-breakdown, her touch of craziness, is typical of the responses of her real-life counterparts. Borden's despair was at times boundless: "There is War on the earth—nothing but War, War let loose in the world, War—nothing left in the whole world but War—War, world without end, amen" (62). In a particularly bitter moment, she writes, "It is all carefully arranged. Everything is arranged. It is arranged that men should be broken and that they should be mended" (124). Bitterness, hopelessness, and even mental breakdowns were evidently not unusual. In a study of the memoirs of Voluntary Aid Detachment nurses in World War I, Sharon Ouditt writes, "These texts, having begun with an enthusiastic response to the call of their country, typically became dominated by images of alienation, dislocation and even madness—motifs of literary modernism" (Ouditt 37–38).

6

The Later Short Fiction: *Men without Women* (1927) and *Winner Take Nothing* (1933)

MEN WITHOUT WOMEN

Men without Women, an uneven collection of 14 short stories, was published October 14, 1927, and had sold 19,000 copies by the following April. Critics Edmund Wilson and Dorothy Parker commented positively on the work, but many of the reviewers were disgusted by its vulgar characters and subject matter. Virginia Woolf reviewed the collection, not very favorably, for the New York *Herald-Tribune* in 1927 and objected to what she saw as Hemingway's "self-conscious virility" ("Essay," 90). Reviewing Hemingway's work may have helped her to formulate her declaration in *A Room of One's Own* that a writer should never be conscious of his or her sex. Hemingway biographer Kenneth Lynn points out that Woolf criticized a publisher's blurb for which Hemingway should not have been held responsible: "The softening feminine influence is absent—either through training, discipline, death or situation" (qtd. in Lynn 369). But Hemingway uses almost those exact words in a letter written to his editor, Maxwell Perkins, on Valentine's Day, 1927.

In a letter to F. Scott Fitzgerald, Hemingway complained that he couldn't find a Bible in Gstaad, Switzerland, and when he finally did, he could not find a good quote that had not already been used as a title. He joked rather unpleasantly that he expected the collection to sell well among gays and graduates of Vassar, a women's college—presumably Hemingway's way of referring to lesbians—although it's puzzling that he felt they would be especially interested in a book titled *Men without Women*.

"IN ANOTHER COUNTRY"

Written in the fall of 1926, "In Another Country" was first published in *Scribner's Magazine* in April 1927. The title is taken from a line in Elizabethan playwright Christopher Marlowe's *The Jew of Malta* that T.S. Eliot quoted as an epigraph to his poem "Portrait of a Lady":

> Thou hast committed—
> Fornication: but that was in another country,
> And besides, the wench is dead. (IV.1.40–42)

The term "fornication" refers to sexual intercourse outside marriage, and the quotation works much better as a gloss on *A Farewell to Arms*—where the narrator does commit fornication in a country other than his own, and Catherine does die at the end of the novel—than on this story, despite Hemingway's drawing on it for his title. Written after Hemingway and his first wife, Hadley, had separated, the story is about both war and marriage, and its themes echo those of *A Farewell to Arms*. The story's first sentence is one of the most famous opening sentences in literature and has justifiably earned the respect of readers and fellow writers.

Plot Development

"In Another Country" is a retrospective narrative, told long after the war is over: "But this was a long time ago, and then we did not any of us know how it was going to be afterward" (*MWW* 35). The story is set in a hospital in Italy during World War I. The doctor tries to reassure the narrator that he will play football again despite a bad leg wound and encourages another patient, an Italian major whose hand injury has cost him his skill at fencing, with photographs of people who had recovered from similar injuries. Neither man is persuaded, however, although both persist with their rehabilitative exercises on what the narrator ironically refers to as "the machines that were to make so much difference" (*MWW* 33).

The narrator recalls his own foolishness for dismissing Italian as an easy language until the major, who believes in following traditional rules and maintaining a certain discipline, dryly suggests that he try using the language correctly for a change. The major asks him what he plans to do when the war is over, if it ever ends, and demands that he "speak grammatically!" (*MWW* 37). When the narrator tells the major that he hopes to be married, the major responds angrily that he must not marry: "If he is to lose everything, he should not place himself in a position to lose that. He should not place himself in a position to lose. He should find things he cannot lose" (*MWW* 37).

After making a telephone call, the major later apologizes for his outburst and explains that his wife has just died. "I am utterly unable to resign myself," he says, crying and biting his lip (*MWW* 38). After he leaves the hospital, the narrator learns from the doctor that the major's wife had died unexpectedly of pneumonia. Ironically, the major had married her only after his injury exempted him from further service—presumably because he did not want to marry her until he was sure he would not be killed in the war.

Character Development

Because "Now I Lay Me," a story about Nick Adams, was tentatively titled "In Another Country—Two," this story's unnamed narrator has generally, if not very justifiably, been assumed to be Nick Adams. Like Nick, he is an American wounded while serving in Italy during World War I. The narrator is isolated from the other young men his age because he received medals solely because he was an American, while they earned theirs for their accomplishments in battle. He calls them "hunting hawks" and recognizes that he is different from them; presumably frightened by his injury, he worries how he will behave if he is sent back to the front. He is naïve in his assurance that Italian is an easy language; as the major makes clear, the young man finds it easy only because he ignores its rules.

His friend the Italian major evidently feels a certain affection for the narrator, for he takes an interest in him, tries to improve his knowledge of Italian, and finally warns the young man against what he now believes was his own mistake in falling in love and marrying. The major is a sensitive man who is devastated by the loss of his wife. Unable to accept her death, he turns his face away to stare out the window at the end of the story, an action that signals his utter hopelessness.

Themes

This story anticipates *A Farewell to Arms*, and like the novel, its themes have to do with love and war. First, it suggests that the damage caused by the war is not as easily repaired as the doctor would like his patients to think—and that damage includes more than simply physical injuries. What these men have lost in the war is not only hope but also any sense of community. The other young war veterans, whom the narrator calls hunting hawks, reject the narrator when they learn that he had not genuinely earned his medals as they had, and each of the story's characters seems isolated and can communicate with the others only superficially (Halter 528).

A second theme, best expressed by the major's warning to the narrator, is that love is dangerous, because it creates the possibility of loss. The major, devastated by his wife's illness, warns the narrator not to marry because loving a wife means that a man has left himself vulnerable to losing her—an unthinkable possibility. When the major loses his wife, he cannot resign himself to his loss; he cannot accept her death. When he returns to the hospital, he goes through the motions but has lost all hope. His unwise advice would doom the narrator to a similar fate, an emotionally sterile life empty of love and therefore of meaning.

"HILLS LIKE WHITE ELEPHANTS"

Written in May 1927, "Hills Like White Elephants" first appeared in the August 1927 issue of *transition*. Much like a one-act play, the story consists almost entirely of dialogue with a handful of expository sentences describing the characters' movements and the story's setting. Often anthologized, the story is generally considered a masterpiece.

Plot Development

"Hills Like White Elephants" is unusual in that its two central characters argue about a subject—abortion—that is never explicitly named in the story but referred to only as "it." The American tries relentlessly to persuade his girlfriend, Jig, to agree to have an abortion, but Jig resists. The story's train station setting and its prominent two lines of tracks become a metaphor for their transient life and the two directions their lives can take from this critical turning point in their relationship. On one side of the station is a fertile landscape with fields of grain, a river, and trees—symbols of the possibilities having the baby could bring this couple; the other side, dry and empty, indicates the barrenness of their life if they choose to go through with the abortion.

Within the station, the girl is particularly interested in a bamboo bead curtain painted with an advertisement for a brand of liquor. Just as the American promises her that the unwanted pregnancy is "the only thing that's made us unhappy" (*MWW* 41), she fingers the curtain's beads, prompting some critics to compare her gesture to the Catholic practice of praying with a rosary.

Character Development

The story has only two characters who speak, Jig and the American, an expatriate couple who are apparently unmarried. The many stickers on their luggage indicate a peripatetic existence and suggest that they drift aimlessly from one location to another. The American does not come off well. He seems selfish and heartlessly determined to get his own way. Although he professes to love Jig, he cares little about her feelings and pushes her not only to do what he wants but to do it on his terms: She must say that she wants the abortion herself. He seems naïve in his assumption that the abortion will carry no consequences and have no lasting effect on their relationship.

Jig can be seen as either caring (emotional in a positive and stereotypically feminine sense) or hysterical (emotional in a negative and stereotypically feminine sense). Hemingway refers to Jig as "the girl" throughout the story, perhaps to suggest her immaturity. She is clearly at the mercy of her traveling companion since she doesn't speak the language, while he does.

Unlike the American, she is profoundly skeptical that after an abortion they could resume their relationship as if nothing had happened. When he insists that he has known people who have had abortions, she responds with bitter sarcasm: "And afterward they were all so happy" (*MWW* 41). She has evidently become disenchanted with the emptiness and transience of their life together: "That's all we do, isn't it—look at things and try new drinks?" (*MWW* 40). It is likely that the ugliness of his behavior has caused her to become disenchanted with the American, too.

Themes

One important theme of "Hills Like White Elephants" is conveyed by the story's poetic title. The expression "white elephant," which originally referred to a literal elephant given as a present by the King of Siam (later Thailand), gradually came to mean a gift that entailed great care and expense. Eventually, it evolved to refer to something unwanted, as in "white elephant sale," meaning a sale of secondhand goods, much like a rummage sale or yard sale. Both of these meanings aptly describe a newborn baby, who also entails great care and expense, and in this case may be unwanted. Certainly the man with whom Jig argues does not seem to want a child. But Hemingway is suggesting that the baby would be a gift as well as a burden, a possibility that the American is unwilling or unable to recognize.

Readers often speculate about what happens after the story's ending. Some argue that Jig, aware of the difficulties she would face as a single and presumably unwed American mother adrift in Europe in the 1930s, unhappily gives in and agrees to have the abortion, but that she will end the relationship. Other critics suggest that she sacrifices the pregnancy to preserve her relationship with the American man.

More recently, Hemingway scholar Stanley Renner has argued that the American comes around finally to Jig's point of view and in shifting the bags to the other side of the platform signals his eventual acceptance of the child. In this reading, Jig's otherwise inexplicable smile near the end of the story, as the American moves their bags, indicates that she is acknowledging his change of heart. Another critic, Hilary K. Justice, contends that the manuscript versions of the story confirm Renner's unorthodox interpretation.

It is perhaps more logical, however, to read Jig's final smile as a conventional gesture of polite thanks, much as she smiles at the Spanish barmaid two sentences earlier to thank her for alerting them of the coming train. The American's silent observation that the other people in the station "were all waiting reasonably for the train" suggests that he is contrasting them with his tiresome traveling companion, who seems to him completely *un*reasonable. Jig's final insistence that there is nothing wrong with her and that she feels perfectly fine indicates that she in turn places the blame for their argument squarely on *his* unreasonableness. The characters seem as much at odds with each other as ever.

"THE KILLERS"

In his private letters, an interview with George Plimpton of the *Paris Review*, Hemingway's 1938 preface to *The First Forty-Nine Stories*, and his 1959 essay "The Art of the Short Story," Hemingway claimed to have written three stories—"The Killers," "Today Is Friday," and "Ten Indians"—all in the same day, May 16, 1926, but the evidence of the manuscripts does not support this extraordinary claim (Smith, *Reader's Guide* 139). Hemingway originally titled the story "The Matadors," which in Spanish means "The Killers," but later changed his mind, perhaps because the Spanish title suggested confusing associations with bullfights. The story was first published in the March 1927 issue of *Scribner's Magazine*.

"The Killers" was later made into a successful 1946 film starring Burt Lancaster and Ava Gardner, the only film of his work that Hemingway liked ("Art" 139). It was remade less successfully in 1964; the remake starred Angie Dickinson and Ronald Reagan.

Plot Development

The two hit men of the story's title, Al and Max, enter a small-town diner, tie up the cook and Nick Adams in the kitchen, hold the diner's boss at gunpoint, and wait for the arrival of Ole Andreson, a Swedish prizefighter who evidently double-crossed the mob (*MWW* 55). They plan to execute him for his apparent betrayal but are disappointed when he does not show up. After they give up and leave, George, who runs the diner, sends an alarmed Nick to warn Ole Andreson of their threats. Nick is frightened to see Andreson's passivity and resignation in the face of his impending murder. Nick returns to the diner and in the face of George's casual lack of concern determines to leave Summit, the Illinois town in which the story's events take place.

Character Development

Al and Max may sound clichéd to twenty-first-century readers, but that's because Hemingway pioneered a trend that continues today of writing sharply sarcastic and even comic dialogue for gangster characters. Hemingway compares them to a vaudeville comedy team; indeed, Max advises George to go to the movies so that he'll know what to expect from mobsters. What is perhaps most disturbing about the gangsters is that they find their murderous assignment so boring that they have to joke around to keep themselves entertained while they wait. As Hemingway biographer Carlos Baker observes in his book *Hemingway: The Writer as Artist*, "with 'The Killers,' Hemingway solidly dramatized the point of view towards human life which makes fascism possible" (123).

Sam, the cook, seems preoccupied with his own safety and advises Nick to stay out of the whole business. When Nick returns from warning Andreson and tells George what happened, Sam is so determined to stay out of it that he refuses to even listen to what Nick has to say. George asks Nick to warn Andreson but once that's accomplished casually instructs Nick not to think about what will happen to the boxer. He seems only mildly concerned about the threat to Andreson's life. Andreson himself is a man in profound despair, unwilling to even try to protect himself but at the same time unable to bring himself to leave his room in the rooming house because he knows that going out will mean almost certain death.

Only Nick seems shocked and disturbed by what happens. Clearly young and naïve, he refuses to believe that the situation could be hopeless and is utterly conventional in his responses. His first thought is that Andreson should call the police, and when Andreson dismisses that idea, Nick assumes the Swede must know the threats are a bluff. Nick is bewildered when Andreson tells him that he knows that the gangsters aren't bluffing. He cannot understand the Swede's passive fatalism.

Historical and Social Context

In the 1920s, when "The Killers" was first written and published, organized crime exerted a powerful hold on American society. Fueled by profits from illegal liquor during Prohibition, organized crime grew in strength and both fascinated and repelled law-abiding Americans. The "mob" was particularly powerful in Chicago, home of notorious mobster Al Capone and the city where Hemingway spent time as a young man. The gangsters could retreat temporarily to the Chicago suburb of Summit when Chicago itself became too dangerous for them. Despite his knowledge of the city's organized crime, Hemingway omitted much of that background from the story, preferring to leave it as the submerged part of the iceberg. "That story probably had more left out of it than anything I ever wrote," Hemingway once commented about "The Killers" ("Art" 139–40). "I left out all Chicago, which is hard to do in 2951 words."

Themes

Cleanth Brooks and Robert Penn Warren, in their classic 1943 discussion of this short story in their book *Understanding Fiction*, argued that the focus of the story was not on Ole or the title characters but rather on Nick and his "discovery of evil." Following in their footsteps, most critics have read the work as an initiation story in which Nick Adams moves from innocence to experience, for as Paul Smith observes, Nick is the only dynamic character, the only character who changes in the course of the story's events.

Edward Sampson was the first to note the comedy of errors underlying the story's surface: Henry's lunchroom is run by a man named George, the meals that appear on the menu aren't available, the killers order for each other rather than each ordering for himself, the clock is 20 minutes fast, and Hirsch's boarding house is run by Mrs. Bell. Nothing is as it seems in this story.

These odd divergences from what might reasonably be expected, coupled with the vaudevillian performances of Al and Max, enhance the surreal, almost slow-motion quality of the story and enable the reader to experience the eerie sense of disbelief—that "This can't be happening" feeling—that Nick must have felt as the events of the story took place. These details also indicate an underlying theme of the story, the failure of the parents of the Lost Generation to provide their children with the means to cope with the violence and senselessness of twentieth-century America: "just as menus, clocks, signs, and names mislead the trusting people who accept them and rely upon them, so too the moral and spiritual code passed down from previous generations will prove an inadequate and deceptive guide to Nick's troubled twentieth-century generation" (Fleming, "Hemingway's 'The Killers' " 313).

"NOW I LAY ME"

In one of its manuscript versions, "Now I Lay Me" was titled "In Another Country—Two." Hemingway wrote the story near the end of 1926, and it was first published in *Men without Women* in 1927. As its title would suggest, the story is a profoundly religious one, in which the protagonist regularly relies upon prayer to keep his night terrors at bay.

Plot Development

As this short story opens, Nick Adams, who has been wounded in the war, does not want to fall asleep because he is afraid that if he falls asleep he will die. In "Now I Lay Me," Hemingway first describes the frightening out-of-body experience he remembered during his own wounding, an experience he later drew upon in *A Farewell to Arms*: "I myself did not want to sleep because I had been living for a long time with the knowledge that if I ever shut my eyes in the dark and let myself go, my soul would go out of my body. I had been that way for a long time, ever since I had been blown up at night and felt it go out of me and go off and then come back" (*MWW* 129).

Like the Nick Adams of "Big Two-Hearted River," this story's protagonist deliberately concentrates on the details of trout fishing in order to hold himself together and keep from breaking down mentally and emotionally. He also finds solace in prayer, trying to remember everyone he has ever known so that he can pray for them individually. The story's title is taken from the traditional children's prayer:

> Now I lay me down to sleep.
> I pray the Lord my soul to keep.
> If I should die before I wake,
> I pray the Lord my soul to take.

In a neat parallel to Nick's emotional state, the prayer's closing couplet has frightened many children into fearing that they will die during the night.

In working through his memories of a safer past, Nick recalls the time his mother, in a cruel moment of housekeeping zeal, burned all Nick's father's Indian artifacts while his father was away on a hunting trip. In an earlier draft of the anecdote, the boy is called "Ernie"—a fact that has prompted many critics to read the anecdote as factually autobiographical. Whether it applies to the Hemingways or not, the disturbing anecdote suggests that Nick is the son of a couple whose marriage has severely deteriorated.

Eventually, Nick has a brief conversation with John, an older man with whom he shares a room. An Italian-American from Chicago who had been abruptly drafted into the Italian army while he was in Italy visiting his family, John was assigned to serve as Nick's orderly because he could speak English. John advocates marriage as an answer to Nick's insomnia, but the story's final line—"he was very certain about marriage and knew it would fix up everything" (*MWW* 137)—ironically implies that marriage has no power to solve Nick's problem.

Character Development

Nick is a lieutenant (*Tenente*) in the Italian army. Intensely sensitive, he cannot use salamanders or crickets for bait because he cannot bear to see them reacting to the hook. The severity of his insomnia worries John, who tells him, "You haven't slept nights ever since I been with you" (*MWW* 134).

Like Nick, John too is traumatized by the war. He describes himself as "nervous" (*MWW* 134) and judging by his insomnia is apparently suffering from shell shock (or what we might now call posttraumatic stress syndrome), although his case seems markedly less severe than Nick's. The father of three girls, he is married to a woman who can successfully run the family business despite being unable to read English.

Themes

John's facile suggestion that marriage would solve Nick's problems points readers to one of this story's themes: the understanding that no other person can solve Nick's emotional problem, or indeed *anyone* else's emotional problems. No external solution is possible; Nick must work through his fear himself, and perhaps time more than anything else will gradually alleviate his anxiety.

The anecdote detailing Nick's mother's cruelty in burning his father's artifacts suggests a second theme: the dangers of an unhappy marriage. Nick's memory of this revealing moment in his parents' marriage doesn't bode well for John's suggestion that Nick marry someone who doesn't even speak English. Nick's confession in the story's final paragraph that he is still not married, despite the passage of time since the events of the story took place, may indicate that his parents' marriage has soured him on the institution, or alternately that he was too damaged by the war to sustain a romantic relationship.

Yet another theme of this story involves the healing power of ritual, even invented, nonsensical rituals such as Nick's imaginary trout-fishing trips. Hemingway was himself powerfully attracted to ritual, from the rites of the Catholic Church to the pre-Christian tragedy of the bullfight. Nick's reliance on ritual to sustain him perhaps explains his capacity for recovery.

WINNER TAKE NOTHING

Winner Take Nothing was published October 27, 1933. Hemingway wrote the collection's epigraph himself, although he attributed it to an invented seventeenth-century text about gaming (Baker, *Life* 241). By January of 1934, the book had sold over 13,000 copies (Reynolds, *1930s* 163). Despite the inclusion of some of Hemingway's best stories, it is generally considered the weakest of Hemingway's three major short story collections.

"A CLEAN, WELL-LIGHTED PLACE"

Hemingway wrote "A Clean Well-Lighted Place" in the fall of 1932, and the story was first published in the March 1933 issue of *Scribner's Magazine*. In his essay "The Art of the Short Story," Hemingway wrote, "Another time I was leaving out good was in 'A Clean, Well-Lighted Place.' There I really had luck. I left out everything" (140). Despite having everything "left out" of it, the story is arguably Hemingway's finest work.

Plot Development

The plot of this story seems slight: Two waiters, one young and one older, wait for an elderly man to leave an outdoor cafe. Because the older waiter is aware that the combination of alcohol, bright lights, and cleanliness helps to stave off depression temporarily, the older waiter is reluctant to rush the old man. Nevertheless, the younger waiter abruptly refuses to take the old man's order of another brandy and instead sends him on his way.

Perhaps the most startling moment in the story occurs after the cafe is closed and the younger waiter departs, when the older waiter recites to himself parodies of the Lord's Prayer and the Hail Mary: "Our nada, who art in nada . . ." and "Hail nothing full of nothing; nothing is with thee" (*WTN* 17). "Nada" means "nothing" in Spanish, so the parodic prayers indicate the man's lack of faith in God or in much of anything. As the end of the story reveals, he is very like the old man, for he, too, knows what it is like to be tormented and unable to sleep.

Character Development

The old man is deaf and, the waiters surmise, at least 80 years old. He drinks until he is drunk every night but is meticulously tidy. His suicide attempt, his alcoholism, and his pathetic eagerness to stay at the deserted café as long as he can indicate that he suffers from depression—perhaps because of his intense loneliness now that he no longer has a wife.

Although he recognizes the old man's plight, the younger waiter is nevertheless unsympathetic and impatient, eager for the customer to leave so that he himself can go home to his wife. Exhausted, he complains that he never gets enough sleep. He is so insensitive that he behaves cruelly to the old man, telling him that he should have succeeded in killing himself (and knowing the old man's deafness will prevent him from hearing these words). The younger waiter seems wholly unable to recognize that financial difficulties are not the only motive for suicide, and the narrator pronounces him stupid. But the younger waiter willingly concedes that drinking at home is very different from drinking in the café: "He did not want to be unjust. He was only in a hurry" (*WTN* 16).

The older waiter's reaction is more complex. He empathizes with the old man, who apparently tried to kill himself in a moment of depression. As the story's ending reveals, the older waiter also dreads going home and prefers a well-lit café. He needs a light at night and lies in bed for hours, futilely trying to fall asleep. He has only his job to give his life meaning and hates to close up the café when he knows there might be others who need the comfort of its relative conviviality. He envies his colleague's youth and confidence. When he asks the younger waiter whether he isn't afraid to go home early, he is jokingly hinting that his colleague's wife may be unfaithful. His rather lame joke perhaps indicates why he himself is alone.

Themes

Many literary critics see this story as an illustration of the philosophical concept of existentialism. Existentialists reject the possibility of a deity and believe that the individual must give meaning to his or her own life. Through his parodic prayers, the older waiter rejects faith in God, just as the older man's suicide signals his rejection of the teachings of the Catholic Church. Both the waiter and the old man are profoundly aware of their isolation in a world that seems disturbingly empty and meaningless. Confronted with nothingness, each of them tries to establish his own small circle of cleanliness, light, and order to hold back the surrounding darkness.

Literary Devices

Hemingway scholars have debated vigorously and at length the question of which waiter is saying which lines of the story's dialogue. During Hemingway's lifetime, the text of the story read:

"His niece looks after him."
"I know. You said she cut him down." (*WTN* 15)

Later, in response to literary critic John Hagopian's argument that it should have been the older waiter who knows about the old man's attempt to hang himself, Scribner's changed the lines to read:

"His niece looks after him. You said she cut him down."

"I know."

The earlier reading makes more sense, since, if Hemingway is following the conventions of writing dialogue, it is the younger waiter who first reports the suicide and then, in answer to his colleague's questions, insists that the old man must have been in despair about nothing because he is financially well off. But the dialogue is nevertheless confusing, since a page earlier it seems to be the younger waiter who is asking questions about the customer's attempt to hang himself. Critic David Kerner has contended that two succeeding lines of dialogue were spoken by the same character, an unorthodox practice termed antimetronomic dialogue, because unlike a metronome, this dialogue does not alternate back and forth evenly. While it's possible to see Hemingway as experimenting with a new technique, the more likely explanation is editorial sloppiness on Hemingway's part.

"THE SEA CHANGE"

First published in *This Quarter* in 1931 before its 1933 appearance in *Winner Take Nothing*, "The Sea Change" is a neglected short story among Hemingway's work, perhaps because of its controversial subject matter. Like "Cat in the Rain," "Out of Season," "A Canary for One," and "Hills Like White Elephants," "The Sea Change" focuses on a turning point in an unhappy romantic relationship. Its unusual love triangle recalls the story "Mr. and Mrs. Elliot" from *In Our Time* and anticipates the complex relationships among David, Catherine, and Marita in Hemingway's *The Garden of Eden*. The posthumous publication of that novel in 1986 provoked renewed critical interest in this otherwise relatively obscure short story.

Plot Development

Although he claimed in a letter to his Scribner's editor, Maxwell Perkins, that he had invented the plot of "The Sea Change," in 1954 Hemingway told an associate, A.E. Hotchner, that the story was based on a conversation he overheard in a bar in Saint-Jean-de-Luz, France (Hotchner 139–40). As he wrote cryptically in his essay, "The Art of the Short Story": "In a story called 'A Sea Change,' everything is left out. I had seen the couple in the Bar Basque in St. Jean de Luz and I knew the story too well. . . . So I left the story out. But it is all there." (131).

In "The Sea Change," Phil tries to persuade an unnamed "girl," with whom he has evidently had a romantic relationship, to stay with him, while she tries to make him understand that she cannot. It eventually becomes evident that she wants to leave him for a romantic relationship with another woman. Like the couple in "Hills Like White Elephants," the couple in "The Sea Change" never refer directly to the event that is causing their argument, perhaps because, like abortion, a woman leaving a man for a lesbian relationship was an unspeakable subject for 1930s Americans.

Hemingway was somewhat more open-minded, counting Gertrude Stein and Sylvia Beach among his lesbian friends. His first wife, Hadley, had once been accused of lesbianism by her mother (Diliberto 24), and he was good friends with Jinny Pfeiffer, an avowed lesbian and the sister of his second wife, Pauline. There are also persistent unresolved questions about the intimate relationship between Grace Hall Hemingway, Ernest's mother, and the much younger Ruth Arnold, a former music student of Grace's who became a part-time mother's helper. Both Ernest and his father evidently believed the relationship was a sexual one (Lynn 100–101).

Character

Phil is a weak man who resorts to bitterness and sarcasm in an unsuccessful attempt to keep his girlfriend. He longs to resort to violence but cannot, since his rival is a woman. His whole sense of self-worth is predicated upon having a beautiful, tanned blonde on his arm, and once she is gone, his sense of self collapses. He seems genuinely bewildered by his girlfriend's defection, as if he cannot imagine any woman preferring another woman to him.

Stereotypically feminine, Phil's "girl" is so eager to please him that even while she is breaking off their relationship, she repeatedly apologizes and promises to come back to him. She is offended when he first asks her to prove her love and then calls her behavior "vice" and "perversion," traditional labels for homosexual behavior in a society that considered it sinful and unnatural. She values politeness and harmony over the harshly stated truth.

Their relationship is apparently superficial. She leaves him happily when he says she can, even though she knows that he has said so unwillingly and only because he has no other choice. He focuses primarily on her beauty and seems upset over her loss, more because of what it says about him than because of any genuine feelings for her. Their relationship was also apparently an unequal one, for when he mentions wanting to have his own way, she tells him that he did for a long time. The implication is that Phil has controlled the relationship, so that her decision to leave him must be especially startling, since it switches their roles and robs him of his power in the relationship.

Themes

One important theme of the short story concerns homophobia. The quotation that Phil half-remembers was taken from Alexander Pope's *An Essay on Man*: "Vice is a monster of so frightful mien, / As, to be hated, needs but to be seen; / Yet seen too oft, familiar with her face, / We first endure, then pity, then embrace" (II.iii.217–20). Pope seems to be saying that while the mere sight of "vice" (a code word here that suggests homosexuality, which would have been considered immoral to mainstream readers in most Western cultures in the 1930s) is hateful, repeated exposure to it prompts us to first tolerate it, then to feel sorry for those engaged in it, and finally to welcome it into our own lives. Some critics have taken this quotation to indicate that Phil, who is tolerating his girlfriend's lesbianism (or as he puts it, her "perversion"), may soon be driven to adopt homosexuality himself. These critics observe that the story's title is an allusion to the song Ariel sings in Shakespeare's *The Tempest*:

> Full fathom five thy father lies
> Of his bones are coral made;
> Those are pearls that were his eyes;
> Nothing of him that doth fade
> But doth suffer a sea-change
> Into something rich and strange. (I.ii.396–401)

The allusion suggests transformation and possibly corruption, but it is unclear whether Hemingway meant the title to refer to Phil or the "girl." Certainly the reference to embracing perversion could suggest that, like David Bourne of *The Garden of Eden*, Phil would be willing to resume a relationship with a woman who had indulged in a lesbian affair.

Although there is some speculation among critics that at the end of the story Phil himself has elected to become a homosexual, there is little evidence within the story to support such a contention. (It is a dubious possibility anyway, given the increasing evidence that homosexuality is genetic rather than chosen.) Some critics have further proposed that the two men at the bar are gay. On the contrary, they promptly strike up a nervous conversation with the barman the moment they hear the word "perversion" (*MWW* 41), and when Phil later mentions "vice" to the barman (*MWW* 43), the two men promptly slide down the bar away from him in a comic moment of homophobic anxiety.

Another important theme in the story is the importance of a superficial, unequal relationship in supporting a man's inflated sense of himself. "Women have served all these centuries as looking-glasses possessing the magic and delicious power of reflecting the figure of man at twice its natural size," Virginia Woolf writes in *A Room of One's Own* (35). "That serves to explain in part the necessity that women so often are to men." Phil looks at the bar mirror three times after the girl leaves. His apparent obsession with his own reflection at the end of the story suggests that because he no longer has a girlfriend to reflect his image back to him at twice his natural size, he must unfortunately rely instead upon the greatly diminished image of himself he sees in the mirror behind the bar.

"A WAY YOU'LL NEVER BE"

First published in *Winner Take Nothing*, "A Way You'll Never Be" is a disturbing but compelling psychological study of shell shock. Its title is said to be a reassuring comment to Jane Mason, a Havana friend and probable lover who later attempted suicide and was eventually hospitalized for mental illness. In *Papa Hemingway*, Hemingway associate A.E. Hotchner recalls Hemingway telling him in 1955 about writing "A Way You'll Never Be" more than two decades earlier:

I had tried to write it back in the Twenties, but had failed several times. I had given up on it but one day here, fifteen years after those things happened to me in a trench dugout outside Fornaci, it suddenly came out focused and complete. Here in Key West, of all places. Old as I am, I continue to be amazed at the sudden emergence of daffodils and stories. (Hotchner 177–78)

Although the story has autobiographical roots, Hemingway himself never sustained the kind of head wound from which Nick Adams suffers.

Plot Development

This relatively neglected Nick Adams story is set in Italy during World War I. It opens with a vivid description of the aftermath of battle. Nick Adams travels through a landscape littered with casualties. Surrounding the grotesquely decaying dead bodies of the soldiers are their weapons, ammunition, and papers—prayer books, photographs, and letters from home. Nick in this story is doubly damaged: He has sustained a serious head wound that was evidently treated improperly, and he is psychically wounded as well by the combat he has witnessed.

Nick is visiting the Italian front wearing his American uniform in hopes of persuading the Austrian enemy that American troops will soon be arriving to reinforce the Italians. He knows the Italian battalion commander, Captain Paravicini, and asks to see him when a soldier challenges his identity. Nick confesses to the captain that he was so frightened before each attack that he had to get drunk in order to force himself to participate. Disappointed by his own lack of self-control, Nick recalls that during an attack that reduced many of those with whom he served to hysterics, he himself wore his chin strap tightened to prevent his teeth from chattering. Paravicini, alarmed by Nick's deterioration, advises him to rest, but when Nick lies down, the pressure on his head wound presumably increases (Smith, *Reader's Guide* 273), contributing to his hysterical breakdown. His memories of the attack abruptly become a vividly realized flashback.

After his rest, Nick experiences a second and more serious breakdown and launches into a surrealistically absurd lecture on the grasshopper, or (as he explains with the precision of an amateur naturalist) the American locust. Concerned by Nick's overwrought state, Paravicini is reluctant to let his obviously unwell friend bicycle back to Fornaci alone and only gives in when Nick becomes a bit more lucid and asks him for that "mark of confidence" in Nick's stability (*WTN* 59).

Character Development

Nick is clearly a sensitive young man. Since the attack, he is unable to sleep at night without a light, and when he does sleep, he has nightmares from which he awakens terrified and drenched in sweat. He wants to be well and is disappointed when he reacts so badly during his visit to his old friend Paravicini on the front lines.

Good friends, Nick and Paravicini call each other "Para" and "Niccolo." Formerly an architect, Paravicini is evidently intelligent and speaks excellent English. Instead of being a captain commanding a company, as Nick remembers him, Paravicini is now an acting major commanding a battalion, a promotion that perhaps indicates the extent of the battalion's casualties in its most recent engagement. Although he probably has little time to spare, he treats Nick kindly and generously, becoming stern only when he sees what a danger Nick has become to himself and others.

Themes

In concluding his impromptu lecture, Nick ends with a quotation from Sir Henry Hughes Wilson, who was Britain's director of military operations during World War I and in 1918 became chief of the Imperial General Staff: "Gentlemen, either you must govern—or you must be governed" (*WTN* 57). Nick evidently sees the world in the hierarchical terms of British imperialism. The only alternatives are to dominate or be dominated—as if life were a zero-sum game in which one either wins all or loses all. His words also have equally disturbing personal implications: "Either Nick must govern his thoughts and actions, or someone else will have to control his activities" (Johnston 433).

"FATHERS AND SONS"

One of his most autobiographical works, "Fathers and Sons" reflects Hemingway's attempt to come to terms with his father's suicide. Hemingway took the story's title from the title of an 1861 novel by Russian writer Ivan Turgenev, whom Hemingway repeatedly mentioned when listing the authors who influenced his work (although Hemingway usually singled out Turgenev's *Sportsman's Sketches*, not *Fathers and Sons*). That novel also dealt with intergenerational conflict. Although the story was given the working titles "Indian Summer" and "Long Time Ago Good," its original title was "The Tomb of My Grandfather."

Plot Development

"Fathers and Sons," a meditative story about the relationships between three generations in the same family, chronicles a cross-country road trip the narrator takes with his young son. That journey parallels Hemingway's real-life road trip from Key West, Florida, to Piggott, Arkansas, in 1932 with his oldest son, Jack, nicknamed Bumby. As the story opens, the story's protagonist, 38-year-old Nick Adams, decides not to follow a sign indicating a detour but—"believing it was some repair which had been completed"—to instead drive straight through the town. He notices the heavy trees "that are a part of your heart if it is your town and you have walked under them, but that are only too heavy, that shut out the sun and dampen the houses for a stranger" (151). Hemingway's metaphor suggests that Nick believes that he has repaired the emotional damage caused by his father's suicide and can safely pass through his memories of his father. Like those small-town trees, his memories of his father are a part of his heart, although they might seem dark and depressing to anyone else.

Meanwhile, he recalls his troubled relationship with his father and tries to come to terms emotionally with both his sometimes disappointing memories of his father and his anguish over his father's eventual suicide. He recalls with gratitude his father teaching him to hunt and fish and remembers both his father's extraordinarily keen eyesight and his comically useless sexual advice. Repulsed by his father's smell, he had once as a boy deliberately lost the hand-me-down long underwear that his father had given him. After he was punished for lying, he secretly aimed a shotgun at his father and angrily thought about killing him.

In the midst of his reverie, Nick is abruptly interrupted by his young son, who had been sleeping alongside him. Earnest and enthusiastic, the boy wants to pay his respects to his grandfather as his French friends do, by visiting his grandfather's tomb.

Character Development

Nick is a writer who—like Hemingway—regularly exorcises painful experiences through his work: "If he wrote it he could get rid of it. He had gotten rid of many things by writing them" (154). As he drives, he recalls sleeping with his Indian girlfriend Trudy Gilby as a teenager and hypocritically objecting when her older half-brother says he's going to sleep with Nick's sister.

Nick's unnamed son is curious and persistent. He longs to be old enough to have his own shotgun. His questions reveal that he is particularly interested in people—the Ojibway, the grandfather he barely remembers—and what they are like. He seems morally uncomfortable that he has never visited his grandfather's grave. Nick's equivocal responses to his son's insistent requests suggest that despite his assurance in the story's first paragraph, Nick has not fully reconciled himself to his father's death. He has not yet forgiven his father for committing suicide, or himself for letting it happen.

Nick's father is an expert outdoorsman whose skill his son admires even long after his father's death. However, Nick describes his father's character in much more ambivalent terms: "Then, too, he was sentimental, and, like most sentimental people, he was both cruel and abused" (152). Certainly Nick's father is utterly conventional when it comes to human sexuality, refusing with typically Victorian prudishness to explain even "mashing"—a slang term for what we might now term sexual harassment.

Themes

Part of what Nick has to contend with during his reminiscences is his own guilt. He recalls once as a child wanting to kill his father and remembers the sick sense of remorse he experienced immediately afterward. He evidently believes that, along with the rest of his family, he somehow let his father down. Nick thinks to himself about his father, "He had died in a trap that he had helped only a little to set, and they had all betrayed him in their various ways before he died" (153). He is haunted by his father's memory and tries to remember the good times they shared, but instead he dwells on the undertaker's reconstruction of his father's face.

But despite Nick's anguish, it is not just sons who betray fathers. Another important theme of this story concerns the myriad ways in which fathers betray their children—for example, Nick's father betrays Nick by beating Nick over the rejected underwear, incompletely answering his questions about sex because the topic makes him uncomfortable, and ultimately killing himself. Nick in turn betrays his own son by incompletely answering his questions about his own father because the topic makes him uncomfortable. Even his responses to his son's questions about Indians—a topic that is much less emotionally wrenching—are not very forthcoming. "Despite the detour sign and the flashing red lights, despite the warning signals from the past, Nicholas Adams, figuratively speaking, is going down the same street, the same road, as did his father" (Johnston 185).

As both father and son in the story, Nick partially understands these cycles of repetition with which, as a father himself, he is necessarily involved. It is not coincidental that the war veteran's father gives his grandson an air rifle and a flag—emblems of violence and nationalism that reveal that the grandfather imagines that his grandson will be raised to be an eager and patriotic soldier, just as Hemingway himself was—even though Hemingway's *In Our Time* and *The Sun Also Rises* reflect the writer's abrupt change of heart regarding the sentimental Victorian notions of duty and honor that his father espoused. Sometimes erroneously considered a warmonger, Hemingway sought instead to break this treacherous father-son cycle of violence. During World War II, when he edited the anthology *Men at War: The Best War Stories of All Time*, he dedicated the book "To John, Patrick, and Gregory Hemingway," his three sons, and wrote bluntly in his "Introduction" to the collection, "This book has been edited in order that those three boys, as they grow to the age where they can appreciate it and use it and will need it, can have the book that will contain truth about war as near as we can come by it, which was lacking to me when I needed it most" (xxiii).

The African Stories

Hemingway traveled to Africa twice—once in the mid-1930s and again in the mid-1950s. He later said that the times he spent in Africa were among the happiest times of his life. His first safari became the basis for *Green Hills of Africa* and inspired what have come to be acknowledged as two of his finest short stories, "The Short Happy Life of Francis Macomber" and "The Snows of Kilimanjaro." His second African journey prompted the creation of the massive manuscript which was edited by his son Patrick into *True at First Light*, a fictional memoir published in Ernest's centennial year, 1999. That second safari ended in near-disaster, and Hemingway never recovered from the ill effects of the two plane crashes that marked the conclusion of that journey.

GREEN HILLS OF AFRICA

In 1933 Hemingway began planning an African safari, inspired by Theodore Roosevelt, America's 26th president, and his 1909 safari, described in his 1910 book, *African Game Trails*. Hemingway's second wife, Pauline, and his friend Charles Thompson accompanied Ernest on the trip, which Pauline's uncle, Augustus Pfeiffer, financed (Reynolds, *1930s* 150). Philip Percival, a British guide who had worked on Roosevelt's safari, agreed to lead the Hemingways into East Africa. Their hunting was extraordinarily successful, although intense competitiveness between Hemingway and Thompson sometimes created unpleasant tensions in the group.

A severe case of amoebic dysentery cut Hemingway's stay short and required that he be flown out to Nairobi for several days of treatment before he could resume hunting (Reynolds, *1930s* 162–64); the experience of waiting all day in miserable health for the plane to arrive perhaps inspired "The Snows of Kilimanjaro." The safari itself became the subject matter of *Green Hills of Africa*, which Hemingway began writing in the spring of 1934 (Baker, *Life* 259). He gave the book the working title of *The Highlands of Africa* (Baker, *Life* 260). As Hemingway himself explained in the book's unpaginated foreword, "The writer has attempted to write an absolutely true book to see whether the shape of a country and the pattern of a month's action can, if truly presented, compete with a work of the imagination."

Although much of what he wrote was factual, he changed the names of the people involved. The narrator refers to Pauline as "P.O.M." (for "Poor Old Mama") throughout most of the book, although the Africans call her "Memsahib." "Pop" and "Mr. J.P." in the book refer to Philip Percival, their British guide. He is one of three people to whom Hemingway dedicated the book. Also among those three is Charles Thompson, the friend whom Hemingway depicts in the book as Karl.

Green Hills of Africa was first published in serial form in *Scribner's Magazine* from May to October of 1935. It was accompanied by line drawings of animals and hunters by Edward Shenton, drawings that also appeared in the book version, which was published in October of 1935.

In Part I of *Green Hills of Africa*, "Pursuit and Conversation," Hemingway describes the hunting of kudu and recalls discussions of writing and writers with Kandinsky, an eccentric Austrian who recalls reading Hemingway's poetry in an obscure German literary magazine. Hemingway's party happens to run across Kandinsky unexpectedly in the bush when his car breaks down. In the ensuing discussion of American literature with Kandinsky, the narrator is harshly critical of Edgar Allan Poe, Herman Melville, Ralph Waldo Emerson, Nathaniel Hawthorne, John Greenleaf Whittier, and Henry David Thoreau, reserving his highest praise, on the other hand, for Mark Twain, Stephen Crane, and Henry James. He also mentions British Nobel Prize winner Rudyard Kipling and French novelist Gustave Flaubert in favorable terms.

As Part I ends, Hemingway shoots a lion that he and his party have been tracking, but inexplicably it is his wife whom the natives credit with the kill. Although P.O.M. knows she didn't shoot the lion, she nevertheless enjoys the ensuing fuss.

In Part II, "Pursuit Remembered," Hemingway describes hunting for rhino and introduces the theme of competition between himself and Karl, his friend on the safari. Karl has shot the best buffalo and the best waterbuck, as well as a lion and a leopard (63). Hemingway successfully and skillfully shoots a rhino only to learn, upon reaching camp, that Karl has stumbled across and sloppily shot a much larger rhino. Hemingway also describes his own wounding of an African buffalo.

In Part II, as in Part I, the narrator discusses writing, although he focuses on European literature this time, referring favorably to Leo Tolstoi, Fyodor Dostoyevsky, James Joyce, Ivan Turgenev, and Stendhal before describing his successful quests to shoot a buffalo, an oryx (a kind of antelope), and ducks. Hemingway also catalogues petty disagreements that exacerbate the friction between himself and Karl.

Part III, the aptly named "Pursuit and Failure," chronicles various disappointments and mishaps as their safari winds down. After the flashback of Part II, Part III returns the reader to where the action paused at the end of Part I. Rain ruins the salt lick where Hemingway had hoped to find a kudu. He is disgusted by what he sees as the pretentious theatricality of the guide he nicknames David Garrick after the great eighteenth-century British stage actor. He is further infuriated when his trusted tracker, M'Cola, neglects to clean Hemingway's rifle, which consequently begins to rust. As this part of the book ends, an anxious Hemingway, knowing he must leave Africa the next day, decides to follow the old guide to a place the old man describes as better country for hunting.

Part IV concerns Hemingway's successful hunt for a kudu in the "unhunted" country to which the old man leads him (218). It also describes Hemingway's less successful hunt for sable; he shoots two, but one is a cow, and the other, a bull that he has "gut-shot," is badly wounded but ultimately eludes them. Elated by the huge kudu he has shot, he returns to camp only to make the bitter discovery that Karl has shot a kudu with even larger horns.

Green Hills of Africa ends with a self-reflexive scene in which the narrator promises to write the book the reader has just read. The book's strengths are its flashes of humor and its vivid, sometimes lyrical descriptions of animals, Africans, and Africa itself—for example, the marvelous passage about the hyena happily munching its own intestines (37–38), the description of the beauty of the dead kudu bull (231), and the narrator's memory of the Masai runners easily keeping pace with the car (219).

Despite its strengths, however, the book's reviews were largely (although not exclusively) negative, and its sales were disappointing after the successes of Hemingway's earlier books. Critics objected to the book's pace; although Hemingway claimed to find the story exciting, few of his readers agreed. Edmund Wilson, for example, pronounced *Green Hills of Africa* "the only book I have ever read which makes Africa and its animals seem dull" (rpt. in Meyers, *Critical Heritage* 217). Many reviewers objected to the unpleasant portrayal of the book's central character, the narrator. The narrator pontificates obnoxiously about literature, brags about his skill at tracking and shooting, dreams up ways to hurt a native guide he finds unlikable, and behaves with unsportsmanlike hostility toward his friend Karl when their competitiveness gets out of hand and becomes what the narrator himself calls an obsession when he sees it in Karl (152). Pop perhaps puts it best: " 'We have very primitive emotions,' he said. 'It's impossible not to be competitive. Spoils everything, though' " (293). Another kind of primitive emotion, anger or the desire for revenge, may also have influenced the bad reviews, for throughout the work Hemingway condemned literary critics and their destructive impact on the artist's confidence and ability.

In her book *Playing in the Dark: Whiteness and the Literary Imagination*, Toni Morrison, a best-selling novelist and the first African-American woman to win the Nobel Prize for Literature, has written critically of what she sees as Hemingway's racism. Hemingway's casual use of the word "niggers" in *Green Hills of Africa* is admittedly disturbing and, like the references in *In Our Time*, has provoked speculation about the extent of Hemingway's prejudice (82). He depicts the native African characters in very sketchy, dismissive, and often stereotypical terms and generally seems interested only in their usefulness to him. Biographer Michael Reynolds has acknowledged Hemingway's "benign racism," apparently meaning by this odd term that Hemingway was casually racist in his language and ideas but neither violent nor particularly active in promoting such attitudes. Scholar Toni Knott has suggested that Hemingway consciously used racial slurs to call them into question, thus forcing his readers to recognize the ways in which our society so blithely categorizes and then dismisses people. Like the anti-Semitism reflected in his work, however, the instances of racism are difficult to explain away.

Twenty-first-century readers are also apt to find the relentless emphasis on killing animals disturbing. Hemingway seems determined not simply to shoot animals, but to kill as many as possible within the legal limits, trying only to avoid shooting the females. Critic Philip Young, who argued that Hemingway sustained emotional trauma from the violent deaths he witnessed in World War I, theorized that "he spent a great deal of time killing animals and fish in order that he might not kill himself" (166). As Hemingway himself explains, with suspicious defensiveness, "I did not mind killing anything, any animal, if I killed it cleanly, they all had to die and my interference with the nightly and seasonal killing that went on all the time was very minute and I had no guilty feeling at all" (272). Yet it is also Hemingway who a dozen pages later in the same book anticipates the damage that his hunting and traveling have begun to cause:

A continent ages quickly once we come. The natives live in harmony with it. But the foreigner destroys, cuts down the trees, drains the water, so that the water supply is altered and in a short time the soil, once the sod is turned under, is cropped out and, next, it starts to blow away as it has blown away in every old country and as I had seen it start to blow in Canada. The earth gets tired of being exploited. (284)

His ecological schizophrenia has led some readers—including Rose Marie Burwell and Terry Tempest Williams—to conclude that with the passing of time, Hemingway grew increasingly sensitive to environmental concerns and more interested in observing animals than in ending their lives.

"THE SNOWS OF KILIMANJARO"

"The Snows of Kilimanjaro" was first published in the August 1936 issue of *Esquire*. Hemingway wrote the story earlier that year and originally titled it "The Happy Ending" (Smith, *Reader's Guide* 349). Later, in his essay "The Art of the Short Story," he claimed to have been inspired to write "The Snows of Kilimanjaro" after a wealthy woman invited the Hemingways to travel to Africa at her expense. He speculated about what might have happened had he accepted her offer: "So I invent how someone I know who cannot sue me—that is me—would turn out, and put into one short story things you would use in, say, four novels if you were careful and not a spender" (136). A reference in the *Esquire* version to "poor Scott Fitzgerald" caused Fitzgerald to write to Hemingway asking him not to refer to him in print (qtd. in Bruccoli 191); in later publications of the story, Hemingway changed the name to "poor Julian."

"The Snows of Kilimanjaro" was made into a film by Darryl Zanuck in 1952. The film starred Gregory Peck, Susan Hayward, and Ava Gardner. Disgusted by the way in which the ending of the story was changed in the film, Hemingway derisively referred to the movie as "The Snows of Zanuck" (Reynolds, *Final* 260).

PLOT DEVELOPMENT

Harry, a writer and the story's protagonist, visits Africa on safari. He sustains a scratch that becomes infected, poisoning his blood. The gangrene is threatening his life as the story opens, and he and Helen, who is presumably his wife, await the plane that will carry them out of the bush back to civilization, where he can receive proper medical treatment. In the meantime, Harry reflects on his life, and what he remembers isn't pretty. Neither is his behavior, as he shifts from acknowledging on the one hand how he has squandered his own talent to making bitter accusations on the other hand, blaming his wealthy wife and her equally rich and spiritually vapid friends for corrupting him and seducing him away from his work.

The story's form is unusual, for Hemingway incorporates within the story Harry's flashbacks to the experiences he wanted to use as raw material for his writing. For the deceptive surprise ending of the story Hemingway owes a debt to Ambrose Bierce's classic 1891 short story "Occurrence at Owl Creek Bridge" (Young 197).

CHARACTER DEVELOPMENT

In an earlier draft of the story, Harry's last name is Walden, linking him to the famous nonfiction work in which Henry David Thoreau describes his two-year sojourn in a cabin on Walden Pond in Massachusetts. The allusion is an interesting one, for Thoreau was attempting to simplify his life, observe nature and, above all, live deliberately. What Thoreau does voluntarily, Harry finds himself compelled to do against his will.

Harry despises himself for betraying himself as an artist and takes his self-hatred out on his wife, a cruelty that makes him hate himself even more. He alternates between reviling Helen and placating her with dishonest apologies. He confesses to himself, although not openly to Helen, that she had little to do with his failure to achieve his promise as a writer and that it was his own choices in life that have led him to this place to die without ever having written what might have been within his power to write. Consumed with bitterness and regret for what he has thrown away with both hands, he is haunted by reminiscences, represented by the italicized passages interspersed throughout the text of the story.

Like Hemingway's wife, Pauline, Helen is wealthy, and it is her family's money that finances their safari—a fact that Harry repeatedly throws in her face. Her wealth has not protected her from a tough life, however. Widowed just after her grown children had left the house, she turned to alcohol and lovers for solace until the accidental death of one of her children. Determined to create a new life, she did so successfully with Harry—unaware of his emotional hollowness and insincerity.

Despite Harry's hateful accusations, there is every reason to believe that Helen genuinely cares for him. As she herself tells him plaintively, "I'm only a middle-aged woman who loves you and wants to do what you want to do" (*SS* 63). Deeply upset by his illness, she worries about him and urges him not to drink because of the threat it poses to his health. She hunts for game far from camp so that she will not frighten away the animals he loves to watch. His vicious accusations move her to tears, and she is obviously frightened and upset by his lack of response at the end of the story.

THEMES

The story's theme centers on the writer who compromises his art, who runs out of time before he is finished writing the stories he believes he was born to write. Harry is rotting from within, and the gangrene that is killing him suggests his corruption and moral decay. He has chosen financial comfort over faithfulness to his artistic calling. Biographer Carlos Baker has suggested Henry James' short story "The Lesson of the Master" as a possible source for the story's conflict between materialism and artistic integrity (*Writer* 192).

The story's italicized passages sound very much like the memories Hemingway later describes in *A Moveable Feast*, his memoir of the 1920s. Hemingway himself frequently complained bitterly that his second wife Pauline's wealth and her rich friends had corrupted his art, so "The Snows of Kilimanjaro" is in part autobiographical. Its very existence and its high quality, however, challenge the notion that by the 1930s Hemingway had destroyed his own talent.

A second theme of the story is the deadening effect of Harry's inability to love. Like Harold Krebs in the short story "Soldier's Home," Harry is emotionally detached; he denies that he loves Helen, just as Krebs denies that he loves his mother. Further, Harry, like Krebs, then lies that he did not mean his denial. Hemingway's choice of the name "Harry" recalls the name of the protagonist, Harold, of "Soldier's Home," and the name "Helen," too, echoes the name of Harold's favorite sister—parallels that suggest the thematic similarity of the two works.

Like Krebs, Harry is too emotionally exhausted to connect with anyone: "with the women that he loved he had quarreled so much they had finally, always, with the corrosion of the quarrelling, killed what they had together. He had loved too much, demanded too much, and he wore it all out" (*SS* 64). Now mired in what is for him a superficial relationship with a woman whom he does not love, it is little wonder that Harry so often associates her with death.

LITERARY DEVICES

Hemingway endows this story with a wealth of symbols. Harry envisions death not in the conventional medieval terms of a skeleton carrying a scythe, but as a bicycle policeman and (more memorably) as a foul-breathed hyena crouching heavily on his chest. The image of the story's title perhaps suggests both the Christian concept of heaven and the artistic heights Harry could have ascended. The story's epigraph introduces the enigmatic metaphor of the leopard frozen on the slopes near Kilimanjaro's summit, the leopard whose presence, the narrator tells us, no one has been able to explain. It is tempting to see the leopard as a metaphor symbolizing the writer, who died before reaching what would have been the summit of his career. Critics have suggested unconvincing sources for the leopard in both Dante's *Inferno* and the Book of Revelations in the Bible. After noting that in the original version of the anecdote the leopard was seeking a mountain goat, Paul Smith rather dryly points out that "the leopard's natural instincts were motivated by precisely those that Harry believes corrupted him, the instinctual desire to feed well" (*Reader's Guide* 354).

HISTORICAL AND SOCIAL SETTING

"The Snows of Kilimanjaro" takes place in Tanganyika, now Tanzania, in the shadow of Mount Kilimanjaro, the tallest mountain in Africa. As the story's epigraph indicates, the Masai (the African tribe native to that area) saw the western summit of the mountain as the House of God. "While critics have sought to explain what the leopard was seeking near the western summit of 'Ngaje Ngai,' the House of God, they have ignored the plight of the Africans laboring below on the East Plains of Africa and Harry's relation to them," comments Hemingway critic Debra Moddelmog. While Harry and Helen believe they have stripped themselves of luxuries, they nevertheless have several black servants at their beck and call (Moddelmog 107).

Moddelmog sees critics' reactions to the story as founded upon the imperialistic assumption that Africa and Africans are interesting only as a backdrop to the actions and interests of white people. Like the critics Moddelmog critiques, Harry and Helen see Africa purely in terms of its usefulness to them: "As in so much American and British literature written by white men, Africa thus becomes the stage for the white male's drama of individuation, in which black African natives serve as stage hands without histories or scripts of their own" (Moddelmog 109).

"THE SHORT HAPPY LIFE OF FRANCIS MACOMBER"

According to a letter to his Scribner's editor, Maxwell Perkins, Hemingway finished writing "The Short Happy Life of Francis Macomber" in April 1936. It was first published in *Cosmopolitan* in September 1936 and was included in *The First Forty-nine Short Stories*, published in 1938. The story later became the basis of the 1947 film *The Macomber Affair*, starring Gregory Peck and Joan Bennett.

PLOT DEVELOPMENT

"The Short Happy Life of Francis Macomber" is possibly the most controversial short story in American literature. It has only three characters: Francis and Margot Macomber, a wealthy husband and wife on safari, and their guide, Robert Wilson. The story is set in Kenya, formerly a British colony. Critic Debra Moddelmog argues that the characters in this story share the imperialistic assumptions of those in "The Snows of Kilimanjaro": They see Africa as their playground and Africans purely as servants. As the story opens, the three characters are returning to camp after Francis has ignobly bolted in fear upon confronting his first lion, an experience related in flashback.

Unnerved by the lion's roaring, to which Margot is oblivious, Francis shoots badly. Wilson insists that they must track the wounded lion and kill it. A reluctant Francis forces himself to try but panics and runs when they discover the lion. After Wilson shoots the lion, Margot pulls away from her husband and kisses Wilson in front of her husband.

Margot, an aging beauty, at first seems emotionally devastated by the revelation of her husband's cowardice, but when she recovers from her initial reaction, she quickly launches an affair with Wilson and taunts her husband with her infidelity. After Francis shoots the buffalo, she, too, undergoes an abrupt transformation. Wilson interprets it as her frightened awareness that she has lost the upper hand in her marriage. Yet she also seems genuinely sickened by the violence of hunting and repeatedly scoffs at their vaunted heroism, contrasting it with the helplessness of their prey (SS 30, 33). It's possible, and perhaps even likely, that she identifies with their victims.

The next day, after chasing the buffalo in the motor car, Francis abruptly loses his fear and, in Wilson's eyes, finally achieves manhood. Margot recognizes the change in her husband and seems uneasy. When Francis and Wilson track the wounded buffalo, it charges Macomber: " . . . Mrs. Macomber, in the car, had shot at the buffalo with the 6.5 Mannlicher as it seemed about to gore Macomber and had hit her husband about two inches up and a little to one side of the base of his skull" (SS 36). Wilson tells her that the newly courageous Macomber *would* have left Margot and asks coldly why she didn't poison her husband; he does not relent until she begins to beg him to stop.

CHARACTER DEVELOPMENT

The Macombers are based in part on Jane and Grant Mason, a couple who spent time with the Hemingways in Key West: "In appearance, Margot Macomber with her perfect oval face and hair drawn back in a knot at the nape of her neck is without doubt modeled after Jane," who, like Margot, was featured in a magazine advertisement for facial cream (Kert 275). Years later, in a rambling essay titled "The Art of the Short Story" that was not published until after his death, Hemingway explained, "I invented her complete with handles from the worst bitch I knew (then) and when I first knew her she'd been lovely.

Not my dish, not my pigeon, not my cup of tea, but lovely for what she was and I was her all of the above which is whatever you make of it" ("Art" 134).

The last name of Hemingway's fictional husband and wife suggests the respectful title *Bwana M'Kumba*, a Swahili term combining "sir" with a word for leader or superior (Smith, *Reader's Guide* 334). Hemingway had earlier used the title ironically in *Green Hills of Africa* when P.O.M., mocking her husband's obnoxious habit of lecturing his guest, observed of Kandinsky, "He didn't have a chance to talk after B'wana M'Kumba started" (29). The Macombers' marriage is a troubled one, which has nearly ended three times already.

Francis Macomber is tall, dark, and handsome. At 35, he is physically fit and very rich. He is also understandably nervous about confronting dangerous game and as the story opens has just run from a lion, an action that bitterly disappoints his wife and convinces Robert Wilson that he is a coward. Wilson sees Francis as strangely boyish until by successfully shooting buffalo he abruptly loses his fear. Only at that point, very near the end of the story, does Macomber achieve both bravery and happiness.

Robert Wilson, the white hunter the Macombers have hired to lead them, has a ruddy complexion and icy blue eyes. Given his reference to England at the end of the story and his fondness for Shakespeare, he is presumably British, although in *True at First Light* Hemingway's son Patrick suggests he was based on Baron Bror Blixen, who was Swedish. Although Wilson rationalizes to himself that he has principles that govern his behavior, his professional principles seem extraordinarily flexible: He threatens the Africans with lashes although he admits whippings are against the law. Chasing the buffalo in cars, he admits, is also illegal and could cost him his license. His personal behavior is no better: He despises Margot but sleeps with her nevertheless. "He is, in effect, a moral whore" (Whitlow 61).

Hemingway's own equivocations about white hunters do not make Wilson's character any easier to read. In *True at First Light*, for example, the "fictional memoir" discussed later in this chapter, Hemingway writes that he respected Philip Percival more than he respected his own father, yet later in the same work, he refers to the "white hunter" in general as a soulless fellow who caters to the whims of his women clients.

THEMES

The interpretation of theme depends on Margot Macomber's guilt or innocence. Does Margot shoot her husband accidentally or on purpose? Is she trying to save him from the buffalo by shooting the charging animal? Or is Wilson right? Is she trying to save herself by shooting the newly emboldened husband who seems suddenly capable of leaving her? Is she guilty of murdering her husband, either consciously or unconsciously?

One group of readers and critics contends that Margot either deliberately or "accidentally on purpose" murders her husband. She is dependent upon him economically and probably emotionally as well. "They had a sound basis of union," Hemingway explains. As he writes in a sentence of such biting irony and nicely balanced parallelism that it is worthy of Jane Austen, "Margot was too beautiful for Macomber to divorce her and Macomber had too much money for Margot ever to leave him" (*SS* 22). Once Francis gains courage, he could easily abandon her for a younger and less contentious wife, leaving Margot without the money and status their marriage brings her. In this reading, her nemesis Wilson is an admirable character, the one man who sees through her scheme to kill her husband and keep his wealth for herself.

Another group more convincingly argues that Margot shot at the buffalo and killed her husband accidentally. The narrator specifically says that she shot at the buffalo. There is, after all, no reason to shoot her husband when he will momentarily be killed by a charging buffalo anyway. In this reading of the story, Margot—however unpleasant her behavior—is a victim, a woman trying desperately to save her husband, perhaps because his abrupt development of courage has attracted her to him once again, and Macomber, ironically, gains his courage only to lose his life. Wilson is a moral whore who sees the world—and the hapless Margot—in the darkest possible terms and condemns her out of sexism and an easy willingness to believe the worst. He has, after all, been wrong before; he pronounced the buffalo dead the moment before it charged (Flora, *Ernest* 80). Certainly his domination of Margot at the end of the story—when he prefers to see her crying and begging, almost literally groveling—is unpleasant and suggests that Margot isn't the only character in the story who has sadistic impulses. As first critic Anne Greco and then Hemingway biographer Kenneth Lynn have suggested, it is also possible that Wilson behaves as he does at the end of the story because he fears that Margot will reveal that he was permitting the Macombers to chase the animals using automobiles, a violation of the law that could cost him his license. Thus he implicates her as a murder suspect in order to blackmail her into telling his version of the events so that his livelihood will be protected.

LITERARY DEVICES

The most important literary device in the story is Wilson's allusion to a line from Act III, Scene 2 of Shakespeare's *Henry IV, Part II* (*SS* 32): "By my troth, I care not; a man can die but once; we owe God a death and let it go which way it will, he that dies this year is quit for the next." Hemingway cited the same quotation approvingly in the anthology he edited, *Men at War: The Best War Stories of All Time*, going on to comment: "That is probably the best thing that is written in this book and, with nothing else, a man could get along all right on that" (xii). The point of the quotation is that, since a man will die eventually anyway, there's no reason for him to fear death. At least if he dies, he will get it over with. Ironically, in Hemingway's story, his protagonist loses his fear of death—and promptly dies.

It's possible to read the story as Hemingway's *Turn of the Screw*. A novella by Henry James, *The Turn of the Screw* is a complex story in which the reader is never sure whether the ghosts that the narrator, a repressed Victorian governess, sees are real or the projections of her fevered imagination. The long and vigorous controversy over this aspect of the story has prompted some critics to suggest that the author (despite comments made elsewhere that seem to indicate the ghosts were meant to be genuine) deliberately introduced the ambiguity into the story and intended for its meaning to be ultimately indeterminate. Very much like James's novella, Hemingway's "The Short Happy Life of Francis Macomber" (despite comments made elsewhere by its author that seem to indicate that Wilson's view of Margot is an accurate one) also seems at times a deliberately ambiguous work whose meaning is ultimately indeterminate. As Hemingway wrote in "The Art of the Short Story," "No, I don't know whether she shot him on purpose any more than you do. I could find out if I asked myself because I invented it and I could go right on inventing. But you have to know where to stop" (135). Hemingway listed *The Turn of the Screw* in a list of recommended fiction; mentioned James in *The Sun Also Rises*, *Torrents of Spring*, *Death in the Afternoon*, *True at First Light*, and many of his private letters; and in his written response to receiving the Nobel Prize lamented that Henry James had never received the honor.

TRUE AT FIRST LIGHT

Look, a large-format glossy photo magazine that competed with *Life* magazine, offered to pay $15,000 of the expenses for a second African safari if Hemingway would let one of the magazine's photographers accompany him to document the safari in pictures. Hemingway would also have to write captions for the photos *Look* chose to publish. The magazine would pay more if he would write an article to accompany the pictures (Mary Welsh Hemingway, *How It Was* 321).

In 1953 Hemingway and his fourth wife, Mary Welsh Hemingway, accepted the generous offer and, after a planned detour through Europe, arrived in Africa in August and stayed until January 1954. Hemingway was particularly interested in seeing an elephant, since he had not seen one during his earlier safari (Reynolds, *Final* 261). Philip Percival, his guide on that 1933–1934 expedition, agreed to lead the Hemingways on this new excursion (Reynolds, *Final* 266).

It is this trip on which Hemingway based the 850-page typed manuscript that his son Patrick edited into *True at First Light* by cutting nearly half its content. Hemingway drafted the work quickly during 1955 (Reynolds, *Final* 285). The manuscript, traditionally referred to as the "African book" or the "African journal," was for many years available only to scholars who visited the Kennedy Library in Boston, where many of Hemingway's papers are preserved. Excerpts from the manuscript were published in the January 25, 1954, and April 20 and 27, 1954, issues of *Look* magazine and in three consecutive weekly issues of *Sports Illustrated* beginning December 20, 1971. The excerpts published in *Sports Illustrated* were titled "The African Journal," although Hemingway's son Patrick takes issue with the term "journal," preferring to call the work "a fictional memoir." Patrick Hemingway chose the book's final title from a passage that he also used as the book's epigraph:

In Africa a thing is true at first light and a lie by noon and you have no more respect for it than for the lovely, perfect weed-fringed lake you see across the sun-baked salt plain. You have walked across that plain in the morning and you know that no such lake is there. But now it is there absolutely true, beautiful and believable. (189)

Patrick's choice of title suggests that he felt the book was more fictional than earlier readers had believed. In a presentation at the centennial conference at Oak Park, Hemingway's birthplace, Patrick Hemingway indicated that influences on *True at First Light* included Olive Schreiner's *The Story of an African Farm*, Isak Dinesen's *Out of Africa*, and Doris Lessing's *Children of Violence* series of five novels, as well as D.H. Lawrence's later work, and specifically his unorthodox theories regarding religion.

The book was published in 1999 to mark the hundredth anniversary of Hemingway's birth on July 21, 1899, and quickly became a bestseller. In a piece in the *New Yorker* shortly before its publication, writer Joan Didion criticized the Hemingway family's decision to publish work Hemingway chose not to publish during his lifetime. She felt that it was unfair to an author and morally reprehensible to publish work that had never been completed to the author's satisfaction.

The reviews of *True at First Light* have largely been negative. Kenneth Lynn's comments, although harsh, are nevertheless representative of the general disappointment of the critics: " . . . this 'fictional memoir' of the first phase of the 54-year-old Hemingway's final visit to East Africa in 1953–54 reflects a marvelous writer's disastrous loss of talent" (Lynn, "Hemingway Ltd." 50). Compared to his other works, this book is slow moving and self-indulgent.

PLOT DEVELOPMENT

True at First Light has little narrative structure and is rambling and unfocused. What plot there is centers on Hemingway's fourth wife, Mary Welsh Hemingway, and her determined quest for a lion; his semi-official responsibilities as an honorary game warden; and his involvement with Debba, a Masai woman whom he designates his fiancée. A potential subplot concerning Mau Mau jail escapees fizzles soon after it is launched.

Mary, who is generally referred to in the text as either Miss Mary or Memsahib, seeks a lion in order to outdo Pauline, Hemingway's second wife, who shot a lion on their 1933–1934 safari. Miss Mary compares the lion to the Holy Grail and the Golden Fleece; she is so persistent that the Africans on the safari are puzzled. Hemingway mockingly attributes her determination to her religion in order to persuade the Africans to understand the importance of what is essentially her jealous whim. In an echo of Santiago's attitude toward the marlin in *The Old Man and the Sea*, Mary tells her husband that she loves and respects the lion that she is nevertheless determined to kill, and the narrator also echoes the character of Santiago in that novella when he tells his wife that their goal is to move the lion "a little too far out" so that he will make a mistake that will allow her to kill him (132).

Yet perhaps Hemingway's attitude had changed in the 20 years between the two safaris. In referring to another lion, whom Mary wants to own, he advocates letting the lion belong not to them but to the lion himself, because that's what the lion would want. Unlike his blithe disregard for wildlife conservation throughout most of *Green Hills of Africa*, Hemingway's attitude about hunting seems primarily defensive in this book. He repeatedly justifies killing the animals he hunts. For example, because the lion that Miss Mary is tracking has killed cattle belonging to Masai villagers, killing it is not only permitted but sanctioned. The leopard he hunts has killed 16 goats, eight of them belonging to Debba's family, and was therefore reclassified as vermin. Clearly Hemmingway is aware that hunting is a less widely approved pursuit than it used to be. Elsewhere in the book, after briefly mentioning what he calls "baboon control," he sarcastically adds, "In order neither to sadden nor enrage baboon lovers I will give no details" (132).

Hemingway creates suspense by describing his patronizing concern that Miss Mary's erratic shooting skills expose her to danger. When she kills a wildebeest, he discovers that she had shot it 14 inches higher than she had aimed. Only much later in the book, after she has killed another wildebeest on her own, does she discover how poor her aim has been, with a shot that sounds startlingly like Margot Macomber's. Hemingway speculates that because she cares about animals, her conscience causes her to flinch at the last moment, causing her wildly inaccurate shooting. Nevertheless, Mary semi-successfully shoots her lion halfway through the book.

Hemingway's position as an acting game ranger apparently entails primarily whatever responsibilities he invents for himself. Although he has only a limited command of Swahili, which he shamefacedly acknowledges he can neither write nor speak correctly, the Africans, he writes, treat him like a ruler. The Informer tells him that he and G.C. are the law, and that the narrator's age gives him an edge in authority. A young police officer asks for his advice in capturing escaped prisoners and calls him "governor" (52–53). Using the magic of Western antibiotics, which apparently are rare or nonexistent in Kenya in the mid-1950s, the narrator plays doctor and provides medical care upon demand to various African natives. Hemingway's portrayal of his status in the community is unpleasantly self-congratulatory.

His status seems to be primarily what attracts Debba to him; he portrays her as priding herself on how his behavior makes her look. Typically, Hemingway insists that he did not initiate his involvement with Debba, but rather that "It started itself" (64). He frequently seemed passive in his relations with women and portrays his affair with Pauline in similar terms in the memoir *A Moveable Feast*. Only the Interpreter Hemingway uses to converse with Mr. Singh has the nerve to ask the narrator pointedly whether he can justify taking an African as his mistress and to tell him that in doing so, he is committing a sin. True to form, the narrator returns her to her family only when Keiti (whom Patrick Hemingway compares to the butler in *The Remains of the Day*) insists that the proprieties be observed (265).

Like most of his other works, *True at First Light* is intensely nostalgic: Hemingway reminisces about Paris cafés (147–49), Michigan cider (161–62), eagle hunting near Lame Deer (207–11), and traveling through Spain (213). Rose Marie Burwell has suggested, "The Paris book that became *A Moveable Feast* begins to take its form here" (146).

CHARACTER DEVELOPMENT

The chief "characters" in this work are Hemingway himself and his wife, Miss Mary. Early in the book, Hemingway writes, "I never knew of a morning in Africa when I woke that I was not happy" (17). Yet Hemingway frequently alludes to his own serious depression. The Spanish words he and Debba repeat to each other, "*No hay remedio*," mean "There is no remedy." After Mary tells him he utters this despairing message in his sleep, Hemingway says "I'm not a no hay remedio boy, really;" she insists that he is (72). Disgusted by the way the men horse around, she tells him, "There's death in every joke" (75). He is evidently very moody; when he jokingly tells Mary that jumping in and out of bottomless pits will be an event in the next Olympic Games, she responds that then he would win it. Some of the references foreshadow his eventual suicide as, for example, when he tells G.C. that he isn't hopeless now but that the day he does lose hope, G.C. will know it.

More than once the narrator mulls Fitzgerald's line about his own battle with depression, which Hemingway struggles to remember and finally recalls: "In a real dark night of the soul it is always three o'clock in the morning" (172). The narrator tells G.C. that he thinks Fitzgerald was referring to despair, and when G.C. asks him if he has ever experienced despair, he responds that he hasn't yet. But he later concedes that he *is* afraid, and his heavy dependence on alcohol is apparent throughout the book. More than once he mentions drinking early in the morning, and he jokes about alcoholism. He attributes the drinking to a need to dull his highly developed sensitivities and then immediately punctures his own pretensions.

On several occasions throughout the book Hemingway briefly mentions his previous marriages, and he seems especially bitter about his third wife, Martha Gellhorn. Given his conservative Christian upbringing, Hemingway's three divorces no doubt contributed to his depression. His marital troubles are perhaps not surprising, however, given the attitudes he elucidates in this memoir. He believes fidelity (for the husband, at least) is impossible after the first marriage, and announces, "Love is a terrible thing that you would not wish on your neighbor" (262).

Now in his fourth marriage, Ernest is perpetually offering his wife heavy-handed and condescending advice, which Mary (understandably) resents and resists. She is tartly disapproving of his sometimes silly sense of humor and complains that he and G.C. "just do devilish things to show off to each other" (224). She also tires of his commanding manner. She objects to his domineering, his yelling, even his clichés: "Don't say listen and don't whisper. And don't say on your own two feet and when the chips are down" (122). In one particularly angry outburst, she complains that she is perpetually watched over as though she were a child and concludes, "Sometimes you're preposterous" (86). Ironically, however, despite his condescending attitude toward his wife, Hemingway staunchly refuses to kill the lion and give her credit for the kill; his ethics prompt him to insist that she kill the animal herself, despite the urgings of others on the safari.

His "great friend and teacher Philip Percival," who guided Hemingway's earlier safari, also guides this one. In the book's opening paragraph, the narrator tells readers that he respected the man he calls Pop "as I had never respected my father" (13). Hemingway insists that Mary follow the ethical standards for hunting that Hemingway had learned from "Pop," even though Hemingway himself admits that the standards must have seemed "too rigid and slightly murderous" to Mary's gunbearer, Charo (47), who has been attacked by animals because of the Hemingways' strict adherence to these challenging standards. Hemingway also subscribes to Pop's theory that a man really shows his mettle when shooting at a dangerous animal at very close range. Like Hemingway's own father, and Dr. Adams in "Indian Camp," Pop is demanding. Worse yet, he is uncommunicative, leaving Ernest to work out on his own what Pop's expectations are.

At the same time, however, Hemingway mocks the way in which the women on a safari predictably fall for the great white hunter, whom he scorns as "that iron-nerved panderer to what a woman expects" (89). He also writes scathingly of the Great White Hunter's hypocrisy and his eagerness to exploit tourists; what seems like conservationism is really the white hunter's desire to preserve his way of making a living.

On the other hand, Bwana Game, or G.C., cares deeply about the preservation of African wildlife. G.C., which stands for "Gin Crazed," is Hemingway's nickname for the white man his son Patrick identifies as the area's game warden. G.C. is slightly older than Hemingway's oldest son Jack, and some of the book's most successful touches of humor occur in the comic exchanges between the narrator and G.C.

Less entertaining is the Informer. The narrator concedes that everyone else hates the Informer (69). In the "Cast of Characters" section at the end of the book, Patrick Hemingway suggests that his father, who had participated in undercover work himself, might have identified with the reviled Informer.

The final important figure in the work is Debba, although she has very little presence of her own in the book; invariably chaperoned by her mother, known as the Widow, Debba is primarily portrayed as a sexual object, a dream girl who asks for nothing but attention and fondles the narrator's pistol holster in various sexually suggestive ways. In defending his father's ability to portray women, Patrick Hemingway suggests that readers "should pay attention to Debba" (316). But *True at First Light* offers the reader very little substantial information about Debba's character; she seems to wriggle with ecstasy over the power the narrator possesses because of his wealth, but we know little else about her.

Miss Mary is surprisingly relaxed about this woman who might be supposed to be her sexual rival, presumably dismissing Debba as a genuine threat to the Hemingways' marriage because of Debba's color. Mary has prepared a speech for any woman who steals her husband's affection, but after she recites it to Hemingway, she tells him that the speech only applies to white women, not to

Debba. Her casual racism here reflects her confidence that while Hemingway might be physically attracted to Debba, she is the wrong color to entice him to divorce Miss Mary and marry her.

THEMES

One possibly inadvertent theme of this work involves the swaggering boast-fulness that many Americans associate with Hemingway, an attitude that occasionally appears in this book. For example, Hemingway implies, not very convincingly, that he has taken part in wartime atrocities and rape and rather crudely suggests that he has enjoyed the sexual favors of Marlene Dietrich. He also makes repeated homophobic references to homosexuality. When Mary asks him to show off, he swats his neck to show where he will shoot a Tommy ram and then makes the stunning shot, in a move reminiscent of Babe Ruth's legendary feat at Chicago's Wrigley Field in the 1932 World Series, first gesturing to where he then promptly hit a home run. But because Hemingway kills the animal instantly, its meat cannot be eaten by the Muslims on the safari, who can eat meat only if the animal has its throat properly cut by a practicing Muslim (33). Mary tells him that the accomplishment is a little too frightening, adding, "When I told you to show off I didn't mean that far off" (62). Yet Hemingway's much vaunted attitude toward masculinity seems to have softened a bit later in life. In this memoir, he seems to have shifted his focus from the difficulty of becoming a man to the need to preserve the childlike qualities of the boy.

Although Hemingway is less given to pontificating in this book than he was in *Green Hills of Africa*, the difficulties of writing well and being a famous writer remain important themes of *True at First Light*. On the second page of the text, the narrator complains that he has read "with distaste" books about himself and his work (14) and later makes a glancing unfavorable reference to Philip Young's study of his writings. He jokingly alludes to *The White Goddess* by Robert Graves, mentions reading the detective fiction of Georges Simenon, describes Mary as reading *The Prince* by Machiavelli, and praises the novels of D.H. Lawrence, whom he regrets never having met. Many of the book's references to secrets and tribal laws (for example, on pages 17, 78–79, 128, 213, and 307) may owe something to D.H. Lawrence's "cerebral mysticism" and "dark mysteries" (35–36). Hemingway also mentions in passing a host of other writers, including James Thurber, James Joyce, Henry James, C. Day Lewis, Dante, and John O'Hara. He makes a condescending reference to a paranoid George Orwell, comments briefly on Emily Brontë's *Wuthering Heights*, and harshly criticizes the novels of South African writer Alan Paton. He is particularly entertaining on the subject of *The Consul at Sunset*, by Gerald Hanley.

Less attractively, he tends to name-drop, mentioning for example "Berenson" (the art critic Bernard Berenson), "Marlene" (film star Marlene Dietrich), and Princess Aspasia of Greece (230, 276).

Hemingway implicitly accuses other writers of stealing from his work but acknowledges that there is a certain dishonesty inherent in the art of writing fiction. He himself is not writing in Africa, despite his wife's encouragement. He is perhaps discouraged by the criticism his recent works have received; he seems unduly bothered by the letter sent by an irate woman reader from Iowa, and his attempts at mocking humor demonstrate the emotional immaturity of which she accuses him. His vindictive response to her letter is grotesquely out of proportion to its significance, suggesting that perhaps his perceptions are already distorted and his responses exaggerated by mental illness.

HISTORICAL AND SOCIAL CONTEXT

Religion and its practice play an important role in *True at First Light*. Hemingway carefully notes which members of the safari are Muslim and cannot drink alcoholic beverages; he points out again and again the importance of the halal, the ritual killing that must be performed in order for devout Muslims to eat an animal's meat. He compares his work as a game ranger to a religious pilgrimage, wonders about the soul, and skeptically refers to the medieval notion of the church as a sanctuary. He comically attempts to explain Christianity to the Informer and gradually outlines a pseudo-religion he has invented to explain any aspect of his behavior the Africans don't understand.

ALTERNATE READING: POSTCOLONIALISM

A postcolonialist reading asks readers to examine a work from the point of view of the colonized and oppressed people it represents, rather than from the point of view of the privileged oppressors. Such a reading helps readers understand the biased assumptions that underlie the work and the ways in which it supports or subverts imperialism. While Hemingway was not British, the nationality that colonized the part of Africa he visits on this safari, he was white, extraordinarily wealthy (especially by African standards), and sometimes racist, making his sensibility closer to that of the British rulers than of the Africans they ruled. Both Mr. Singh and his interpreter see Hemingway as European and refuse to distinguish Americans from colonizers.

Hemingway enjoys a little too much the respect the Africans give him for what are essentially the trappings of his privileged status as an American rather than genuine character attributes: his wealth and his limited knowledge of first aid. The antibiotics he brings earn him near-reverence among the fever-ridden Africans. Very early in the book he admits he loves command, although he dissembles that he especially loves self-command. He refuses to criticize the Empire when Mr. Singh asks him how well it functions, yet he observes with a certain condescension that primitive people enjoy playing with their own appearance—a particularly ironic point given his own experiments with dying his hair and his wish to have his ears pierced. Hemingway is not, however, wholly oblivious to his own privilege. He contrasts the material luxuries enjoyed by the Americans with what he ironically identifies as the African luxury of enduring hardship stoically.

In contrast to his attitude on his earlier trip to Africa, on this safari Hemingway demonstrates a new self-consciousness about his attitudes regarding race. Some might pejoratively label this change "political correctness," while others might more favorably describe it as an increased racial sensitivity. "Once they had been the boys," he observes regarding the Africans working on the safari. Neither he nor the Africans had thought anything of the term when he used it 20 years earlier, Hemingway maintains. Philip Percival still uses the term, but then "Pop" had known them all long enough to recall them as boys. Although Hemingway insists that "no one would have minded if I had used the word," he nevertheless concedes, a little unwillingly, "the way things were now you did not do it" (16).

He pays attention to more than just the changes in language, however. Although he ordinarily works alongside the Africans, he refrains from doing so in town for the sake of appearances. Presumably working alongside the black Africans in town would suggest to the townspeople that he was not properly maintaining white superiority. He mocks the Moslem missionary's anti-white sermon but later tells Ngui, with apparent seriousness, that he prays for "Africa for Africans" and writes, "the white man always took the other people's lands away from them and put them on a reservation where they could go to hell and be destroyed as though they were in a concentration camp" (209). Through his use of the words "reservation" and "concentration camp," Hemingway links the European colonization of Africa with two historical examples of genocide: the European Americans' treatment of Native Americans and the murder of six million Jews in Nazi Germany.

The participants in this safari occasionally mock the tradition of British imperialism in Africa. As Mary points out ironically, "we didn't come out here to bring order into Africa" (115). When the officious young policeman says, "In a way, governor, we're the last of the Empire builders. In a way we're like Rhodes and Dr. Livingstone," Hemingway replies dryly, "In a way" (126). Hemingway mentions what he calls "the White Man's Burden Act" (189), invoking Rudyard Kipling's famous (and notoriously controversial) 1899 poem advocating imperialism and calling for white men to accept paternal responsibility for the care of people of color.

The black Africans of the book get relatively short shrift compared to the whites. Hemingway spends much less time describing the appearance and character of Charo, Keiti, Mwindi, Nguili, Msembi, Mbebia, Mthuka, Ngui, Mwengi, Arap Meina, and Chungo than he does depicting "G.C." or even Pop, who is not even present throughout much of the action. Yet it is the labor of the black Africans that makes this comfortable and luxurious safari possible. Only occasionally—as for example when Hemingway is embarrassed that he has asked Mwindi for a towel that is already at hand—does Hemingway indirectly reveal the extent of their service. They track animals, load and drive the car, clean the guns, fold and lay out the Hemingways' clothes, haul their bath water, carry their messages, prepare meals, bring them tea and drinks, and even awaken them in the morning. The blacks are expected to remain subordinate; even saying "no" without adding the courtesy title "Bwana" is considered insulting (238).

Hemingway recognizes that "ndio," the Swahili word for "yes," "is what the African always says to the White Man to get rid of him through agreement" (42). Elsewhere he ironically describes his own pomposity as the know-it-all White Man, yet at the same time he insists that he is no longer white. He knows he is a stranger in Africa but rejects that knowledge. When he says he wants to become a member of the Kamba tribe, a skeptical Mwindi responds, "Maybe" (242). Hemingway likes to think that the distinctions of race and class vanish during the hunt and talks first of becoming a blood brother of the Africans and later of rejoining the white race. Thus, although Hemingway admittedly recognizes that black Africans treat white foreigners in certain characteristic ways, he prefers to think of himself as the exception to those rules of behavior. Isn't it pretty to think so?

8

For Whom the Bell Tolls
(1940)

Immediately after its publication, *For Whom the Bell Tolls* was Hemingway's most acclaimed novel. The *New York Times*, for example, called *For Whom the Bell Tolls* "the best book Ernest Hemingway has written" and "one of the major novels in American literature" (Adams "New Novel" 1). What attracted many readers was the novel's affirmative quality, especially compared to his earlier work; the suspense of the main character's mission, and the moving and dramatic love story.

Hemingway began writing the book in March 1939 and finished it in the summer or fall of 1940, basing the events of the story on what he had learned from reporting on the Spanish Civil War for the North American Newspaper Alliance in 1937 and 1938. He took the title for his novel from a passage by John Donne in *The Oxford Book of English Prose* and quoted the passage for his novel's epigraph (Baker, *Life* 348). He dedicated the book to Martha Gellhorn, his third wife.

For Whom the Bell Tolls was a critical success and an enormous bestseller. It was chosen as the Book-of-the-Month Club selection for November 1940 (Hanneman 52). Paramount Pictures bought the film rights for $110,000 (Reynolds, *Final* 28). The popular 1943 film starred Gary Cooper and Ingrid Bergman, who both became friendly with Hemingway.

PLOT DEVELOPMENT

The events of the novel take place during three days at the end of May 1937. Robert Jordan, an American university professor who has volunteered to fight to support the Spanish government against the fascist forces, arrives at the mountain camp of a small group of Spanish guerrilla fighters. He has just accepted a difficult mission to work with them behind fascist lines to blow up a bridge. The partisans include Anselmo, an old man; the peasant Agustín, who cannot finish a sentence without uttering an obscenity; Primitivo; the brothers Andrés and Eladio; Fernando; Rafael, the gypsy; the dour Pablo; and two women, Pilar and Maria. Robert and Maria are immediately attracted to each other. Robert soon learns that she has been gang-raped by fascist soldiers. After a brief reconnaissance mission, he plans the demolition of the bridge. That night, Maria comes to his sleeping bag, and they make love.

The next day, the band notices a disturbing number of planes overhead—an ominous foreshadowing of later events. Robert, Maria, and Pilar walk to a meeting with El Sordo, a real-life historical figure and the leader of a neighboring band of guerrillas. On their way they stop to rest, and Pilar tells her horrifying story of how the violence of the civil war played out in a small farming village. Once they reach their destination and meet briefly with El Sordo, he agrees to sell Robert dynamite and to try to provide horses and men to support the mission. On the way back, after briefly alluding to her jealousy, Pilar leaves them, and Robert and Maria make love. Afterward, Robert is overwhelmed by emotion, afraid that his time with Maria will be cut short because of his hopeless mission. In a cynical moment he describes his task to himself as "co-ordinating two chicken-crut guerrilla bands to help you blow a bridge under impossible conditions, to abort a counter-offensive that will probably already be started" (167). As they return to camp, it is snowing. That evening, after a tense confrontation with Pablo, Robert is asked by the band to kill Pablo at the first opportunity.

Robert recalls, in a flashback, his last trip to Madrid and his stay at the Hotel Gaylord's. He is disillusioned by the corruption and dishonesty of the military leaders and disappointed by their stupidity concerning military strategy. Back at the cave, Pilar tells the others that Robert's predecessor, Kashkin, had been shot by Robert because he was too badly wounded to survive. The group wonders whether Kashkin's obsession with making sure he would be shot rather than be left alive to be tortured by the enemy signaled a premonition of his own death. Robert is skeptical, but Pilar describes the smell of death that she says surrounds those who are about to die. That night, Maria again comes to Robert's sleeping bag.

On the following day, Robert awakens when he hears a horse coming and shoots and kills a cavalryman who stumbles upon their camp. The guerrillas watch silently as more cavalrymen pass through later, probably searching for the one Robert shot. Afterwards, Robert and the others hear the firing as El Sordo's group of six guerrilla fighters is killed and beheaded by the fascist forces. The story of El Sordo's last stand, as Hemingway envisions it in Chapter 27, is generally considered one of the strengths of the novel. That night, as they curl up together in his sleeping bag, he and Maria daydream about the future.

When Anselmo reports increased fascist activity, a worried Robert Jordan sends Andrés to General Golz with a message alerting him that the surprise attack is anticipated and should be called off, but by the time the persistent Andrés finally reaches Golz's chief of staff with the message, it is too late to stop the attack. Hemingway is particularly savage in his depiction of André Marty, a historical figure who was chief commissar of the International Brigades, a man whom Hemingway despised. In the meantime, Robert discovers that Pablo has left with two horses and part of their dynamite. Furious, Robert returns to his sleeping bag and gradually calms down as he holds Maria. When she wakes, he makes love to her one last time. Afterwards, when they have joined the others for breakfast, Pablo unexpectedly returns with more men and more horses. He had thrown the explosives into a gorge but regretted leaving the group.

Although the bridge is successfully blown, Anselmo and Eladio are killed in the effort, and Fernando is critically wounded. Robert Jordan's injury, incurred as the partisans attempt to escape, prevents him from leaving with them. Instead, he sends an unwilling Maria off with Pablo and Pilar and steels himself to remain conscious despite the pain of a badly broken leg. Strongly tempted to kill himself as his father did, he fights off what he sees as cowardice, knowing that if he can hold off the soldiers even briefly, perhaps by killing their officer, he may give the others the time they need to escape to safety. Ironically, the officer he must attempt to kill is Lieutenant Paco Berrendo, a devout Catholic from Navarre who ordered the beheading of El Sordo and his band to prove their defeat.

Increasingly, as the story progresses, Hemingway gives his protagonist the feeling of being trapped on an endlessly revolving wheel. Robert Jordan experiences a sense of déjà vu, "feeling it all moving in a circle" (212), and describes the sensation of riding around and around on a great, nightmarish merry-go-round or Ferris wheel (225) that one critic has compared to the traditional image of the wheel of fortune. Jordan ultimately believes he has escaped the cycle: "But I am off that wheel, he thought. And nobody is going to get me onto it again" (226). Yet the novel itself is essentially circular, ending, as it began, with a scene in which Robert Jordan lies full-length on a bed of pine needles. What Hemingway has shown us in the intervening pages is that, as Robert Jordan himself speculates, "it is possible to live as full a life in seventy hours as in seventy years" (166).

CHARACTER DEVELOPMENT

Robert Jordan, tall, thin, and blond, is a college Spanish teacher from Montana and the author of a 200-page book about Spain (248). The partisans call him

"Roberto" or sometimes "*Inglese*," because he speaks English as well as excellent Spanish. A semi-autobiographical figure, Robert, like Hemingway, is discomfited by his father's pious Victorian sentimentality and haunted by his suicide. He is tormented by what he sees as his father's cowardice in killing himself and feels closer to his grandfather, whose bravery he admires. Both of Hemingway's grandfathers had fought for the Union Army in the Civil War (Baker, *Life* 1–2); similarly, Robert recalls his grandfather's stories about his Civil War service and hopes anxiously to live up to that legacy.

The first test of his courage is his encounter with Pablo, an illiterate peasant whose physical strength has won him the command of the small band of partisans. Pablo has killed many people, as Pilar reveals in her atrocity tale, and the killings have taken a toll, leaving him alcoholic, hopeless, and weary of war. He is, as the others insist to Robert, very smart, and his skills are needed to bring the survivors to safety after the bridge is successfully blown. But war has brutalized him, and he is so sick of violence that he has become mentally unstable. He is also jealous of Roberto's intimacy with Maria, to whom Pablo is also attracted. Robert Jordan repeatedly considers killing him for the good of the group, so the reader is not surprised when Pablo betrays the band by stealing the exploder, detonators, and some of the dynamite from Jordan.

Pablo's abrupt return *is* surprising, however. He himself attributes his return to his loneliness; he could not bear the isolation of leaving the band. He brings with him men to replace Sordo's band but kills them after the bridge is blown so that there will be enough horses for his own band to escape, an act that brands him a murderer in Jordan's mind. Nevertheless, it is the intelligent if amoral Pablo who recognizes that Jordan's broken leg dooms him to die in the mountains, and Pablo, along with Pilar, is the one Jordan trusts to ensure Maria's safe escape.

Maria is a beautiful 19-year-old Spanish woman. She has witnessed the murders of her parents, killed by the fascists when her father, the mayor of the village, would not renounce the Republic. She herself is the victim of a brutal gang rape by the fascists. Her golden brown hair is very short because it was shaved while she was imprisoned by the rebels. She escaped when the train she was on was blown up by Pablo's band of partisans and has since let her hair grow out. Immediately after the escape, she was still deeply traumatized as a result of her experiences, unable to speak or stop crying and fearful of anyone's touch. It is only through Pilar's stubbornness that the nearly helpless Maria was not left behind to die.

Roberto and Maria would like to be married and already consider themselves husband and wife. At least one Spanish reader objected to what he saw as the immorality inherent in Hemingway's portrayal of a naïve young Spanish woman willingly participating in a sexual relationship with a foreigner she barely knows. But Hemingway points out, via Agustín, that Maria is a virtuous woman, and that she does not take lightly her unorthodox relationship with Robert, a relationship that would never have occurred had it not been for the social disruption caused by the revolution. Nevertheless, Maria is one of Hemingway's weaker heroines and seems more stereotypical than Brett Ashley, Catherine Barkley, or Pilar.

Pilar, a heavyset 48-year-old peasant woman, is one of Hemingway's most interesting woman characters. As she herself says, she is so simple that she is complicated (156). A woman of integrity, she is both intelligent and powerful. When Pablo tries to resist Jordan, Pilar confronts him publicly, accusing him of cowardice. When she takes Jordan's side, the others in the band immediately join her, thus sparing Jordan the necessity of killing Pablo to prevent his sabotaging their mission. All of the partisans are half admiring and half afraid of her. Jordan, too, finds much to admire in Pilar, telling himself, "She is a damned sight more civilized than you are" (168).

The name Pilar was Hemingway's pet name for his second wife, Pauline, and he christened his beloved boat *Pilar*. In Spanish, it refers to the Virgin Mary, who, according to Catholic tradition, miraculously appeared to Saint James in Zaragoza in 40 A.D. The stone pillar on which she stood became first a venerated shrine and later the site of a cathedral established in her name. Her appearance is celebrated during the Pilar Festivals with parades and bullfights.

Pilar came to Pablo only after her five-year relationship with a matador ended with his death after too many gorings in the bullring. She often reminisces about their relationship and about the bullfights she has witnessed. She believes that a woman is beautiful only when she is loved by a man; no longer loved, Pilar becomes ugly even to herself. By the end of the novel, she has come to care deeply for Robert Jordan.

Many scholars believe she is based in part on Hemingway's former friend, the lesbian modernist writer Gertrude Stein. Pilar is evidently sexually attracted to both Robert and Maria. She tells Maria and Robert Jordan that she is jealous and, despite Maria's protests that "there is nothing like that between us," acknowledges, "There is always something like something that there should not be" (154). Pilar evidently believes that even though both she and Maria are heterosexual, there is a homoerotic element, a same-sex attraction, in their friendship and in every friendship. Thomas E. Gould notes that an earlier draft of the novel was more explicit about Pilar's sexual attraction to Maria (73–75). There is also a direct allusion to Stein in the novel. Echoing Stein's famous line, "A rose is a rose is a rose," Jordan thinks to himself, first, "An onion is an onion is an onion" and then, "a stone is a stein is a rock is a boulder is a pebble" (289). (*Stein* is a German word meaning "stone.") Although his words sound like nonsense, he seems to be belittling Stein rather literally, reducing her from a *Stein*, or stone, down to the tiniest of pebbles.

Of the remaining partisans, the one who leaves the deepest impression on both Robert and the reader is Anselmo, the old man who guides Robert to the cave. Anselmo, who is 68, is afraid he will run if a battle begins. Yet when asked to stay and tally the passing cars, he follows orders despite the discomfort of an unexpected snowstorm. While he remains at his post, he experiences profound guilt and remorse over the killings that he acknowledges are necessary under the circumstances of the war. The deeply moral old man cries after killing the sentry who guards the bridge they must demolish. His values are echoed by Robert Jordan and endorsed by the novel as a whole; he believes that after the war, those who killed, even in a just cause, must somehow try to atone for what they have done. He is convinced that afterwards there must be a public ceremony of penance to cleanse the people of the sins they have committed. A humane idealist, he hopes for a Republican Spanish government that will reform and educate the defeated fascists rather than simply executing them. His fate at the end of the novel saddens both Robert Jordan and the reader.

THEMES

One important theme of the novel is the question of whether a short but intensely lived three days can be as full and as valuable as a lifetime—whether the quality of a life matters more than the quantity of its days. Aware that his sacrifice will deprive him of years of potential happiness with Maria, Robert must decide both whether the sacrifice is worth the cost and whether they can make the three days they will have together as good as the years of marriage they might have had. What makes his decision simpler is the immortality afforded us by love—another important theme of the novel. At the same time as the novel hints at the deaths to come, it also celebrates the redemptive power of human sexuality. Immediately attracted to Robert Jordan (as he is to her), Maria quietly comes to his sleeping bag the first night and asks him to make love to her to help her erase her memories of the gang rape she suffered at the hands of the fascists. They make love three times during the course of the novel, and twice "the earth moved" for both of them (160), an experience that Pilar says happens only three times in a lifetime. Although the expression has since become a laughable cliche, at the time the novel was published, it was a fresh and romantic way to describe the overwhelming power of sexual love. Some of the most beautiful passages in the novel describe the relationship between Robert and Maria, including the experimental lyricism of Hemingway's description of their last night together. At the end of the novel, Roberto insists that he will survive through Maria. Some readers have suggested that in addition to keeping him alive through her memories, the text suggests the possibility that she might be pregnant with his child—thus creating a different kind of immortality for Robert.

A third important theme of the book is the value of sacrificing oneself for others, a theme that Hemingway specifically links to Christ. Allusions to Christianity pepper the novel. Robert Jordan jokingly asks Maria to dry his feet with her hair, as Mary Magdalene does for Christ (Luke 7:38). Jordan compares the war to a crusade, or holy war, and links the feeling his participation in the war gives him to the feeling of a First Communion, the Catholic ceremony welcoming a young child into the community of the Church. Robert also muses that his own surname evokes the biblical river Jordan (438). Many of the characters pray throughout the novel, including Robert, Maria, Anselmo, and Lieutenant Berrendo, among others.

Like Christ, Robert willingly gives up his own life for others, knowing full well that his sacrifice may not save those he loves. Also like Christ, Robert knows what will happen to him and accepts his fate with open eyes, not wanting to die but willing to do so if it will help defeat the forces he regards as evil. The thought of a future with Maria is the strongest temptation to evade his fate, but with great effort he is able to reject that temptation. Like the biblical messiah, Robert, too, is betrayed by a member of his own band. Pilar compares Pablo, who temporarily betrays the group, to Judas Iscariot, betrayer of Christ (391). "I didn't think you had experienced any complete conversion on the road to Tarsus, old Pablo," Robert thinks when he realizes that Pablo has recruited others to join them but plans to betray them as well. He is referring to Pablo's namesake, the biblical figure of Paul, a Jew from Tarsus who experienced an abrupt conversion to Christianity on the road to Damascus (Acts 9:1–22).

In an uncharacteristically religious moment, Jordan thinks to himself of the war, "It gave you a part in something that you could believe in wholly and completely and in which you felt an absolute brotherhood with the others who were engaged in it," and as a consequence of this feeling of community, "your own death seemed of complete unimportance" (235). Perhaps the central theme that makes this novel so meaningful for so many readers is its testament to the importance of community. Robert Jordan knows that he is risking his life in fulfilling the orders he has been given, but he freely accepts his own individual risk for the good of the community.

While war can occasionally bring out the best in people, as it does for Robert Jordan, it more commonly destroys people. Ironically, it is the enemy officer Lieutenant Berrendo who utters another important theme of Hemingway's novel: "What a bad thing war is" (322). Hemingway is preoccupied in this novel with the way in which war brutalizes human beings and eventually renders both sides (however innocent initially) capable of horrific atrocities, like those

Pilar describes. After all, it is war that leads Berrendo to order the beheadings of El Sordo and his gang, Pablo to murder the men whose horses he needs, and even the gentle Anselmo to kill the sentry guarding the bridge. Robert, too, succumbs to the temptation to commit violent acts without regret, although he recognizes and fears his own all-too-ready willingness to participate: "You took to it a little too readily if you ask me, he told himself. And what you will be like or just exactly what you will be suited for when you leave the service of the Republic is, to me, he thought, extremely doubtful" (165). Like Anselmo, Hemingway seems convinced that actions committed during the war will require an extraordinary penance afterward if those who participated in the war are ever to return successfully to normal, everyday, peacetime life.

LITERARY DEVICES

Hemingway adopts various unusual tactics to approximate for English-speaking readers the effect of hearing Spanish spoken. For example, he often uses Spanish syntax with English words. Rather than fighting to include in the published novel the various profane and obscene expressions that a rough band of guerrilla fighters might be expected to use, he uses terms like "un-nameable," "unprintable," "obscenity," and "filth," relying on readers to mentally replace those terms with the appropriate four-letter words. Spanish, like many languages, has two forms of the pronoun "you": one formal and polite, for use with strangers, and one informal and familiar, for use with family and friends; Hemingway uses the archaic English words "thee" and "thou" to suggest the second form of "you."

Hemingway has Robert refer to Maria as "rabbit," which is somewhat disturbing given that the Spanish word for rabbit is a vulgar slang term for a woman's genitals. Citing this point as well as a number of errors Hemingway made in his use of Spanish in the novel, former Hemingway Society president Allen Josephs once argued that Hemingway's poor Spanish severely damages his credibility for many readers. However, in "On Language," an appendix to his book-length discussion of the novel, Josephs modified his position to conclude about Hemingway, "Even if he did throw an occasional wild pitch in Spanish now and then, he won the game" (*Undiscovered Country* 160).

In this work, as in *A Farewell to Arms*, Hemingway was at least partially inspired by other literary works, perhaps the two most prominent being the writings of Lawrence of Arabia and the 1902 novel *The Virginian* by Owen Wister (Plath, "Shadow Rider"; Price; Adair, "Seven Pillars"; Hodson). T.E. Lawrence, better known as Lawrence of Arabia, was a British citizen who lived in Saudi Arabia, joined the Arab revolt against the Turks from 1916 to 1918, and published an account of his experiences, *Seven Pillars of Wisdom*, in 1926. His work with explosives may have inspired Hemingway's creation of Robert Jordan's mission. *The Virginian*, a very different work, is the classic Western novel that immemorialized the line, "When you call me that, *smile!*" (22). Its repeated showdown scenes seem to have contributed to Robert Jordan's confrontations with the sometimes nefarious Pablo.

As John Teunissen and Dean Rehberger (in Rena Sanderson's essay collection) have noted, Hemingway also alludes in this novel to the American legends about George Custer, the American general who led the Seventh U.S. Cavalry to a defeat at the hands of the Sioux and Cheyenne at Little Bighorn, Montana, in 1876. Robert Jordan recalls the commercialized print he has seen of a romanticized painting of Custer's last stand. Robert's attitude about Custer is ambivalent: As a child, he admired the Custer of mythic grandeur but was less impressed when his grandfather abruptly deflated the myth (and the boy's hero) by pointing out the idiocy of Custer's military tactics (339). Custer's last stand is echoed and transformed, first in Chapter 27, in which Hemingway details El Sordo's last stand, and then in the novel's climactic confrontation between a guerrilla band and a cavalry squadron.

As in *A Farewell to Arms*, Hemingway foreshadows throughout the novel what is to come. For example, Robert knows from the moment he meets Pablo that Pablo has lost heart and is likely to betray the cause. Ominously, Robert relates very early in the novel that Kashkin, Jordan's Russian predecessor who had helped the group blow up the train carrying Maria, committed suicide after being captured by the enemy, although later Jordan admits that he shot Kashkin when he was wounded too seriously to escape after completing their last assignment. Pablo immediately poses to Jordan the question of whether he would be willing to be left behind if he were wounded during the mission. After reading Robert's palm shortly after their first meeting, Pilar refuses to tell him his fortune, insisting that she sees nothing in his hand, but Robert does not believe her. He fully anticipates his own death.

HISTORICAL AND SOCIAL CONTEXT

The Spanish Civil War began in mid-July 1936 when General Francisco Franco led Spain's army in an uprising against its democratically elected government. The General's rebel forces, known as the Nationalists, were supported by the Catholic Church, the extreme right wing, and Hitler and Mussolini, "whose fascist governments used the war to field-test their new weapons systems" (Reynolds, *1930s* 262). On the other side, the Loyalists (or Republicans) defending the leftist government of the Spanish Republic included the country's socialists and communists, as well as five volunteer international brigades under the leadership of Russian advisers. America, Britain, and France stayed out of the conflict, unwilling to side with communists. In February 1937 in a letter Hemingway wrote to the family of his second wife, Pauline, he described the Spanish Civil War as a dress rehearsal for the coming war in Europe—more than two and a half years before World War II began.

On April 26, 1937, German troops supporting the rebels bombed the Spanish village of Guernica, leaving a third of the civilian population killed or wounded (Reynolds, *1930s* 265)—inspiring Picasso's famous painting *Guernica*, now in the Prado, Madrid's world-renowned art museum. The war ended when Madrid fell to General Franco's forces on March 28, 1939, so Hemingway knew when he wrote the novel that the Loyalists, with whom the novel's protagonist fought, had been defeated. Robert Jordan's hopes for international aid, then, are particularly ironic. He thinks to himself that if only the French would leave the border open and America would send planes, the Spanish would fight forever—but even these relatively meager hopes will not be fulfilled.

When Pilar asks Robert if he is a communist, he says he is not, that he is instead an antifascist. He later tells himself that he has no politics and acknowledges that although he is fighting with the communists, he does not believe in Marxism. Similarly, Hemingway opposed the fascism of the Nationalists but was not himself a communist. He remained skeptical of politics throughout his life.

In a series of articles and a forthcoming book, *Investigating Hemingway*, scholar William Brasch Watson has carefully documented the experiences on which Hemingway drew for the novel, including what he learned in Spain about explosives and demolition, and describes the four days Hemingway spent observing the guerrilla operations of a group of partisans in Alfambra. Watson believes that the author was deliberately recruited by the communists to support the Republic and that he was more actively involved in the war than has generally been acknowledged.

Hemingway knew that neither side in this conflict had a monopoly on evil. Although the reader's sympathies are clearly meant to be with the partisans, Pilar's atrocity tale (99–129) demonstrates that the partisans are as capable of evil as the fascists. Roberto kills a cavalryman who stumbles upon the partisans; afterwards, he experiences guilt as he learns from the man's papers that he is a 21-year-old from Navarra and reads the letters the boy received from his sister and his fiancée. The novel was condemned by many communist readers, in part for its emphasis on individual experience and personal suffering rather than communal experience and the common good. Communists also objected that in *For Whom the Bell Tolls* Hemingway described Republican atrocities in Pilar's tale yet did not emphasize strongly enough the many atrocities committed by the fascists. Jordan is less biased: "He liked to know how it really was; not how it was supposed to be. There was always lying in a war" (230).

ALTERNATE READING: JUNGIAN

Swiss psychoanalyst Carl Gustav Jung, initially a colleague of Sigmund Freud, eventually rejected what he saw as Freud's overemphasis on sexuality in human life and evolved his own distinctive theory of the human psyche. According to Jung, human beings have two selves, the public self of which they themselves are aware and which they show to others, and a shadow self of which even the individual is not fully conscious. The goal of Jungian psychoanalysis is to integrate the two divided selves of the personality into one healthy, unified whole.

Applying Jungian psychoanalytic techniques to literature enables readers to see the themes that resonate in us as readers because we are struggling with those issues in our own psyches, whether we are fully conscious of our struggles or not. We participate vicariously in Robert's struggle to unite the divided halves of his personality—the hopeful half that loves Maria and carries out the bombing of the bridge because it may help the cause he believes in, and the pessimistic half that knows his love affair is doomed and that he will not survive this mission. On the last page of *For Whom the Bell Tolls*, Hemingway writes of Robert Jordan, "He was completely integrated now . . ." (471), suggesting that Robert has achieved psychic wholeness through what he experiences during the three days before his death.

It is possible to see the ruthless, despairing Pablo as a double for Robert, an incarnation of Robert's shadow self. Like Robert (but unlike the other partisans, including Pilar), Pablo recognizes immediately the futility of blowing the bridge; he also apprehends instantly the implications of Robert's injury. He is, like Robert, highly intelligent (despite his illiteracy), skilled at planning guerrilla military operations, and profoundly pessimistic about the outcome of the war. He also shares with Robert a deep depression and a conviction that their actions are futile—attitudes that Hemingway experienced again and again during his life. When Robert and Pablo unite to work together, Hemingway has dramatized the integration of Robert's public and shadow selves.

Jung also believed in the importance of archetypes—certain roles or life patterns that recur again and again in human experience and that all human beings inherit as part of what he called a "collective unconscious." He believed that art that drew on these persistent life patterns appealed to the reader's unconscious awareness of these roles and helped them work out their own relationships to these universal human situations. According to one classic archetype Jung identified, a hero must participate in a cycle in which he departs from his ordinary existence to enter an underworld of death and then return to life. For Robert Jordan, the cave represents an underworld into which he must descend before he can reemerge—the symbolic death he must undergo before he can be reborn.

The cave has a second meaning that also draws on mythic archetypes. As Roberto and Anselmo are returning to the cave in which the partisans have made camp, Roberto refers to it as Pablo's palace and "the cave of the lost eggs" (199). The word "eggs" in Spanish has a slang meaning of testicles, so Robert's reference suggests that Pablo is so fearful that he is no longer a man. But eggs simultaneously suggest female fertility. Along with the many references throughout the novel to dead rabbits and bad or black milk, this and other mentions of eggs together give an impression of blighted maternity and destroyed fertility (Tyler, "Dead Rabbits" 130).

Hemingway draws heavily on folklore and superstition in this novel, from the ominous palm reading that Pilar refuses to discuss to the famous passage in which Pilar describes in outlandish and grotesque detail the smell of death (251–56). Perhaps most interesting are Roberto's multiple references to the "mysteries," evoking the Eleusinian mysteries of ancient Greece, mysteries revealed only to initiates into the cult of Demeter.

Jung has suggested that the ancient Greek myth of Demeter reveals profound truths about the female psyche. According to Greek mythology, Demeter is the goddess of vegetation, whose daughter, Persephone, is kidnapped and raped by Hades, god of the underworld. When Demeter learns from the witch-goddess Hecate that Persephone has become queen of the dead and is unable to return from the underworld, Demeter, as goddess of vegetation, creates a famine upon the earth. The human suffering that results is so severe that Zeus, king of the gods, intervenes, compelling Hades to allow Persephone to return to her mother each spring for part of the year.

For more than 2000 years, the ancient Greeks celebrated the Eleusinian mysteries, a secret practice that honored the maiden, mother, and crone of the myth. Initiates engaged in mystical rituals they were forbidden to discuss with others and were promised immortality as a result of their participation in the cult. It is possible to interpret Robert's many references to Pilar's secrets and mysteries as allusions to the myth and cult of Demeter, and his ultimate insistence to Maria of his own immortality—e.g., "As long as there is one of us there is both of us" (463)—as a sign of his initiation into these rituals.

Like Persephone in the Eleusinian myth, Maria is raped and brought back from the dead, in her case by Pilar, a loving maternal figure rather than her literal mother. Also like Persephone, Maria is associated with both vegetation and fertility. Hemingway repeatedly compares her hair to fields of wheat (for example, on pages 23, 158, 345, and 346). Even her nickname, "rabbit"—Spanish slang for a woman's genitals—emphasizes her connection to fertility. Her losses—her parents' death, her gang rape, and finally her loss of

Robert—parallel Spain's. Like Persephone, Spain, too, has unwillingly been taken by force into an underworld of violence and death. But Hemingway ends the novel with Robert's sacrifice, which offers the reader hope.

9

The Old Man and the Sea
(1952)

The Old Man and the Sea was first published in the Sept. 1, 1952, issue of *Life* magazine (Hanneman 63), and more than 5 million copies of the issue, which featured a black and white photo of Hemingway on the cover, sold out within 48 hours (Baker, *Life* 504). Adriana Ivancich, the Italian woman who inspired the character of Renata in Hemingway's novel *Across the River and Into the Trees*, designed the original cover for the book (Reynolds, *Final* 250). The deceptively simple novella reassured the public that after several disappointing books, Ernest Hemingway was still capable of artistic excellence.

The Book-of-the-Month Club chose *The Old Man and the Sea* as part of a two-book selection in September 1952. Hemingway's wife, Mary Welsh Hemingway, recalls that more than 50,000 copies of the book were sold in its first two weeks (306). The 27,000-word novella eventually spent 26 weeks on the *New York Times Book Review*'s bestseller list (Hanneman 64). "Before the year was out, translations appeared in nine European languages," and the number had reached 26 languages by 1957 (Reynolds, *Final* 258). Novelist William Faulkner, Hemingway's Nobel Prize-winning contemporary, praised the book as Hemingway's best work. *The Old Man and the Sea* won the Pulitzer Prize for fiction in 1953 and was specifically mentioned in the award citation when Hemingway received the Nobel Prize for Literature in 1954.

The book was made into a 1958 film starring Spencer Tracy as the old man. Hemingway spent time with the producer, screenwriter, and Tracy and tried unsuccessfully to land a marlin to provide footage for the film. But he was ultimately disgusted with the finished movie. The novel was later remade into a 1990 made-for-TV movie starring Anthony Quinn and a 2000 large-format film that won an Oscar for Best Animated Short Film.

Initially Hemingway's hugely popular little book was widely regarded as a masterpiece for its simple prose, richly evocative symbolism, and affirmative message. Some later critics have been less favorable, however, complaining about the story's sentimentality, its affected prose, and the boy's excessive hero worship of the old man, who suspiciously resembles Hemingway. The book is still regularly taught in both high school and college literature classes.

Hemingway first learned how to fish for marlin in Cuba in 1932 (Baker, *Life* 228). He wrote about the experience in an article, "Marlin Off Cuba," that appeared in *American Big Game Fishing*, a 1935 limited edition book edited by Eugene V. Connett (Morton 52). In addition to his own experiences with marlin fishing, he based *The Old Man and the Sea* on a story he had first described in a 1936 article published in *Esquire* magazine (*By-Line* 239–40) and later recounted to his editor, Maxwell Perkins, in a 1939 letter outlining several writing projects he had in mind (*SL* 478; Bruccoli, *Only Thing* 273). Hemingway wrote the first draft of the novella in six weeks (Reynolds, *Final* 238).

PLOT DEVELOPMENT

As *The Old Man and the Sea* opens in September, Santiago, an old Cuban fisherman, has gone an astonishing 84 days without catching a fish. Manolin, the boy who has fished with him since Manolin was five, is forbidden by his family to go fishing any longer with such a spectacularly unlucky fisherman. So a lonely Santiago sails out alone, ventures out too far, and hooks a magnificent marlin, more than twice the size of his tiny skiff. Despite exhaustion and physical pain, Santiago fights the marlin for three days and finally succeeds in landing him, only to lose him to sharks that attack the fish's bleeding body as he tries to return home with it lashed to the side of his skiff. Defeated but not destroyed, Santiago returns to his village bearing only the skeleton of his massive catch, but the impressive skeleton is enough to convince Manolin to defy his family and resume what he sees as his rightful place fishing alongside Santiago.

CHARACTER DEVELOPMENT

The story's protagonist is an old man named Santiago, which in Spanish means Saint James, the patron saint of Spain. Wrinkled and weather-beaten, Hemingway's Santiago nevertheless remains physically strong. Once he was known as *El Campeon* (Spanish for "the champion") because he could beat anyone at arm wrestling. Despite being so poor that he sometimes goes hungry and often wears patched clothes, he has great dignity. He is lonely, misses his wife, and repeatedly wishes that Manolin were still with him (45, 48, 50, 51, 56, 62, 83). In his loneliness, he has begun to talk to himself, the birds, and even the fish he hopes to catch. Perhaps in a subconscious effort to console himself for his misfortunes, he often dreams of Africa, especially of lions playing together like cats on a beach at dusk. Despite his long spell of failure, he remains optimistic and persists in trying. The other fishermen of the village either ridicule him or pity the old man.

Manolin, the boy, is devoted to Santiago, who has been teaching him the art of fishing since the boy was five years old. The boy's age is unclear and has been the subject of much debate, with proponents of every age from 10 to 22. The fact that he is still an apprentice suggests that he is young, but his ultimate decision to defy his family indicates that he is no longer a child. It perhaps makes the most sense to assume he is a teenager, perhaps 15 or 16.

Manolin leaves Santiago unwillingly to fish from another boat only because his family has ordered him to do so to avoid what they see as Santiago's permanent bad luck. He wishes to serve the old man and berates himself for thoughtlessness when he doesn't anticipate all of Santiago's needs. Although Santiago is too proud to ask for help himself, Manolin asks others in the village for food so that he can ensure that Santiago has enough to eat. The two of them use polite fictions to avoid acknowledging unpleasant truths about Santiago's poverty and thus let the old man save face. When Santiago returns at the end of the novel, Manolin cries for all the old man has suffered. The boy insists that he will fish with Santiago despite his family's wishes. His change of heart suggests that Santiago's triumph has taught Manolin how to become a man.

THEMES

One important theme of *The Old Man and the Sea* has to do with luck and the laws of chance. Santiago thinks to himself that while it's important to be lucky, it is also important to be exact so that he can take advantage of his luck when it comes. He and the boy discuss lucky numbers and lottery tickets, and it is the old man's reputation for bad luck that costs him his apprentice. Santiago believes that he "violated" his luck by fishing too far out and briefly wishes he could buy some luck before adding, "Luck is a thing that comes in many forms and who can recognize her?" (116–17). Certainly for Santiago what seems like good luck—successfully catching the fish—eventually becomes misfortune.

Baseball figures prominently in *The Old Man and the Sea*. Hemingway's theme here is that sports like baseball and marlin fishing parallel life, and that one's performance in both sports and life depends on luck and skill. Santiago muses that Joe DiMaggio would persist in trying to catch the fish just as he himself does. Joseph Paul DiMaggio, familiarly known to baseball fans as the "Yankee Clipper" and "Joltin' Joe," was a center fielder for the New York Yankees whose play twice won him the Most Valuable Player award and eventually earned his admission to the Baseball Hall of Fame. DiMaggio was later remembered not only for his baseball career but for his marriage to Marilyn Monroe and his commercials for coffeemakers. He was also memorialized in the Simon and Garfunkel song "Mrs. Robinson" in the classic 1967 Dustin Hoffman film *The Graduate*.

Ironically, DiMaggio was a pampered athlete who didn't have to play if he were hurt or felt ill, while Santiago persists heroically in the face of great suffering. His right hand is cut by the fishing line, his left hand cramps into a claw, and his back begins to hurt as the fish pulls hard enough to tow the boat along behind him for two days and two nights. His left hand is later cut by the fishing line as well, and he sees spots before his eyes from faintness and dizziness. But "pain does not matter to a man," he tells himself (84). Exhausted, he thinks, "I am tireder than I have ever been" (89) and counsels himself, "Keep your head clear and know how to suffer like a man" (92).

Perhaps in part because of its theme of the redemptive value of suffering, *The Old Man and the Sea* has sometimes been read as a Christian allegory. (An allegory is a story in which the characters, setting, and plot points all represent larger truths.) For example, it is possible to see Santiago, a humble fisherman, as a Christ figure. Christ called on his disciples to become fishers of men (Mark 1:16–17 and Matthew 4:18–19), and Santiago himself recalls that Saint Peter, whom he calls San Pedro, was a fisherman. Santiago's humility is a Christian virtue. Hemingway refers rather pointedly to the crucifixion of Christ: When the sharks come, Santiago utters a sound that the author describes as "just a noise such as a man might make, involuntarily, feeling the nail go through his hand and into the wood" (107). Near the end of the book, when Santiago struggles to climb uphill bearing the mast on his back, he recalls Christ's struggle to bear the cross to Calvary (John 19:17). When the old man sleeps, he stretches out his arms with the palms up, paralleling the position of Christ on the cross.

Although the old man does not believe he is religious, he prays, reciting both the Our Father and the Hail Mary prayers of his Catholic faith. *The Old Man and the Sea* is sometimes described as a parable, a story told to illustrate a moral point. The stories Christ is described as telling in the New Testament are parables. The moral and thematic point of the novella might be Santiago's famous declaration: "A man can be destroyed but not defeated" (103). Christians believe that Christ was destroyed—physically killed—but not defeated, since He is resurrected.

It is also possible to see in the work an allegory about Hemingway's own experience as an author. "Perhaps the old man is Hemingway himself, the great fish is this great story and the sharks are the critics. Symbolism won't match up to real life here though: there is absolutely nothing the sharks can do to this marlin," according to the editorial accompanying the story in *Life* magazine ("Great American Storyteller" 20). The sharks who attack Santiago's catch, leaving him with only the bare bones of his once-splendid marlin, bear a certain resemblance to the critics who savaged Hemingway's *Across the River and Into the Trees*, and Hemingway's written remarks in his response to winning the Nobel Prize for Literature echo remarks uttered by Santiago about the need to go out very far alone. But it's perhaps also important to remember Hemingway's own disclaimer: In a skeptical letter to a friend, he disingenuously insisted that the sea was just the sea, the old man an old man, the boy just a boy, and the fish a regular old fish, and he specifically stated that there was no symbolism at all in the book (*SL* 780).

ALTERNATE READING: ECOFEMINIST

Ecofeminism, a critical approach which evolved from both feminism and environmentalism, suggests that human beings tend to perceive the environment and women in similar ways. European and American cultures in particular have long seen the earth as something that human beings should dominate and subdue, and women have traditionally been relegated to a similar fate. Consider for example the biblical book of Genesis, in which "man" is given dominion over the animals, and Eve is told that her husband will be her master. In an ecofeminist interpretation, a reader pays close attention to the way in which nature and female characters are perceived and treated, and then examines the fairness of those perceptions and that treatment. Thus, an ecofeminist reading of a novel can tease out the work's implications for both gender relations and the environment.

An important passage for this kind of interpretation occurs in *The Old Man and the Sea* on page 30 when Santiago insists that the sea is feminine: ". . . the old man always thought of her as feminine and as something that gave or withheld great favours, and if she did wild or wicked things it was because she could not help them. The moon affects her as it does a woman, he thought" (30). From an ecofeminist standpoint, Santiago reveals here a deep distrust of women and nature, both of which he believes are at the mercy of the moon and helpless to control their own wildness and wickedness. Given his condescending and misogynistic attitude, it's perhaps not surprising that he hides the photo of his wife. Similarly, the deep scorn revealed by the narrator of the text for the uncomprehending woman tourist of the novel's final two pages also verges on misogyny; if she doesn't speak the language, her error is after all an innocent and understandable mistake.

Santiago's attitude towards nature is equally unsympathetic. He has witnessed cockfights and knows that he could not endure losing an eye and still continue to fight as the fighting cocks do—but he does not seem particularly repulsed by a sport that causes such pain, commenting only, "Man is not much beside the great birds and beasts" (68). He recalls the marlin who swam circles around his boat after he had killed the marlin's mate. Whether real-life marlins are likely to exhibit this behavior or not, the passage suggests that Santiago perceives emotion in these fish and chooses to ignore that perception in order to continue killing them for money. As he puts it, "we begged her pardon and butchered her promptly" (50).

Yet in his epic fight with the marlin of this story, Santiago identifies with the fish. He begins by feeling sorry for him but gradually links himself more closely with the marlin: "Now we are joined together and have been since noon. And no one to help either one of us" (50). Soon he is expressing warmer feelings, but they are undercut by his deadly intention: " 'Fish,' he said, 'I love and respect you very much. But I will kill you dead before this day ends' " (54). "He is my brother," the old man thinks to himself (59). He even wishes he *were* the fish. He later calls the fish his friend and finally, after acknowledging that the fish may kill him, declares, "I do not care who kills who" (92). Once the fish is dead, Santiago compares its eye to a mirror. It is clear that the old man sees himself in the fish, that he recognizes how akin he and the fish are, yet he kills the fish despite their kinship.

Santiago recognizes the immorality of killing the fish but rationalizes his decision to do so. Hemingway claims the old man feels the fish's pain: "When the fish had been hit it was as though he himself were hit" (103). Even after the fish is dead and lashed to his skiff, the old man wonders, "is he bringing me in or am I bringing him in?" He thinks to himself, "If you love him, it is not a sin to kill him. Or is it more?" (105).

It is, as Santiago suggests, more. Santiago's sin is pride. He thinks he can somehow successfully catch a fish that he knows from the outset is two feet larger than his skiff and return safely to shore with it despite the sharks. He even admits to himself, "You killed him for pride . . ." (105). His behavior recalls the hubris of Icarus of Greek myth, who despite repeated warnings flew too near the sun with the wings his father, Daedalus, made for him. The wax holding the wings together melted, and Icarus fell to his death. In a similar act of hubris, only after the sharks have cost him the catch of a lifetime does Santiago concede that he went too far out. No wonder he has a cramped hand resembling the claw of an eagle and dreams of lions. He identifies with the two creatures that traditionally symbolize pride.

Santiago is well aware that if he truly regards the fish as his brother, then killing him is unquestionably a sin, particularly since his motives are entirely selfish and mercenary: "But what a great fish he is and what he will bring in the market if the flesh is good" (49). The old man also longs to restore his reputation as *El Campeon*, and even the skeleton of the fish helps to accomplish that, earning him the admiration and sympathy of his fellow villagers. But Santiago does not want to face his own immorality in killing the marlin. "Do not think about sin. It is much too late for that and there are people who are paid to do it," he thinks (105). He likes to think he is smarter than the fish but eventually admits that he is "only better armed" (103) and acknowledges, "I am only better than him through trickery and he meant me no harm" (99).

Yet he rationalizes to himself that fishing is what he was born to do and that it is somehow not wrong to kill the fish if he cares about it while he kills it. Readers working from an ecofeminist perspective might see Santiago not as the saintly, idealized Christ figure of the traditional allegorical interpretation described earlier, but as a surprisingly violent man who murders living creatures while piously (but insincerely) claiming to respect their right to live and be free of human intervention. In this reading, Santiago's humiliating defeat at the hands of the sharks is a richly deserved comeuppance for his arrogance in going out too far.

10

The Posthumous Works: *A Moveable Feast* (1964), *Islands in the Stream* (1970), and *The Garden of Eden* (1986)

Since Hemingway's death in 1961, his heirs have chosen to publish a selection of his letters and several works he left unfinished, including *A Moveable Feast* in 1964, *Islands in the Stream* in 1970, unpublished short fiction in *The Nick Adams Stories* in 1972, *The Dangerous Summer* in 1985, *The Garden of Eden* in 1986, and *True at First Light* in 1999, to mark the centennial of his birth. (*True at First Light* is discussed in Chapter 7.) While all of these works are worth reading, they should be read with the understanding that Hemingway was not fully satisfied with them and would very likely have continued to revise his work had he lived longer. Readers should also recognize that these posthumous writings have been edited and in some cases cut extensively and that these changes might not be consistent with Hemingway's vision of his work.

More of Hemingway's work is expected to appear in the future. The Ernest Hemingway Foundation and Society have already announced preliminary plans to support the publication of a multivolume edition of Hemingway's letters and an uncut edition of the African journal, a heavily edited version of which was published as *True at First Light*. Scholars hope to see a complete text of *The Garden of Eden* manuscripts someday as well.

All three of the books discussed in this chapter (along with *The Old Man and the Sea*) emerged at least in part from what Hemingway had earlier envisioned as a trilogy encompassing novels on the sea, air, and land (Reynolds, *Final* 256–57). His working titles for the trilogy were *The Sea When Young* (for the work that apparently became both *A Moveable Feast* and *The Garden of*

Eden), *The Sea When Absent* (which became *Islands in the Stream*), and *The Sea in Being* (which became *The Old Man and the Sea*) (Baker, *Life* 488–89).

A MOVEABLE FEAST

A Moveable Feast, the last book Hemingway worked on before his death, may also have had its origin in two other events—his alleged discovery at the Ritz of a trunk of manuscripts he had left there in 1930 (Reynolds, *Final* 301), and a request from *Atlantic Monthly* to contribute to a special issue celebrating its hundredth anniversary. There is conflicting evidence concerning the story of the trunks, however, and Hemingway eventually sent two short stories rather than an autobiographical sketch to *Atlantic*. Regardless of what inspired its creation, Hemingway finished most of a first draft of *A Moveable Feast* within six months (Reynolds, *Final* 310). Literary critic Tom Dardis speculates that this resurgence of Hemingway's talent may have been the direct result of a drastic reduction in Hemingway's drinking, a cutback advocated by his physician in an attempt to lower his dangerously high blood pressure and soaring cholesterol level.

A memoir of his years in Paris in the 1920s, *A Moveable Feast* was edited for publication by his widow, Mary Hemingway, after his death. "If the reader prefers, this book may be regarded as fiction," the book's preface says. "But there is always the chance that such a book of fiction may throw some light on what has been written as fact." Because there is no handwritten version of the preface, Hemingway scholar Gerry Brenner has suggested that it may have been cobbled together by Mary Hemingway from statements Hemingway had expressed in various drafted fragments. According to Brenner in his article, "Are We Going to Hemingway's Feast?," Mary also shuffled the order of the chapters, restored material Hemingway had cut, and cut material he left in his final typescript, including, for example, a discussion in which he acknowledges that "the rich" were not ultimately to blame for the end of his marriage to Hadley, takes personal responsibility for its failure, and apologizes to her. A skeptical Brenner has pronounced the published version of *A Moveable Feast* "a bastard text" (529). Nevertheless, the book appeared on the *New York Times Book Review*'s bestseller list from May to December 1964 and was in first place for 19 of those weeks. It was a Book-of-the-Month Club selection in June 1964 (Hanneman 74). The book's epigraph identifies its (misspelled) title as a comment Hemingway made to a friend in 1950: "If you are lucky enough to have lived in Paris as a young man, then wherever you go for the rest of your life, it stays with you, for Paris is a moveable feast."

The book in some ways resembles a *Kunstlerroman*, a German term for a novel about the development of an artist. Among the best-known examples of the *Kunstlerroman* in modernist literature are James Joyce's *Portrait of the Artist as a Young Man* and Virginia Woolf's *To the Lighthouse*. Hemingway himself called it an autobiography by "remate," which is a jai alai term for a kill-shot (Baker, *Writer* 375n30). Biographer Carlos Baker suggests that Hemingway may have meant to say "rebote," which refers to a rebound shot, since rather than write about himself directly, he revealed much about himself indirectly, through discussions about his friends and associates.

Hemingway's memoir chronicles the creation of his first novel, *The Sun Also Rises*. The narrator mentions his own work repeatedly, describing his own exhilaration at writing well, discouragement over the rejections he receives, and persistence despite interruptions and distractions. With dismay verging almost on despair, Hemingway realizes that in order to become a successful writer, he must write a novel: "But it seemed an impossible thing to do when I had been trying with great difficulty to write paragraphs that would be the distillation of what made a novel" (75). Hemingway initially seems to have made little progress: "Since I had started to break down all my writing and get rid of all facility and try to make instead of describe, writing had been wonderful to do. But it was very difficult, and I did not know how I would ever write anything as long as a novel. It often took me a full morning of work to write a paragraph" (156). Yet in the next paragraph, he mentions with deceptive casualness that he has received an advance from an American publisher for his collection of short stories, *In Our Time*. By the end of *A Moveable Feast*, he mentions, almost in passing, that he has shown a first draft of his *The Sun Also Rises* to Maxwell Perkins, the New York editor to whom Fitzgerald had introduced him, and Hemingway rejects Fitzgerald's assistance in revising the draft.

In many of the sketches Hemingway presents us with anti-artists, a series of writers who have the talent but lack the necessary commitment to become true artists. Many seem petty and self-destructive in their unhealthy obsessions. For example, Hemingway belittles British novelist Ford Madox Ford, whom he finds physically repugnant, for Ford's comical (and stereotypically British) preoccupation with class. Hemingway depicts the artist Pascin's promiscuity and mentions his suicide almost as an afterthought. Also troubling to the young writer are Ernest Walsh's dishonesty and his terminal illness. Walsh, whose poetry Hemingway implies is overrated, attempts unsuccessfully to con the young writer into believing he will win a major literary prize from the magazine Walsh edits. Hemingway is disgusted by Walsh's fraud and dismayed by his long struggle against consumption (a lung disease more commonly known as tuberculosis and often curable now with antibiotics). Evan Shipman, whose work Hemingway respects, lacks the necessary drive to become an artist, while Ralph Cheever Dunning is evidently addicted to opium. Even F. Scott Fitzgerald has chosen alcoholism over art. Ernest is particularly disturbed by Fitzgerald's confession that he wrote good stories and then deliberately made them worse in order to make them appeal to the *Saturday Evening Post*. Hemingway equates the practice with prostitution and is convinced that it will permanently damage Fitzgerald's ability to write. He is also disgusted by Fitzgerald's hypochondria and wasteful extravagance.

Hemingway could be vicious. Memorably, he compares Wyndham Lewis (who had reviewed his work unfavorably) to "an unsuccessful rapist" (109). Although Hemingway seems to have been more charitable in the manuscript version, his depiction of his friend Fitzgerald in the published book is embarrassing and unkind. Hemingway may have been working out his anger at Fitzgerald for "The Crack-Up," a confessional essay in the February 1936 issue of *Esquire*, in which Fitzgerald publicly described his own bouts with alcoholism and depression.

Hemingway is particularly severe in his criticism of Fitzgerald's wife, Zelda, whom Hemingway regarded, probably with some justification, as a hindrance to her husband's work. He attributed what he saw as her deliberate efforts to sabotage her husband's work to her jealousy of his talent, and Hemingway drew on that quality in his creation of the character of Catherine Bourne in *The Garden of Eden*. Perhaps he also objected to Zelda's sensitivity and intelligence. She once told Hadley that she noticed that Hadley always did what Hemingway wanted. "Ernest didn't like that much, but it was a perceptive remark," Hadley told an interviewer years later (Milford 116).

But Hemingway also remembered others fondly. For example, he writes about Sylvia Beach and her lending library, Shakespeare and Company, with both affection and gratitude. Beach was the first to publish and publicly support the brilliant and controversial novel *Ulysses* by James Joyce, the expatriate Irish writer whom Hemingway recalls seeing occasionally and whose work he consistently praises. He particularly recalls Beach's generosity in extending loans to struggling writers.

In *A Moveable Feast* Hemingway never acknowledges that he and his wife were living off the income from Hadley's trust fund. The couple lived modestly with their new baby in a tiny two-room apartment with no hot water and with only a chamber pot rather than an indoor toilet. Hemingway recalls that he barely allowed Hadley enough money to buy clothes. He describes his own infatuation with betting on horse races and admits he came close to becoming a compulsive gambler.

He particularly exaggerates their poverty in the chapter entitled "Hunger Was Good Discipline." He recalls walking the streets of Paris hungry. In an earlier chapter, Hadley tells him, "There are so many sorts of hunger. . . . Memory is hunger" (56–57). Food becomes a trope in this book for the full-blown enjoyment of life, and Hemingway's hunger further represents both his burning ambition then to become a successful writer and enjoy his life to the utmost, and his heartsick nostalgia in recalling those days nearly 40 years later. Then he was hungry for artistic and financial success, and now he is hungry for the lost past.

The memoir ultimately becomes a lyrical tribute to his first wife, Hadley, the betrayed heroine of the book. "When I saw my wife again standing by the tracks as the train came in by the piled logs at the station, I wished I had died before I ever loved anyone but her" (*AMF* 210). In the novel's closing pages, he describes in almost clinical detail the beginning of the end of his first marriage. Earlier in the work he carefully foreshadows their coming divorce, noting his failure to knock wood after he had said how lucky they always were. When he mentions that he and Hadley were young and in love, he tosses in as an ironic aside, "time would fix that" (15). Hemingway expresses remorse at having left Hadley for his second wife, Pauline, and suggests that the end of his first marriage signaled an insidious moral corruption brought on by his association with the rich and their hangers-on. Typically, he blames his friend the writer John Dos Passos, whom he calls the "pilot fish," in much stronger terms than he reproaches himself, almost as if he were passively and unknowingly led into the affair with Pauline rather than consciously and actively choosing infidelity.

Many readers find Hemingway's self-portrait disturbing. He attacks many writers who had befriended him and promoted his work, including Gertrude Stein and F. Scott Fitzgerald. He sometimes mocks people who had done little to deserve such public humiliation, and some of those he ridiculed were no longer alive to defend themselves. There is an unpleasant element of self-congratulation in the implied contrast between himself and so many failed artists. He consistently depicts himself as unlike other artists because he sacrificed, valued his art above all else, and chose wisely, and his claims seem distastefully self-serving, not to mention too good to be true.

What redeems the work for many readers, however, is the beauty of his prose. In *Hemingway in the Autumn*, a video celebrating Hemingway's years in Idaho, Michael Reynolds confesses that he would forgive a man many sins for a good story, and *A Moveable Feast*, despite the covertness of its plot, is an excellent story, complete with the beauty of 1920s Paris, salacious literary gossip about the sex lives of famous writers, and a bittersweet tale of lost love.

ISLANDS IN THE STREAM

Islands in the Stream, which Hemingway originally called *The Island and the Stream* (Reynolds, *Final* 237), was first published as a complete novel on October 6, 1970. It spent 24 weeks on the *New York Times* bestseller list, and the novel was made into a 1977 film starring George C. Scott. A long excerpt from the "Bimini" section was published in the October 1970 *Esquire*, and the March 1971 issue of *Cosmopolitan* included a long excerpt from the "Cuba" section.

PLOT DEVELOPMENT

Set during World War II, the novel is divided into three parts, titled "Bimini," "Cuba," and "At Sea." Hemingway first visited Bimini, an island 45 miles off the coast of Miami, in 1934 (Baker, *Life* 259). The "Bimini" section is set in the mid-1930s, and the later sections are set in February and March of 1943 or 1944. The book's title refers to Bimini's location in the warm ocean current known as the Gulf Stream.

At a rowdy boys' night out, protagonist Thomas Hudson and his friend Roger Davis look on as their friend Frank Hart jokingly shoots flares at drums of gasoline on the dock. Both object mildly, but neither is successful in stopping the dangerous behavior. A wealthy tourist on another boat first protests the noise and then reemerges later, verbally abusing Roger; Roger responds by knocking him unconscious. He returns later to threaten Roger with a shotgun. Roger afterward reveals to Tom that he had left the west coast because he had nearly killed a man in a fight.

Soon afterward, Thomas Hudson's three sons—Tom, Andrew, and David— arrive to spend the summer with their father. On one of their first outings together of the summer, only quick use of a submachine gun by Hudson's friend Eddy saves David from the attack of a hammerhead shark; Hudson's shots all went wide of the mark. Afterwards, while the boys' own father seems oddly unaffected by the incident, a guilt-stricken Roger asks for hemlock, the poisonous drink used in the execution of Greek philosopher Socrates. His overreaction is probably the result of his own childhood trauma, his brother's drowning.

David hooks a massive fish and plays it for six hours, until he is crying with exhaustion, his arms and back aching, his feet scraped raw and bleeding. Although his brother Tom is agitated by David's suffering, Hudson insists, a little cruelly, "there is a time boys have to do things if they are ever going to be men" (131). As a father, he seems oddly detached and disinterested. He sees David shaking and crying after the fish escapes at the last minute but nonetheless leaves him to Roger and later acknowledges that David is a "mystery" whom only Roger understands. Hudson even concedes to Roger that the responsibility was Hudson's, as the boy's father, and that he delegated it to Roger unfairly.

As Book One ends, Tom receives a telegram stating that David and Andrew, the younger two boys, were killed in a car accident with their mother. In 1933, Hemingway's sons were involved in an accident while riding in the car with Hemingway's friend and lover, Jane Mason (Kert 249), and many years later

Hemingway's second son, Patrick, recalled his father's anxiety about his sons traveling by car with Pauline, Patrick and Gregory's mother and by then Ernest's second ex-wife, whom Ernest remembered as being unable to drive.

Roger, who is arguably the work's most interesting character, disappears from the book completely after Book One. At the beginning of Book Two, which is set in Cuba, Tom Hudson cannot sleep and is dependent on a double Seconal tablet, a sleeping pill. He bestows lavish affection on his cat Boise, nicknamed Boy, who seems to take the place of his sons. The reader learns only belatedly that Tom, his only surviving son, was killed in the war (262)—a development perhaps inspired by the fact that Hemingway's oldest son, Jack, was captured by the Germans in October 1944 and spent more than six months as a prisoner of war (Baker, *Life* 448). Hudson tells Lil that he was always happiest with his children and in despair admits to himself, " . . . you will never have what you want again" (286).

Book Two contains several implausible stories. For example, Hudson launches a desperate and intense shipboard affair with a princess whose husband, a baron, confronts him politely. During their conversation the baron suggests that his wife is mentally ill and kindly warns Hudson off. A second example sounds like the setup for a ribald joke: Tom tells Lil, the aging, overweight prostitute he meets in the bar, about spending a night with three beautiful Chinese girls sent to him by a millionaire friend.

Despite these lurid and unlikely tales, Tom spends much of the novel regretting his divorce from his beloved first wife, a famous actress who is now touring with the USO, the United Service Organization, which provided entertainment for American troops during World War II. Only after he sleeps with her does Hudson tell her the news about their son, and even then, he lies initially and finally confirms the truth only after she somehow guesses what happened. Tom eventually reveals that their son was shot down, but even then he lies that young Tom's parachute didn't burn. The second book of the novel ends with her departure and Hudson's decision, in the face of his losses, to commit himself to duty, serving his country by (somewhat improbably) patrolling for Nazis in the Caribbean.

In Book Three, titled "At Sea," Hudson and his friends masquerade as scientists in order to locate German submarines in the waters around Cuba. He and his shipmates discover a burned village in which all the inhabitants have been shot by bullets from a German Luger. Unable to reach the authorities in Guantanamo, he and his crew prepare for a fight. They capture a German dying of gangrene and repeatedly try to contact the authorities, but their only commands from Guantanamo instruct them to "CONTINUE SEARCHING CAREFULLY WESTWARD" (368). The west, home of the sunset, is here (as it often is in Western literature) a metaphor for death, as becomes clearer when

Hudson muses to himself, "I have her pretty far west . . . I don't think they meant this far west" (384).

Tom and his men track the Germans to their turtle boat, and when Tom and Peters search the boat, Peters and a lone German are both killed. Tom's men are ambushed as they pursue the Germans through a channel, and Tom is shot. In the rush of the action, he continues to give orders, and only when the Germans are all killed does he realize that he is dying.

CHARACTER DEVELOPMENT

The novel's protagonist, painter Thomas Hudson, is "a realist whose canvases are based on those of Winslow Homer," whose work Hemingway and Hadley had admired in the Art Institute in Chicago (Reynolds, *Young* 158). Hemingway, who describes Hudson on the novel's first page as "a good painter" (3), named his character after an eighteenth-century British artist. A semi-autobiographical figure, Hudson, like his creator, has three sons who have two different mothers. Fit and tan, he is a big man with sun-streaked hair. Also like Hemingway, he has spent time on a Montana ranch and in New York on business. A withdrawn man who does not enjoy discussing emotional issues, Hudson prefers to rely on denial as a coping mechanism: "If you don't think about it, it doesn't exist. The hell it doesn't. But that's the system I'm going on, he thought" (258). An angry Willie later accuses him of being "a goddamned grief hoarder" (271).

Hemingway establishes the three boys' characters quickly, if a little clumsily, via a conversation between Thomas Hudson and Joseph, his black house servant. Tom, the oldest, attended expensive schools and has the manners to prove it; David, the middle boy, is very intelligent; and Andrew, the youngest, is known for his meanness (10). Hudson mentally compares David to an otter. Andy, who closely resembles his father physically, resembles his father emotionally, as well, for Hudson believes that like his father, the boy had a quiet, growing wickedness within.

Roger Davis, Thomas Hudson's friend and alter ego, is a writer for Hollywood. In the original manuscript of the "Bimini" section, "Roger Hancock" was the central character and the father of three sons, and Thomas Hudson does not even exist (Fleming, "Roger" 53–54). In the published version, the two men look enough alike to be taken for "kin" (154). Tormented by guilt over a canoeing accident when he was 12, in which he failed to save his 11-year-old brother from drowning, Roger apparently suffers from insomnia and gives Davy the impression that he is unhappy, even "tragic" (161).

In his first appearance in the novel, Willie is described as a dark-complected young man with an artificial eye. Only late in the novel is it revealed that

Willie, whose behavior is erratic and often menacing, received a medical discharge and has a "bad head" (394). He is an emotionally disturbed ex-Marine who loves to kill. Hemingway gives him the novel's marvelous last words: "You never understand anybody that loves you" (466).

THEMES

Perhaps the most important theme of the novel concerns loss, first Tom's loss of his sons to their mothers and then the loss of his sons to death, and the power of work to ameliorate his loneliness and grief. Thomas Hudson dreads the day his sons will leave and tries to cope with loneliness and eventually bereavement by throwing himself first into his work as an artist and later into service to his country during wartime. "Your boy you lose. Love you lose. Honor has been gone for a long time. Duty you do" (326), adding later "Duty is a wonderful thing" (418). He sounds anachronistically Victorian here in his praise of duty—an odd choice given that the Victorians were the generation against which Hemingway and his fellow modernists had so famously rebelled.

As in *The Sun Also Rises*, the ravages of alcoholism are an underlying theme in the novel. Young Tom worries that Eddy may be a "rummy" (91). The whole group acts out an ostensibly comic impromptu sketch for the tourists in which young Tom tearfully pleads with Roger not to drink when he needs to finish his novel, David pretends to have gone on the wagon, and Andrew, the youngest of the three, apparently downs five glasses of gin. The unfunny joke backfires when a young woman is so disturbed by Andrew's apparent drinking that she leaves the bar in tears.

Hudson tries to convince himself that he drinks to avoid seeing the island's desperate poverty and disease but ultimately admits the truth: "You're always drinking against something or for something now, he thought. The hell you are. Lots of times you are just drinking" (246). Although he is sarcastic on the subject of what he calls "rummies," he is aware of his own inconsistency: "And what about yourself? What time of day did you take your first drink this morning and how many have you had before this first one? Don't you cast the first stone at any rummies" (259).

As he does in *To Have and Have Not* and to a lesser extent in *For Whom the Bell Tolls*, Hemingway also depicts the insidious attractiveness of violence while simultaneously seeming to celebrate it. Roger, who seems otherwise intelligent and capable, is (like his creator) all too likely to end up in a brawl with whatever unsavory, belligerent fellow he happens to stumble across. As he admits to Thomas Hudson, " . . . when you start taking pleasure in it you are awfully close to the thing you're fighting" (48). Thomas Hudson is little better: He sleeps with his gun, which he describes in sexually suggestive language.

Later, he and his crew jokingly refer to the guns as children. Hudson favors honesty in describing the role he plays in the war, conceding that: ". . . we are all murderers. . . . We all are on both sides, if we are any good, and no good will come of any of it. . . . But I don't have to be proud of it. I only have to do it well. I didn't hire out to like it" (356). Even Hemingway's beloved pastime of hunting is called into question in this novel, as Tom compares his own injury to those of the animals he and Henry have shot. Both Roger and Hudson come to a growing realization of the immorality of violence, even when it is sanctioned by society.

The novel is also haunted by the idea of suicide. In a conversation with Tom, Roger mentions the suicide of the woman he was seeing the last time he saw Tom, and when Tom insists that Roger could never kill himself, Roger equivocates, suggesting that in the right circumstances, suicide can seem "logical" (156). Once he has lost his sons, Tom, too, flirts with the notion of suicide, imagining himself eating Torpex for breakfast (257). Hemingway scholar Rose Marie Burwell usefully defines Torpex as "a highly explosive powder used in torpedoes, mines, and depth bombs" (207n35). Lil later discusses three Cuban methods of suicide—eating the phosphorus from matches, drinking shoe dye, and the spectacularly gruesome method of setting oneself on fire. Even the pig that is to be delivered to them along with their supplies inexplicably swims out to sea and is drowned—an implausible incident that Hemingway's second son, Patrick, nevertheless remembers as genuine. It is difficult to read the novel today without seeing these references as harbingers of Hemingway's final mental illness and death.

THE GARDEN OF EDEN

William Faulkner once accused Hemingway of artistic timidity, of a failure to experiment with his writings. Hemingway's posthumously published work has proven Faulkner wrong. Novelist E.L. Doctorow's review of *The Garden of Eden* in the *New York Times* was aptly titled "Braver Than We Thought." *The Garden of Eden* is Hemingway's most experimental, innovative work.

Hemingway probably began writing *The Garden of Eden* in the spring of 1948 and stopped working on it in March 1959 (Burwell 97), although Carlos Baker contends Hemingway began work in 1946, set it aside in 1947, and resumed work on the manuscript in 1958 (*Life* 454–55, 540). The massive handwritten draft of *The Garden of Eden* had 48 chapters and was over 200,000 words; Tom Jenks of Scribner's, Hemingway's publisher, edited the sometimes disorganized and often repetitive manuscript into a publishable novel consisting of 30 chapters and 70,000 words (Gajdusek 6). Jenks cut one entire subplot concerning the painters Nick and Barbara Sheldon and the writer Andy

Murray, whose love triangle mirrors that of David, Catherine, and Marita (Burwell 101).

The edited version was first published in May 1986, 15 years after Hemingway's death. David Bourne's African story was also published separately under the title "An African Betrayal" in the May 5, 1986, issue of *Sports Illustrated* (Oliver, *A to Z* 115) and was later included in the Finca Vigía edition of Hemingway's short stories. The novel consists of three books: Book I, which takes place on the Mediterranean coast of France; Book II, which is set in Madrid; and Book III, which returns to the French coastal setting of Book I.

PLOT DEVELOPMENT

Set in the 1920s, *The Garden of Eden* centers on David Bourne, a writer, and his wife, Catherine, Americans who are living in the south of France as the story opens. They have been married only three weeks and are still on their honeymoon, one that at least in its setting parallels Hemingway's own honeymoon with his second wife, Pauline, in 1927. In their sexual life together, David mysteriously metamorphoses into Catherine's "girl," "Catherine," while Catherine transforms herself into "Peter."

Marita, a beautiful young woman, begins a lesbian relationship with Catherine but eventually seduces David away from Catherine. The relationship between David, Catherine, and Marita bears a certain resemblance to the relationship between Hemingway, his first wife Hadley, and his second wife Pauline, at least as that love triangle is depicted in *A Moveable Feast.* In this memoir Hemingway writes that his marriage with Hadley "had already been infiltrated by another rich using the oldest trick there is. It is that an unmarried young woman becomes the temporary best friend of another young woman who is married, goes to live with the husband and wife and then unknowingly, innocently and unrelentingly sets out to marry the husband. . . . [T]he arrangement has advantages until you know how it works out" (209–10).

Marita, whom David and Catherine nickname "Heiress" (120), is initially all blushes but rapidly loses her bashfulness in her relationship with Catherine. All three of them swim together in the nude, and at Catherine's urging, David kisses Marita, who has already told him that she is in love with Catherine and in love with him. Marita surprises them both by telling Catherine that she will be her girl as well as David's. Although Catherine initially balks, she soon gives in, first kissing Marita and then insisting to David that while she loves him, she has to have an affair with Marita. David, uncomfortable but trying to mask his discomfort, jokes that "Perversion's dull and old-fashioned" (120).

He gives in soon enough and confesses to himself that he is in love with both women. Soon afterward, he and Marita become lovers, and Catherine, who initially seems pleased, proposes that Marita marry David, too. She quickly becomes jealous of Marita, however, rather theatrically calling her David's "paramour" (155). Catherine refuses to give David up and decides that she and Marita will take turns and share David.

Setting aside the honeymoon narrative he is writing about his relationship with Catherine, David instead begins working on a short story about his father and himself during his childhood in Tanganyika (now Tanzania), Africa. The story, which stands comparison with Hemingway's best, depicts David as an eight-year-old boy. In the story, David discovers the whereabouts of an aging bull elephant and unwittingly gives the information to his father, who tracks and kills the animal. A distraught David, shocked by what he perceives as his father's betrayal, determines, "Never tell anyone anything ever. Never tell anyone anything ever again" (181).

After Marita reads the honeymoon narrative, David tells both women that he is through with the narrative. Catherine responds with anger. David, after a warning glance from Marita, promises to continue the narrative when he is finished writing the stories. But that is not enough for Catherine, who pleads with him to return to the narrative that chronicles their life together. David's artistic betrayal of Catherine presages his later emotional and sexual betrayal.

In Book Four, everything comes to a head when Marita, evidently preferring to remain faithful to David, asks Catherine to leave her alone, and the three have an unpleasant scene in which Catherine "slyly" tells David that she burned his newspaper clippings (216). David, suddenly frightened, searches his room and discovers that she has also burned the notebooks containing his African short stories—a deliberate act of destruction which recalls Hadley's accidental loss of Hemingway's own early manuscripts in 1922.

After an argument, Catherine takes the train for Biarritz, and David spends the following night in Marita's hotel room. Only the next day does he read the letter Catherine left for him, and he is moved by her apology. Determined to write something new and better than what Catherine has destroyed, David spends hours unable to draft more than a sentence. He and Marita expect to marry eventually, and Marita begins to worry about other women. The next day he tries once again to write, and as the published version of the novel ends, he is rapidly recalling and writing down the stories he had thought were lost forever.

The manuscript version's endings do not correspond with the ending of the published version of *The Garden of Eden*. In one ending, Catherine returns to David after a stay in a Swiss sanatorium, and he becomes her caregiver; there is no mention of Marita. The couple agree that they will commit suicide if Catherine's madness returns (Burwell 105). In another ending, David and Marita are together, and David is able to reconstruct his destroyed short story—but the novel continues for another 39 pages (Burwell 105): "There is no evidence that Hemingway ever considered ending the novel at the point Jenks chose" (Burwell 98).

CHARACTER DEVELOPMENT

David is from Oklahoma but spent time in East Africa as a child. He is the author of two novels: *The Rift*, which is set in East Africa, and a second book about flying in World War II. Throughout most of the novel David seems haunted by remorse over the changes Catherine makes in their relationship but remains curiously passive. He drinks to ease his remorse and tries not to think about what they have done: " . . . if he did not think then everything that was wrong might go away" (151).

Yet David does find Catherine's impulses tempting and seems to participate willingly in her schemes. After her hair is dyed white blonde, he wishes the hairdresser had left Catherine's hair alone and tells himself that what they have done cannot be changed back. Yet when Catherine asks him to have his hair colored, telling him she wants them to be alike, he resists only momentarily before giving in. "We're damned now," Catherine giddily tells him afterwards. "I was and now you are" (178). Confronted by Catherine's letter expressing remorse for her act of destruction, David ultimately concedes his own responsibility for what has happened: "There had been too much emotion, too much damage, too much of everything and his changing of allegiance, no matter how sound it had seemed, no matter how it simplified things for him, was a grave and violent thing" (238). He acknowledges that in rejecting his wife in favor of Marita, he has both made his own life more comfortable and irreparably hurt Catherine.

Critic Rosemary Burwell accurately asserts that "Catherine's is the most complex characterization of the novel, and she is unique among Hemingway's women because she insists upon some accomplishment of her own" (110). Catherine, whose maiden name was Hill, is beautiful and young, only 21 when the novel opens. Hemingway may have based her character in part on F. Scott Fitzgerald's wife Zelda, for Catherine shares Zelda's longing to become an artist in her own right. As Catherine reads David's press clippings, she tells the waiter, perhaps with frustration, that she is not a writer but a housewife and later calls David "the only one who had worked" (40). She tells David, a little plaintively, that she would like to paint or write but knows she lacks the talent. Confronted by the beauty of Spain, she says wistfully, "Now it's just like being hungry all the time and there's nothing you can ever do about it" (53).

Thwarted by her lack of talent, Catherine focuses her creativity on her personal transformation: "Maybe I'd better go back into our world, your and my world that I made up; we made up I mean" (54). Her lapse here is revealing: The world in which they live is one that she and not David has created. She later tells David and Marita that she feels as though she has made them up, too. When she tries to explain why she burned David's manuscripts, he tells her to write whatever she wants to say, and she tells him she can't write stories of her own, adding, "If you were friendly you'd write them for me" (223).

Being a woman complicates her longing to be an artist. She seems to believe that women cannot create art, that art is an exclusively male activity. It would be interesting to compare Hemingway's depiction of her to Judith Shakespeare in Virginia Woolf's *A Room of One's Own*, for Woolf's Shakespeare is a would-be woman writer who goes mad and commits suicide when her artistic impulses are stifled because of her gender. Being a "girl," Catherine bluntly remarks to David, is "a god damned bore" (70); she later insists that being a woman is emotionally difficult. Her inability to conceive the child she wants only adds to her unhappiness, for she saw the possibility of bearing a child almost as a consolation prize for being female: "I thought if I'd be a girl and stay a girl I'd have a baby at least. Not even that" (71). When Marita accuses her of not really being a woman at all, Catherine responds that she knows Marita is right, but David doesn't understand.

Catherine also seems to share Zelda Fitzgerald's mental instability. Zelda experienced repeated episodes of mental illness characterized by hallucinations, depressions, self-destructive behavior, and suicide attempts and was frequently hospitalized for psychiatric care. In the two penultimate chapters of *A Moveable Feast*, Hemingway recalls her intense jealousy of her husband's work, her hostility towards Scott, and one of her more outrageous statements. She spent the last months of her life in a psychiatric hospital in Asheville, North Carolina. Catherine's jealousy of David's work and her profound depression perhaps echo Zelda's behavior. Through allusions in the text (4, 11), Catherine is also linked to Vincent Van Gogh, the nineteenth-century Dutch painter whose bouts with manic depression led him to cut off part of his ear, spend time in an asylum, and eventually shoot himself, despite his brilliance as an artist.

It is also possible (and perhaps ultimately even more persuasive) to see the self-destructive Catherine—an artist thwarted by her mental illness and inability to create, a person given to sexual experimentation and emotional scenes—as an alter ego of her creator. Like Catherine, Hemingway suffered from depressions and writer's block, flirted with sexual games, and argued bitterly with his spouses. Both Catherine and Hemingway destroyed their own marriages (Hemingway more than once), and each experienced suicidal impulses.

Although David seems to enjoy Catherine's sexual games the first couple of times, he soon worries that her behavior is becoming very wild very fast. He becomes increasingly uneasy when Catherine shares what he calls their "night things" with the colonel and when she tells him that she has become a boy during the day (67). When she believes that David has left her because of her lesbian relationship with Marita, her reaction is so extreme that David is frightened. David notes that the transformative episodes that he both enjoys and fears are rapidly coming closer together. When David tells her she's not crazy, she responds, "Not yet maybe" (100).

Quite early in the novel, Colonel John Boyle tells David that he knew Catherine's father: "Very odd type. Killed himself in a car. His wife too" and adds, "Stupid way for grown up people to be killed" (61). Although it's not clear exactly how they died, his phrasing suggests that perhaps her father deliberately caused the accident, and his advice to David—to take care of Catherine and avoid having children—implies that the father's mental illness is hereditary. David quickly begins to see Catherine as mentally ill and himself as her caretaker—a relationship that parallels the one depicted by F. Scott Fitzgerald in his 1934 novel *Tender Is the Night*, which he based in part on his relationship with Zelda. Marita openly acknowledges that David has taken care of Catherine. Even Catherine implicitly recognizes his attitude when she snaps, "I'm not a damned invalid" (135), twice insists that she won't be "shut up" (145, 158), and refuses to see the Swiss doctor that David recommends.

When David tells Marita of Catherine's refusal to go to Switzerland, he wearily adds that he feels as though they had been married for a long time "and never had anything but problems" (161); Catherine in turn tells David she feels very, very old, so old that she is past caring what happens to her. But once again she recovers, telling David she is fine and no longer depressed. By then, however, it has become clear that David and Marita are discussing what they see as Catherine's mental illness behind her back. A hostile David finally tells Catherine that he is sick of her craziness.

Early critics of the novel have tended to label Catherine as an emasculating and dangerous threat and Marita as a nurturing and submissive helpmate. In creating such a reductive dichotomy, they overlook the sympathetic elements of Catherine's character and the disturbing aspects of Marita's. After David and Marita make love for the first time, David alludes to her supposed modesty. But she is not all that modest. At Catherine's insistence, Marita reads the honeymoon narrative that David has begun but temporarily laid aside in favor of the elephant story, and when David asks her about what he calls the part set in Madrid, which presumably involves the sexual transformations, Marita tells David that she understands because she is just like him.

Marita openly admits to Catherine in front of David that she is "trying to study his needs" (122). After initiating the affair with Catherine, Marita confuses Catherine by abruptly and hypocritically rejecting her lesbian advances two days later, and soon afterwards Marita turns on Catherine, protesting that they cannot in good conscience make David go to Madrid when he is in the middle of writing his story. She becomes extraordinarily solicitous of David's work; David himself calls his writing "his own country, the one that Catherine was jealous of and that Marita loved and respected" (193)—an idea he echoes later. But there are ominous signs that Marita, too, may eventually develop into a less subordinate figure as, for example, when she asks if she can read the elephant story for herself "so I can feel like you do and not just happy because you're happy like I was your dog?" (203).

THEMES

One theme of *The Garden of Eden* has to do with the fluidity of sexual identity. Hemingway seems to suggest that our sense of ourselves as male or female is not as fixed as we might like to think and that we can choose to emphasize those aspects of ourselves that are more like the opposite sex than our own. Catherine can choose to "become" Peter, David can choose to take a feminine role, and Marita can enjoy affairs with both of them. All three of them are at least initially interested in sexual experimentation.

Yet while he implicitly argues for this fluidity and willingness to experiment, at the same time Hemingway develops the theme that the choice to identify with the opposite sex is unspeakably dangerous and inevitably leads to immorality and eventual madness. As Catherine participates in her sexual experiments, she becomes increasingly unstable. David becomes more and more frightened by Catherine's insistence that they exchange sexual identities, and he responds to his fear by turning to Marita, who despite her initial lesbian interlude with Catherine seems firmly committed to heterosexuality by the time she and David have become lovers.

The story also has to do with the theme of betrayal. David compares Catherine's blond hair to ivory (169)—but his comparison represents an ominous development in their relationship, considering that in the short story he is writing he betrays the elephant, which is then killed for its ivory. The implication is that David will eventually betray Catherine as well—as he does, in a passive way that parallels his betrayal of the elephant. Even at the end of the first chapter, while he is still on his honeymoon, he has already emotionally forsaken her: "his heart said goodbye Catherine goodbye my lovely girl goodbye and good luck and goodbye" (18).

Later in the novel he betrays her more actively, by choosing to write his father-son story set in Africa rather than the narrative based on his honeymoon with her. Catherine in turn betrays David by burning his manuscript. Marita, who is Catherine's lover first, betrays her with David, encouraging him to see Catherine as mentally ill and discussing what they should do about this problem of his sick wife. And David retaliates for Catherine's destruction of his manuscript by leaving her for Marita. None of the three people involved in this almost incestuous triangle seems psychologically healthy, and all three treat each other badly.

LITERARY DEVICES

The Garden of Eden is an interesting example of metafiction—self-reflexive fiction that takes as its subject its own creation. The novel is itself the honeymoon narrative David is writing, and its completion may signal Catherine's ultimate triumph. While it's not clear what their sexual transformations mean, they have proven fascinating and sometimes disturbing to many readers and have prompted scholars to reexamine some of Hemingway's earlier writings for similar themes—including the apparent homosexuality of characters in such short stories as "A Simple Enquiry," "Mother of a Queen," and "The Sea Change" and the fascination with haircutting and with twinned male and female characters in *A Farewell to Arms*, *For Whom the Bell Tolls*, and the posthumously published short story "The Last Good Country."

ALTERNATE READING: INTERTEXTUAL

In an intertextual reading, a reader studies a work in the light of other texts to which it alludes and examines the meanings that the author's allusions to those other texts invoke. The title *The Garden of Eden* is of course an allusion to the biblical story of Adam and Eve in the book of Genesis. Certainly Hemingway casts Catherine as both Eve and the serpent. She is the temptress who destroys the couple's happiness in the paradise of their honeymoon. Very early in the novel Catherine calls herself "the destructive type" (5). David addresses her as "Devil" more than two dozen times, and she calls their sexual transformations "devil things" (29). As her skin color grows darker, she becomes more closely associated with Satan, sometimes known as the Prince of Darkness, and in a passage that confirms this metaphoric reading of her darkness, a bewildered David wonders how dark she will finally become. When the colonel calls Catherine "the darkest white girl I've ever seen" (63), she insists that she is naturally dark, that the sun just brings out the color that is latent within her—as if her wickedness were waiting within to be extracted by the right set of circumstances. David even compares her to a goat, recalling the cloven hooves associated with the medieval figure of the Devil. Catherine tells David that he is both easy and fun to corrupt, although she immediately dismisses what she has said as a joke. Like Harry in "The Snows of Kilimanjaro," David has been corrupted financially as well as morally. Because his wife's wealth has enabled him to live comfortably without working, he has not had economic compulsion driving him to write, and his art has suffered as a consequence.

"All things truly wicked start from an innocence," Hemingway wrote in *A Moveable Feast* (210). Both Catherine and David share an innocent happiness as the novel opens upon their seemingly idyllic honeymoon on the French Riviera. Hemingway suggests that by giving in to Catherine's wish that they transform themselves sexually, David has succumbed to temptation much as Adam did when he ate of the apple Eve offered him. David drinks to avoid confronting what he sees as his own sin in condoning Catherine's behavior. In the manuscript, Hemingway further emphasizes this theme of temptation. The couple are inspired to begin their sexual games only after they see Auguste Rodin's ominously titled *The Damned Women*, a bronze sculpture depicting a lesbian embrace. The sculpture, also known as *Ovid's Metamorphoses*, is part of a series for a larger work titled "The Gates of Hell" (Burwell 102).

It is ironic that while in the biblical book of Genesis, Eve is punished with the pain of childbirth, Catherine is evidently infertile. Instead, in Hemingway's novel, Catherine pays for her sins with her sanity, while David in turn pays for his transgressions by losing his chance of happiness with Catherine, who despite her apparent madness seems somehow more vital than Marita. After their "fall," Catherine in particular seems oddly diminished, unable even to remember exactly what it is that she and David have lost.

The Bible is not the only religious text invoked in *The Garden of Eden*. Critic Tamara M. Powell has compared Catherine to Lilith, Adam's wife in ancient Jewish texts. According to Jewish tradition, God created Adam and Lilith as one androgynous being and divided it into two only after its two halves fought bitterly with each other. When Adam and Lilith then argued about who should be in charge, Lilith fled, and God replaced her with the more submissive Eve. The parallels to Catherine's struggle with David over who should control his writing, her flight, and David's replacement of her with the apparently more submissive Marita are obvious. As Powell observes, "Androgyny is in some way a part of both women's lives. In addition, Catherine and Lilith both want power in their relationships, both lose husbands to meeker women, both are destructive, and both are complex characters" (80).

Hemingway also draws on an even older tradition to make a similar point about Catherine. Colonel Boyle notices her in the Prado art museum admiring a statue of Leda and the swan. Hemingway thus invokes both the ancient Greek myth in which Zeus transforms himself into a swan so that he can take advantage of Leda and the 1924 poem by W.B. Yeats in which the poet asks whether Leda takes on both Zeus' knowledge and his power through their sexual encounter. The allusion reflects on Catherine's own sexual transformation and suggests that what she is after is David's knowledge and power as an artist.

By invoking these traditional religious and mythic texts, Hemingway calls readers' attention to what he sees as the profound moral implications of his characters' unorthodox behavior and at the same time examines the power dynamics of an unconventional marriage. Very much like David, Hemingway himself seems simultaneously drawn to these sexual exchanges and morally discomfited by them. He views Catherine with compassion, yet seems at the same time repulsed by the very mood swings and artistic jealousy he shares with her. *The Garden of Eden* is a rich, contradictory, and intricate work that demonstrates both its author's courage and his complexity.

Selected Bibliography

Note: Abbreviations used in the text appear in parentheses.

WORKS BY ERNEST HEMINGWAY

Hemingway at Oak Park High: The High School Writings of Ernest Hemingway, 1916–1917. Ed. Cynthia Maziarka and Donald Vogel, Jr. Oak Park, IL: Oak Park and River Forest High School, 1993.

Dateline: Toronto—The Complete Star *Dispatches, 1920–24*. Ed. William White. New York: Scribner's, 1985.

In Our Time. New York: Scribner's, 1925.

The Sun Also Rises. New York: Scribner's, 1926.

Torrents of Spring. New York: Scribner's, 1926.

(*MWW*): *Men without Women*. New York: Scribner's, 1927.

A Farewell to Arms. New York: Scribner's, 1929.

(*DIA*): *Death in the Afternoon*. New York: Scribner's, 1932.

(*WTN*): *Winner Take Nothing*. New York: Scribner's, 1933.

(*GHOA*): *Green Hills of Africa*. New York: Scribner's, 1935.

To Have and Have Not. New York: Scribner's, 1937.

For Whom the Bell Tolls. New York: Scribner's, 1940.

"Introduction." *Men at War: The Best War Stories of All Time*. Ed. Ernest Hemingway. New York: Bramhall House, 1955. xi–xxvii.

Across the River and Into the Trees. New York: Scribner's, 1950.

The Old Man and the Sea. New York: Scribner's, 1952.

POSTHUMOUS WORKS

(*AMF*): *A Moveable Feast*. New York: Scribner's, 1964.

By-Line: Ernest Hemingway. Ed. William White. New York: Scribner's, 1967.

The Fifth Column and Four Stories of the Spanish Civil War. New York: Scribner's, 1969.

Islands in the Stream. New York: Scribner's, 1970.

(*NAS*): *The Nick Adams Stories*. Ed. Philip Young. New York: Scribner's, 1972.

The Dangerous Summer. New York: Scribner's, 1985.

The Garden of Eden. New York: Scribner's, 1986.

(*SS*): *The Short Stories of Ernest Hemingway*. New York: Macmillan, 1986.

The Complete Short Stories of Ernest Hemingway: The Finca Vigía Edition. New York: Scribner's, 1987.

"The Art of the Short Story." *Ernest Hemingway: A Study of the Short Fiction*. Ed. Joseph M. Flora. Boston: Twayne, 1989. 129–44.

Complete Poems. Ed. Nicholas Gerogiannis. Lincoln: University of Nebraska Press, 1992.

Ernest Hemingway on Writing. Ed. Larry W. Phillips. New York: Simon and Schuster Trade Paperbacks, 1999.

True at First Light. New York: Scribner's, 1999.

BIOGRAPHIES, MEMOIRS, AND OTHER BIOGRAPHICAL SOURCES

"Back to His First Field." *Kansas City Times* 26 Nov. 1940: 1–2. Rptd. In *Conversations with Ernest Hemingway*, ed. Matthew J. Bruccoli. Jackson: University Press of Mississippi, 1986. 21–24.

Baker, Carlos. *Ernest Hemingway: A Life Story*. New York: Scribner's, 1969.

———. *Ernest Hemingway: Selected Letters, 1917–1961*. New York: Scribner's, 1981.

Brian, Denis. *The True Gen: An Intimate Portrait of Hemingway by Those Who Knew Him*. New York: Grove Press, 1988.

Bruccoli, Matthew J. *Fitzgerald and Hemingway: A Dangerous Friendship*. New York: Carroll & Graf, 1994.

Cowley, Malcolm. "Portrait of Mr. Papa." *Life* 10 Jan. 1949: 86–101.

Diliberto, Gioia. *Hadley*. New York: Ticknor, 1992.

Griffin, Peter. *Along with Youth: Hemingway, The Early Years*. New York: Oxford University Press, 1985.

———. *Less than a Treason: Hemingway in Paris*. New York: Oxford University Press, 1990.

Hemingway, Gregory H. *Papa: A Personal Memoir*. Boston: Houghton Mifflin, 1976.

Hemingway, Leicester. *My Brother, Ernest Hemingway*. Cleveland: World, 1962. 3rd ed. Sarasota, FL: Pineapple, 1996.

Hemingway, Mary Welsh. *How It Was*. New York: Knopf, 1976.

Hotchner, A.E. *Papa Hemingway: A Personal Memoir*. Rev. ed. New York: Bantam, 1966.

Josephs, Allen. "Hemingway's Out of Body Experience." *Hemingway Review* II. 2 (Spring 1983): 11–17.

Lynn, Kenneth S. *Hemingway*. New York: Simon & Schuster, 1987.

Mellow, James R. *Hemingway: A Life without Consequences*. Boston: Houghton, 1992.

Meyers, Jeffrey. *Hemingway: A Biography*. New York: Harper and Row, 1985.

Miller, Madelaine Hemingway. *Ernie: Hemingway's Sister "Sunny" Remembers*. 1975. Holt, MI: Thunder Bay Press, 1999.

Montgomery, Constance Cappel. *Hemingway in Michigan*. 1966. Detroit: Wayne State University Press, 1990.

Nagel, James, and Henry S. Villard, eds. *Hemingway in Love and War: The Lost Diary of Agnes von Kurowsky, Her Letters & Correspondence of Ernest Hemingway*. Boston: Northeastern University Press, 1989.

Parker, Dorothy. "The Artist's Reward." *New Yorker* 30 Nov. 1929: 28–31.

Reynolds, Michael. *Hemingway: An Annotated Chronology, An Outline of the Author's Life and Career Detailing Significant Events, Friendships, Travels, and Achievements*. Detroit: Omnigraphics, 1991.

———. *Hemingway: The American Homecoming*. Cambridge, MA: Blackwell, 1992.

———. *Hemingway: The Final Years*. New York: Norton, 1999.

———. *Hemingway: The 1930s*. New York: Norton, 1997.

———. *Hemingway: The Paris Years*. Cambridge, MA: Basil Blackwell, 1989.

———. *The Young Hemingway*. New York: Basil Blackwell, 1986.

Ross, Lillian. "How Do You Like It Now, Gentlemen?" *New Yorker* 13 May 1950: 36–62. Rpt. in *Hemingway: A Collection of Critical Essays*. Ed. Robert P. Weeks. Englewood Cliffs, NJ: Prentice-Hall, 1962. 17–39.

Sanford, Marcelline Hemingway. *At the Hemingways: With Fifty Years of Correspondence between Ernest and Marcelline Hemingway*. Rev. ed. Ed. John Sanford. Moscow: University of Idaho Press, 1999.

Voss, Frederick. *Picturing Hemingway: A Writer in His Time*. New Haven, CT: Smithsonian National Portrait Gallery, Washington, DC, in association with Yale University Press, 1999.

AUDIOVISUAL SOURCES

Ernest Hemingway: Wrestling with Life. Biography. Introd. Jack Perkins. Narr. Mariel Hemingway. Videocassette. New York: A&E Home Video, 1998.

Hemingway, Ernest, narr. *Ernest Hemingway Reads*. Audiocassette. Caedmon, 1992.

———. *Spanish Earth*. Dir. Joris Ivens. 1937. Videocassette. Hollywood's Attic, 1996.

Hemingway in the Autumn: Ernest Hemingway in Idaho. Prod. and dir. David Butterfield. Narr. Carolyn Holly. Videocassette. Centennial Entertainment, 1996.

Hemingway: Winner Take Nothing. Narr. Margaux Hemingway. Videocassette. MPI Home Video, 1998.

SELECTED GENERAL CRITICISM

Baker, Carlos. *Hemingway: The Writer as Artist.* 4th ed. Princeton, NJ: Princeton University Press, 1972.

Beegel, Susan F., ed. *Hemingway's Neglected Short Fiction: New Perspectives.* Ann Arbor: University of Michigan Research Press, 1989.

———. "Conclusion: The Critical Reputation of Ernest Hemingway." *The Cambridge Companion to Hemingway.* Ed. Scott Donaldson. New York: Cambridge University Press, 1996. 269–99.

Benson, Jackson J. *Hemingway: The Writer's Art of Self-Defense.* Minneapolis: University of Minnesota Press, 1969.

———, ed. *New Critical Approaches to the Short Stories of Ernest Hemingway.* Durham, NC: Duke University Press, 1990.

———. *The Short Stories of Ernest Hemingway: Critical Essays.* Durham, NC: Duke University Press, 1975.

Brasch, James D., and Joseph Sigman. *Hemingway's Library: A Composite Record.* New York: Garland, 1981.

Brenner, Gerry. *Concealments in Hemingway's Works.* Columbus: Ohio State University Press, 1983.

Capellan, Angel. *Hemingway and the Hispanic World.* Ann Arbor: University of Michigan Research Press, 1985.

Comley, Nancy R., and Robert Scholes. *Hemingway's Genders: Rereading the Hemingway Text.* New Haven, CT: Yale University Press, 1994.

Conrad, Barnaby. *Hemingway's Spain.* San Francisco: Chronicle, 1989.

Curnutt, Kirk. *Ernest Hemingway and the Expatriate Modernist Movement.* Detroit: Gale Group, 2000.

Dardis, Tom. "Hemingway: 'I'm no rummy.' " *The Thirsty Muse: Alcohol and the American Writer.* New York: Ticknor & Fields, 1989. 155–209.

Donaldson, Scott, ed. *The Cambridge Companion to Ernest Hemingway.* New York: Cambridge University Press, 1996.

Eby, Carl. *Hemingway's Fetishism: Psychoanalysis and the Mirror of Manhood.* Albany: State University of New York Press, 1999.

Fenton, Charles A. *The Apprenticeship of Ernest Hemingway: The Early Years.* New York: Farrar, Straus, & Young, 1954.

Fleming, Robert E. *The Face in the Mirror: Hemingway's Writers.* Tuscaloosa: University of Alabama Press, 1994.

———, ed. *Hemingway and the Natural World.* Moscow: University of Idaho Press, 1999.

Flora, Joseph. *Ernest Hemingway: A Study of the Short Fiction.* Boston: Twayne, 1989.

———. *Hemingway's Nick Adams*. Baton Rouge: Louisiana State University Press, 1982.

Gajdusek, Robert E. *Hemingway's Paris*. New York: Scribner's, 1978.

Grebstein, Sheldon Norman. *Hemingway's Craft*. Carbondale: Southern Illinois University Press, 1973.

Grimes, Larry. *The Religious Design of Hemingway's Early Fiction*. Ann Arbor: University of Michigan Research Press, 1985.

Hanneman, Audre. *Ernest Hemingway: A Comprehensive Bibliography*. Princeton, NJ: Princeton University Press, 1967.

Hays, Peter L. *Ernest Hemingway*. New York: Continuum, 1990.

———. "Hemingway and London." *Hemingway Review* IV.1 (Fall 1984): 54–56.

———. "Hemingway's Clinical Depression: A Speculation." *Hemingway Review* 14.2 (Spring 1995): 50–63.

Jamison, Kay Redfield. *Touched with Fire: Manic-Depressive Illness and the Artistic Temperament*. New York: Macmillan, 1993.

Johnston, Kenneth G. "Hemingway and Cezanne: Doing the Country." *American Literature* 56.1 (March 1984): 28–37.

———. *The Tip of the Iceberg: Hemingway and the Short Story*. Greenwood, FL: Penkevill, 1987.

Josephs, Allen. "How Did Hemingway Write?" *North Dakota Quarterly* 63.3 (Summer 1996): 50–64.

Kennedy, J. Gerald, and Jackson Bryer, eds. *French Connections: Hemingway and Fitzgerald Abroad*. New York: St. Martin's, 1998.

Kert, Bernice. *The Hemingway Women*. New York: Norton, 1983.

Knott, Toni D., ed. *One Man Alone: Hemingway and* To Have and Have Not. Lanham, MD: University Press of America, 1999.

Larson, Kelli A. *Ernest Hemingway: A Reference Guide, 1974–1989*. Boston: Hall, 1990.

Laurence, Frank M. *Hemingway and the Movies*. Jackson: University Press of Mississippi, 1981.

Lee, A. Robert. *Ernest Hemingway: New Critical Essays*. Totowa, NJ: Barnes & Noble, 1983.

Leff, Leonard J. *Hemingway and His Conspirators: Hollywood, Scribners, and the Making of American Celebrity Culture*. Lanham, MD: Rowman & Littlefield, 1997.

Lewis, Robert W., ed. *Hemingway in Italy and Other Essays*. New York: Praeger, 1990.

Mandel, Miriam. *Hemingway's* The Dangerous Summer: *The Complete Annotations*. Metuchen, NJ: Scarecrow, forthcoming.

———. *Hemingway's* Death in the Afternoon: *The Complete Annotations*. Metuchen, NJ: Scarecrow, 2001.

———. *Reading Hemingway: The Facts in the Fictions*. Metuchen, NJ: Scarecrow, 1995.

Merrill, Robert. "Demoting Hemingway: Feminist Criticism and the Canon." *American Literature* 60.2 (May 1988): 255–68.

Messent, Peter. *Ernest Hemingway*. London: Macmillan, 1992.

Meyers, Jeffrey. "Kipling and Hemingway: The Lesson of the Master." *American Literature* 56.1 (March 1984): 87–99.

———, ed. *Hemingway: The Critical Heritage*. Boston: Routledge & Kegan Paul, 1982.

Moddelmog, Debra A. *Reading Desire: In Pursuit of Ernest Hemingway*. Ithaca, NY: Cornell University Press, 1999.

Moreland, Kim. *The Medievalist Impulse in American Literature: Twain, Adams, Fitzgerald, and Hemingway*. Charlottesville: University Press of Virginia, 1996.

Morrison, Toni. *Playing in the Dark: Whiteness and the Literary Imagination*. Cambridge, MA: Harvard University Press, 1992.

Nagel, James, ed. *Ernest Hemingway: The Oak Park Legacy*. Tuscaloosa: University of Alabama Press, 1996.

———. *Ernest Hemingway: The Writer in Context*. Madison: University of Wisconsin Press, 1984.

Noble, Donald R., ed. *Hemingway: A Revaluation*. Troy, NY: Whitston, 1983.

Oliver, Charles M. *Ernest Hemingway A to Z: The Essential Reference to the Life and Work*. New York: Facts on File, 1999.

———, ed. *A Moving Picture Feast: The Filmgoer's Hemingway*. New York: Praeger, 1989.

Paul, Steve. "On Hemingway and His Influence: Conversations with Writers." *Hemingway Review* 18.2 (Spring 1999 Centennial Issue): 115–32.

Phillips, Gene D. *Hemingway and Film*. New York: Frederick Ungar, 1980.

Plimpton, George. "The Art of Fiction: Ernest Hemingway." *Paris Review* 5 (Spring 1958): 109–29. Rptd. in *Conversations with Ernest Hemingway*. Ed. Matthew J. Bruccoli. Jackson: University Press of Mississippi, 1986.

Raeburn, John. *Fame Became of Him: Hemingway as Public Writer*. Bloomington: Indiana University Press, 1984.

Reynolds, Michael. *Hemingway's Reading 1910–1940: An Inventory*. Princeton, NJ: Princeton University Press, 1981.

Rogal, Samuel J. *For Whom the Dinner Bell Tolls: The Role and Function of Food and Drink in the Prose of Ernest Hemingway*. San Francisco: International Scholars, 1997.

Rosen, Kenneth, ed. *Hemingway Repossessed*. Westport, CT: Praeger, 1994.

Rovit, Earl, and Gerry Brenner. *Ernest Hemingway*. Boston: Twayne, 1986.

Scafella, Frank, ed. *Hemingway: Essays of Reassessment*. New York: Oxford University Press, 1991.

Smith, Paul. "Hemingway's Apprentice Fiction: 1919–1921." *American Literature* 58.4 (December 1986): 574–88.

———. "Hemingway's Early Manuscripts: The Theory and Practice of Omission." *Journal of Modern Literature* 10 (June 1983): 268–88.

———. *A Reader's Guide to the Short Stories of Ernest Hemingway*. Boston: Hall, 1989.

———, ed. *New Essays on Hemingway's Short Fiction*. New York: Cambridge University Press, 1998.

Spilka, Mark. *Hemingway's Quarrel with Androgyny*. Lincoln: University of Nebraska Press, 1990.

Stephens, Robert O., ed. *Ernest Hemingway: The Critical Reception*. New York: Burt Franklin, 1977.

Stoneback, H.R. "In the Nominal Country of the Bogus: Hemingway's Catholicism and the Biographies." *Hemingway: Essays of Reassessment*. Ed. Frank Scafella. New York: Oxford University Press, 1991. 105–40.

Svoboda, Frederic J., and Joseph J. Waldmeir, eds. *Hemingway: Up in Michigan Perspectives*. East Lansing: Michigan State University Press, 1995.

Wagner, Linda W., ed. *Ernest Hemingway: A Reference Guide*. Boston: Hall, 1977.

———. *Ernest Hemingway: Six Decades of Criticism*. Ann Arbor: Michigan State University Press, 1987.

Wagner-Martin, Linda. *A Historical Guide to Ernest Hemingway*. New York: Oxford University Press, 2000.

———. *Seven Decades of Criticism*. East Lansing: Michigan State University Press, 1998.

Waldhorn, Arthur. *A Reader's Guide to Ernest Hemingway*. New York: Farrar, Straus and Giroux, 1972.

Whiting, Charles. *Hemingway Goes to War*. Phoenix Mill, UK: Sutton Publishing, 1999.

Whitlow, Roger. *Cassandra's Daughters: The Women in Hemingway*. Westport, CT: Greenwood Press, 1984.

Williams, Wirt. *The Tragic Art of Ernest Hemingway*. Baton Rouge: Louisiana State University Press, 1981.

Wilson, Edmund. "Hemingway: Gauge of Morale." *The Wound and the Bow: Seven Studies in Literature*. Cambridge, MA: Houghton Mifflin, 1941. 214–42.

Young, Philip. *Ernest Hemingway: A Reconsideration*. University Park: Pennsylvania State University Press, 1966.

IN OUR TIME

REVIEWS

Lawrence, D.H. "*In Our Time*: A Review." *Hemingway: A Collection of Critical Essays*. Ed. Robert P. Weeks. Englewood Cliffs, NJ: Prentice-Hall, 1962. 93–94.

"Preludes to a Mood." *New York Times Book Review* 18 Oct. 1925: 8.

Review of *In Our Time*. *Time* 18 Jan. 1926: 38–39.

Rosenfeld, Paul. "*Tough Earth.*" *New Republic* 25 Nov. 1925: 22–23.

Tate, Allen. Review of *In Our Time*. *Nation* 10 Feb. 1926: 160–62.

CRITICISM

Brogan, Jacqueline Vaught. "Hemingway's *In Our Time*: A Cubist Anatomy." *Hemingway Review* 17.2 (1998): 31–46.

Clifford, Stephen. "Hemingway's Fragmentary Novel: Readers Writing the Hero in *In Our Time*." *Hemingway Review* 13.2 (Spring 1994): 12–23.

Cox, James M. "*In Our Time*: The Essential Hemingway." *Southern Humanities Review* 22.4 (Fall 1988): 305–20.

Hays, Peter L., comp. *A Concordance to Hemingway's* In Our Time. Boston: Hall, 1990.

Mansell, Darrel. "Words Lost in *In Our Time*." *Hemingway Review* 17.1 (Fall 1997): 5–14.

Moddelmog, Debra A. "The Unifying Consciousness of a Divided Conscience: Nick Adams as Author of *In Our Time*." *American Literature: A Journal of Literary History, Criticism, and Bibliography* 60.4 (1988): 591–610.

Reynolds, Michael, ed. *Critical Essays on Ernest Hemingway's* In Our Time. Boston: Hall, 1983.

———. "Hemingway's *In Our Time*: The Biography of a Book." *Modern American Short Story Sequences: Composite Fictions and Fictive Communities*. Ed. J. Gerald Kennedy. Cambridge: Cambridge University Press, 1995. 35–51.

Scafella, Frank. "Imagistic Landscape of a Psyche: Hemingway's Nick Adams." *Hemingway Review* 2 (Spring 1983): 2–10.

Seed, David. " 'The Picture of the Whole': *In Our Time*." *Ernest Hemingway: New Critical Essays*. Ed. A. Robert Lee. Totowa, NJ: Barnes & Noble, 1983. 13–35.

Smith, Paul. "Hemingway's Sense of an Ending: *In Our Time* and After." *Hemingway Review* 12.1 (Fall 1992): 12–18.

Strong, Amy Lovell. "Screaming through Silence: The Violence of Race in 'Indian Camp' and 'The Doctor and the Doctor's Wife.' " *Hemingway Review* 16.1 (Fall 1996): 18–32.

Strychacz, Thomas. "*In Our Time*, Out of Season." *The Cambridge Companion to Hemingway*. Ed. Scott Donaldson. New York: Cambridge University Press, 1996. 55–86.

Tetlow, Wendolyn E. *Hemingway's* In Our Time: *Lyrical Dimensions*. Lewisburg, PA: Bucknell University Press, 1992.

Vaughn, Elizabeth Dewberry. "*In Our Time* as Self-Begetting Fiction." *Modern Fiction Studies* 35.4 (Winter 1989): 707–16.

———. " 'Truer Than Anything True': *In Our Time* and Journalism." *Hemingway Review* XI.2 (Spring 1992): 11–18.

Winn, Harbour. "Hemingway's *In Our Time*: 'Pretty Good Unity.' " *Hemingway Review* IX.2 (Spring 1990): 124–41.

"Indian Camp"

Grimes, Larry. "Night Terror and Morning Calm: A Reading of Hemingway's 'Indian Camp' as Sequel to 'Three Shots.' " *Studies in Short Fiction* 12 (1975): 413–15.

Meyers, Jeffrey. "Hemingway's Primitivism and 'Indian Camp.' " *Twentieth-Century Literature* 34.2 (Summer 1988): 211–22. Rpt. in *New Critical Approaches to the Short Stories of Ernest Hemingway*. Ed. Jackson J. Benson. Durham, NC: Duke University Press, 1990. 300–308.

Wainwright, J. Andrew. "The Far Shore: Gender Complexities in Hemingway's 'Indian Camp.' " *Dalhousie Review* 66.1–2 (Spring-Summer 1986): 181–87.

Wolter, Jurgen C. "Caesareans in an Indian Camp." *Hemingway Review* 13.1 (Fall 1993): 92–94.

"Soldier's Home"

Barron, Cynthia M. "The Catcher and the Soldier: Hemingway's 'Soldier's Home' and Salinger's *The Catcher in the Rye*." *Hemingway Review* 2 (Fall 1982): 70–73.

Boyd, John D. "Hemingway's 'soldier's Home.' " *Explicator* 40 (Fall 1981): 51–53.

Imamura, Tateo. " 'Soldier's Home': Another Story of a Broken Heart." *Hemingway Review* 16.1 (Fall 1996): 102–07.

Kennedy, J. Gerald, and Kirk Curnutt. "Out of the Picture: Mrs. Krebs, Mother Stein, and 'Soldier's Home.' " *Hemingway Review* 12.1 (Fall 1992): 1–11.

Kobler, J.F. " 'Soldier's Home' Revisited: A Hemingway *Mea Culpa*." *Studies in Short Fiction* 30 (1993): 377–85.

Lamb, Robert Paul. "The Love Song of Harold Krebs: Form, Argument, and Meaning in Hemingway's 'Soldier's Home.' " *Hemingway Review* 14.2 (Spring 1995): 18–36.

Monteiro, George. "Hemingway's 'Soldier's Home.' " *Explicator* 40 (Fall 1981): 50–51.

"Big Two-Hearted River"

Adair, William. " 'Big Two-Hearted River': Why the Swamp Is Tragic." *Journal of Modern Literature* 17.4 (1991): 584–88.

Civello, Paul. "Hemingway's Primitivism: Archetypal Patterns in 'Big Two-Hearted River.' " *Hemingway Review* 13.1 (1993): 1–16.

Cowley, Malcolm. "Nightmare and Ritual in Hemingway." *Hemingway: A Collection of Critical Essays*. Ed. Robert P. Weeks. Englewood Cliffs, NJ: Prentice-Hall, 1962. 40–51.

Lamb, Robert Paul. "Fishing for Stories: What 'Big Two-Hearted River' Is Really About." *Modern Fiction Studies* 37 (1991): 161–82.

Plath, James. "Fishing for Tension: The Dynamics of Hemingway's 'Big Two-Hearted River.' " *North Dakota Quarterly* 62.2 (Spring 1994–1995): 159–65.

Schmidt, Susan. "Ecological Renewal Images in 'Big Two-Hearted River': Jack Pines and the Fisher King." *Hemingway Review* 9.2 (Spring 1990): 142–45.

Summerhayes, Don. "Fish Story: Ways of Telling in 'Big Two-Hearted River.' " *Hemingway Review* 15.1 (1995): 10–26.

Svoboda, Frederic J. "Landscapes Real and Imagined: 'Big Two-Hearted River.' " *Hemingway Review* 16 (Fall 1996): 33–42.

Winchell, Mark Royden. "Fishing the Swamp: 'Big Two-Hearted River' and the Unity of *In Our Time*." *South Carolina Review* 18.2 (1986): 18–29.

THE SUN ALSO RISES

REVIEWS

Ashley, Schuyler. Review of *The Sun Also Rises*. *Kansas City Star* 4 Dec. 1929: 8.

Dos Passos, John. "A Lost Generation." *New Masses* 2 (Dec. 1926): 26.

"Hemingway Seems Out of Focus in the 'Sun Also Rises.' " *Chicago Daily Tribune* 27 Nov. 1926: 13.

"Marital Tragedy." *New York Times Book Review* 31 Oct. 1926: 7.

Muir, Edwin. *Nation and Athenaeum* 2 July 1927: 450, 452.

Rascoe, Burton. "Diversity in the Younger Set." *New York Sun* 6 Nov. 1929: 10.

"Sad Young Men." *Time* 1 Nov. 1926: 48.

"Study in Futility." *Cincinnati Enquirer* 30 Oct. 1926: 5.

Tate, Allen. "Hard-Boiled." *Nation* 15 Dec. 1926: 642, 644.

CRITICISM

Adams, Richard. "Sunrise out of the Waste Land." *Tulane Studies in English* 9 (1959): 429–44.

Balassi, William. "Hemingway's Greatest Iceberg: The Composition of *The Sun Also Rises*." *Writing the American Classics*. Ed. James Barbour and Tom Quirk. Chapel Hill: University of North Carolina Press, 1990. 125–55.

Berman, Ron. "Protestant, Catholic, Jew: *The Sun Also Rises*." *Hemingway Review* 18.1 (Fall 1998): 33–48.

Bloom, Harold, ed. *Major Literary Characters: Brett Ashley*. New York: Chelsea House, 1991.

———. *Modern Critical Interpretations: Ernest Hemingway's* The Sun Also Rises. New York: Chelsea House, 1987.

Cheatham, George. " 'Sign the Wire with Love': The Morality of Surplus in *The Sun Also Rises*." *Hemingway Review* XI.2 (Spring 1992): 25–30.

Crowley, John W. "Bulls, Balls, and Booze: *The Sun Also Rises*." *The White Logic: Alcoholism and Gender in American Modernist Fiction.* Amherst: University of Massachusetts Press, 1994. 43–64.

Djos, Matts. "Alcoholism in Ernest Hemingway's *The Sun Also Rises*: A Wine and Roses Perspective on the Lost Generation." *The Hemingway Review* (Spring 1995): 64–78.

Elliott, Ira. "Performance Art: Jake Barnes and 'Masculine' Signification in *The Sun Also Rises*." *American Literature* 67.1 (1995): 77–94.

Goodman, David R. "A Rejoinder to Matts Djos on Drinking in *The Sun Also Rises*." *North Dakota Quarterly* 64.3 (1997): 48–55.

Hays, Peter. "Hunting Ritual in *The Sun Also Rises*." *Hemingway Review* 8.2 (1989): 46–48.

Hemingway, Ernest. "The Unpublished Opening of *The Sun Also Rises*." *Antaeus* 33.1 (Spring 1979): 7–10. Rptd. in *Brett Ashley*. Ed. Harold Bloom. New York: Chelsea House, 1991. 5–8.

Knodt, Ellen Andrews. "Diving Deep: Jake's Moment of Truth at San Sebastian." *Hemingway Review* 17.1 (Fall 1997): 28–37.

Nagel, James, ed. *Critical Essays on Ernest Hemingway's* The Sun Also Rises. New York: G.K. Hall, 1995.

Oliver, Charles M., ed. *Special SAR Issue.* Special issue of *Hemingway Review* VI.1 (Fall 1986): 1–120.

Reynolds, Michael S. The Sun Also Rises: *A Novel of the Twenties.* Boston: Twayne, 1988.

———. "Jake's Odyssey: Catharsis in *The Sun Also Rises*." *Hemingway Review* IV.1 (Fall 1984): 33–36.

Rudat, Wolfgang E.H. *Alchemy in* The Sun Also Rises: *Hidden Gold in Hemingway's Narrative.* Lewiston, NY: Edwin Mellen Press, 1992.

———. *A Rotten Way to Be Wounded: The Tragicomedy of* The Sun Also Rises. New York: Peter Lang, 1990.

Sarason, Bertram D., ed. *Hemingway and* The Sun Set. Washington, DC: NCR, 1972.

Svoboda, Frederic Joseph. *Hemingway and* The Sun Also Rises: *The Crafting of a Style.* Lawrence: University Press of Kansas, 1983.

Thorn, Lee. "*The Sun Also Rises*: Good Manners Make Good Art." *Hemingway Review* VIII.1 (Fall 1988): 42–49.

———, ed. *New Essays on* The Sun Also Rises. New York: Cambridge University Press, 1987.

A FAREWELL TO ARMS

REVIEWS

Canby, Henry Seidel. "Story of the Brave." *Saturday Review of Literature* 12 Oct. 1929: 231–32.

Fadiman, Clifton P. "A Fine American Novel." *Nation* 30 Oct. 1929: 497–98.

Hutchison, Percy. "Love and War in the Pages of Mr. Hemingway." *New York Times Book Review* 29 Sept. 1929: 5.

"Man, Woman, War." *Time* 14 Oct. 1929: 80.

Matthews, T.S. "Nothing Ever Happens to the Brave." *New Republic* 9 Oct. 1929: 208–10.

Ross, Mary. Review of *A Farewell to Arms*. *Atlantic* Nov. 1929: 20.

CRITICISM

Bloom, Harold, ed. *Modern Critical Interpretations: Ernest Hemingway's* A Farewell to Arms. New York: Chelsea House, 1987.

———, ed. *New Essays on* A Farewell to Arms. Cambridge: Cambridge University Press, 1990.

Fetterley, Judith. *The Resisting Reader*. Bloomington: Indiana University Press, 1978.

Gellens, Jay, ed. *Twentieth Century Interpretations of* A Farewell to Arms: *A Collection of Critical Essays*. Englewood Cliffs, NJ: Prentice-Hall, 1970.

Graham, John. *The Merrill Studies in* A Farewell to Arms. Columbus, OH: Merrill Publishing, 1971.

Lewis, Robert W. A Farewell to Arms: *The War of the Words*. New York: Twayne, 1992.

Lockridge, Ernest. "Faithful in Her Fashion: Catherine Barkley, the Invisible Hemingway Heroine." *Journal of Narrative Technique* 18 (1988): 170–78.

Mandel, Miriam. "Ferguson and Lesbian Love: Unspoken Subplots in *A Farewell to Arms*." *Hemingway Review* 14.1 (Fall 1994): 18–24.

Monteiro, George, ed. *Critical Essays on Ernest Hemingway's* A Farewell to Arms. New York: G.K. Hall, 1994.

Nolan, Charles J. Jr. "Catherine Barkley: Hemingway's Scottish Heroine." *Hemingway Review* 7.1 (1987): 43–44.

Norris, Margot. "The Novel as War: Lies and Truth in Hemingway's *A Farewell to Arms*." *Modern Fiction Studies* 40.4 (1994): 689–710.

Oldsey, Bernard. *Hemingway's Hidden Craft: The Writing of* A Farewell to Arms. University Park: Pennsylvania State University Press, 1979.

Oliver, Charles M., ed. *Special Issue on* A Farewell to Arms. Spec. issue of *Hemingway Review*. 9.1 (1989): 1–112.

Reynolds, Michael. *Hemingway's First War: The Making of* A Farewell to Arms. Princeton, NJ: Princeton University Press, 1976.

Wexler, Joyce. "E.R.A. for Hemingway: A Feminist Defense of *A Farewell to Arms*." *Georgia Review* 35 (1981): 111–23.

MEN WITHOUT WOMEN

REVIEWS

Hutchison, Percy. "Mr. Hemingway Shows Himself a Master Craftsman in the Short Story." *New York Times Book Review* 16 Oct. 1927: 9, 27.

Review of *Men without Women. Time* 24 Oct. 1927: 38.

Woolf, Virginia. "An Essay in Criticism." *New York Herald Tribune Books* 9 Oct. 1927: 1, 8. Rptd. in *Granite and Rainbow*. New York: Harcourt, 1958. 85–92.

CRITICISM

"In Another Country"

Halter, Peter. "Indeterminacy in Hemingway's 'In Another Country.' " *English Studies* 71.6 (Dec. 1990): 523–34.

Steinke, James. "Hemingway's 'In Another Country' and 'Now I Lay Me.' " *Hemingway Review* V.1 (Fall 1985): 32–39.

"Hills Like White Elephants"

Abdoo, Sherlyn. "Hemingway's 'Hills Like White Elephants.' " *Explicator* 49.4 (Summer 1991): 238–40.

Coleman, Hildy. " 'Cat' and 'Hills': Two Hemingway Fairy Tales." *Hemingway Review* 12.1 (Fall 1992): 67–72.

Hannum, Howard L. " 'Jig Jig to dirty ears': White Elephants to Let." *Hemingway Review* XI.1 (Fall 1991): 46–54.

Justice, Hilary K. " 'Well, Well, Well': Cross-Gendered Autobiography and the Manuscript of 'Hills Like White Elephants.' " *Hemingway Review* 18.1 (Fall 1998): 17–32.

Kozikowski, Stanley. "Hemingway's 'Hills Like White Elephants.' " *Explicator* 52.2 (Winter 1994): 107–09.

Lanier, Doris. "The Bittersweet Taste of Absinthe in Hemingway's 'Hills Like White Elephants.' " *Studies in Short Fiction* 26 (Summer 1989): 279–88.

O'Brien, Timothy D. "Allusion, Word-Play, and the Central Conflict in 'Hills Like White Elephants.' " *Hemingway Review* 12.1 (Fall 1992): 19–25.

Renner, Stanley. "Moving to the Girl's Side of 'Hills Like White Elephants.' " *Hemingway Review* 15.1 (Fall 1995): 27–41.

Urgo, Joseph R. "Hemingway's 'Hills Like White Elephants.' " *Explicator* 46.3 (1988): 35–37.

"The Killers"

Berman, Ron. "Vaudeville Philosophers: 'The Killers.' " *Twentieth Century Literature* 45.1 (Spring 1999): 79–93.

Brooks, Cleanth, and Robert Penn Warren. "The Discovery of Evil: An Analysis of 'The Killers.' " *Understanding Fiction*. Englewood Cliffs, NJ: Prentice-Hall, 1979. 194–202.

Carter, Steven. "Rosencrantz and Guildenstern Are Alive: A Note on Al and Max in Hemingway's 'The Killers.' " *Hemingway Review* 17.1 (Fall 1997): 68–71.

Fleming, Robert E. "Hemingway's 'The Killers': The Map and the Territory." *Hemingway Review* IV.1 (Fall 1984): 40–43. Rpt. in *New Critical Approaches to the Short Stories of Ernest Hemingway*. Ed. Jackson J. Benson. Durham, NC: Duke University Press, 1990. 309–13.

Monteiro, George. "The Hit in Summit: Ernest Hemingway's 'The Killers.' " *Hemingway Review* 8.2 (1989): 40–42.

"Now I Lay Me"

Phelan, James. " 'Now I Lay Me': Nick's Strange Monologue, Hemingway's Powerful Lyric, and the Reader's Disconcerting Experience." *New Essays on Hemingway's Short Fiction*. Ed. Paul Smith. New York: Cambridge University Press, 1998. 47–71.

WINNER TAKE NOTHING

REVIEWS

Kronenberger, Louis. "Hemingway's New Stories and Other Recent Works of Fiction." *New York Times Book Review* 5 Nov. 1933: 6.

Matthews, T.S. Review of *Winner Take Nothing*. *New Republic* 15 Nov. 1933: 24–25.

Troy, William. "Mr. Hemingway's Opium." *Nation* 15 Nov. 1934: 570.

"A Clean, Well-Lighted Place"

Bennett, Warren. "The Characterization and the Dialogue Problem in Hemingway's 'A Clean, Well-Lighted Place.' " *Hemingway Review* 9.2 (1990): 94–123.

Kerner, David. "The Ambiguity of 'A Clean, Well-Lighted Place." *Studies in Short Fiction* 29.4 (1992): 561–74.

———. "Hemingway's Attention to 'A Clean, Well-Lighted Place.' " *Hemingway Review* 13.1 (Fall 1993): 48–62.

Leonard, John. " 'A Man of the World' and 'A Clean, Well-Lighted Place': Hemingway's Unified View of Old Age." *Hemingway Review* 13.2 (Spring 1994): 62–73.

Ryan, Ken. "The Contentious Emendation of Hemingway's 'A Clean Well-Lighted Place.' " *Hemingway Review* 18.1 (Fall 1998): 78–91.

Smith, Paul. "A Note on a New Manuscript of 'A Clean, Well-Lighted Place.' " *Hemingway Review* 8.2 (Spring 1989): 36–39.

Thomson, George H. " 'A Clean, Well-Lighted Place': Interpreting the Original Text." *Hemingway Review* II.2 (Spring 1983): 32–43.

"The Sea Change"

Bennett, Warren. " 'That's Not Very Polite': Sexual Identity in Hemingway's 'The Sea Change.' " *Hemingway's Neglected Short Fiction: New Perspectives.* Ed. Susan F. Beegel. Ann Arbor, MI: University Microfilms, Inc., 1989. 225–45.

Kobler, J.F. "Hemingway's 'The Sea Change': A Sympathetic View of Homosexuality." *The Arizona Quarterly* 26 (Winter 1970): 318–24.

Tyler, Lisa. " 'I'd Rather Not Hear': Women and Men in Conversation in 'Cat in the Rain' and 'The Sea Change.' " *Notable Women: Female Critics and the Female Voice in Hemingway.* Ed. Gloria Holland and Lawrence Broer. Tuscaloosa: University of Alabama Press, forthcoming.

Wycherly, H. Alan. "Hemingway's 'The Sea Change.' " *American Notes & Queries* 7 (Jan. 1969): 67–68.

"A Way You'll Never Be"

Vanderbilt, Kermit. "Nick Adams Through the Looking Glass: 'A Way You'll Never Be.' " *Explicator* 51.2 (1993): 104–10.

"Fathers and Sons"

Beegel, Susan F. "Second Growth: The Ecology of Loss in 'Fathers and Sons.' " *New Essays on Hemingway's Short Fiction.* Ed. Paul Smith. New York: Cambridge University Press, 1998. 75–110.

McCann, Richard. "To Embrace or Kill: 'Fathers and Sons.' " *Iowa Journal of Literary Studies* 3.1–2 (1981): 11–18. Rpt. in *New Critical Approaches to the Short Stories of Ernest Hemingway.* Ed. Jackson J. Benson. Durham, NC: Duke University Press, 1990. 266–74.

Strong, Paul. "Gathering the Pieces and Filling in the Gaps: Hemingway's 'Fathers and Sons.' " *Studies in Short Fiction* 26 (1989): 49–58.

THE AFRICAN STORIES

GREEN HILLS OF AFRICA

Reviews

Matthews, T.S. "A Hemingway You'll Never Be." *New Republic* 27 Nov. 1935: 79–80.

Review of *Green Hills of Africa. Newsweek* 26 Oct. 1935: 39–40.

Weeks, Edward. Review of *Green Hills of Africa. Atlantic* Nov. 1925: 30.

Criticism

Bredahl, A. Carl, Jr., and Susan Lynn Drake. *Hemingway's* Green Hills of Africa *as Evolutionary Narrative: Helix and Scimitar.* Lewiston, NY: Edwin Mellen Press, 1990.

Gajdusek, Robert. "A Brief Safari into the Religious Terrain of *Green Hills of Africa.*" *North Dakota Quarterly* 60.3 (Summer 1992): 26–40.

Lounsberry, Barbara. "*Green Hills of Africa*: Hemingway's Celebration of Memory." *The Hemingway Review* II.2 (Spring 1983): 23–31.

———. "The Holograph Manuscript of *Green Hills of Africa.*" *Hemingway Review* 12.2 (Spring 1993): 36–45.

Strychacz, Thomas. "Like Plums in a Pudding: Food and Rhetorical Performance in *Green Hills of Africa.*" *Hemingway Review* 19.2 (Spring 2000): 23–46.

———. "Trophy-Hunting as a Trope of Manhood in *Green Hills of Africa.*" *Hemingway Review* 13.1 (Fall 1993): 36–47.

Trogdon, Robert W. " 'Forms of Combat': Hemingway, the Critics, and *Green Hills of Africa.*" *Hemingway Review* 15.2 (Spring 1996): 1–14.

Weber, Ronald. *Hemingway's Art of Nonfiction.* New York: St. Martin's, 1990.

"THE SNOWS OF KILIMANJARO"

Bush, Lyall. "Consuming Hemingway: 'The Snows of Kilimanjaro' in the Postmodern Classroom." *Journal of Narrative Technique* 25.1 (Winter 1995): 23–46.

Friedman, Norman. "Harry or Ernest? The Unresolved Ambiguity in 'The Snows of Kilimanjaro.' " *Creative and Critical Approaches to the Short Story.* Ed. Noel Harold Kaylor, Jr. Lewiston, NY: Edwin Mellen Press, 1997. 359–73.

Herndon, Jerry A. " 'The Snows of Kilimanjaro': Another Look at Themes and Point of View." *South Atlantic Quarterly* 85 (1986): 351–59.

Howell, John, ed. *Hemingway's African Stories: The Stories, Their Sources, Their Critics.* New York: Scribner's, 1969.

Kennedy, J. Gerald. "Figuring the Damage: Fitzgerald's 'Babylon Revisited' and Hemingway's 'Snows of Kilimanjaro.' " *French Connections: Hemingway and Fitzgerald Abroad.* Ed. J. Gerald Kennedy and Jackson Bryer. New York: St. Martin's, 1998. 317–43.

Lewis, Robert W., Jr., and Max Westbrook. " 'The Snows of Kilimanjaro': Collated and Annotated." *Texas Quarterly* 13 (1970): 67–143.

———. "The Texas Manuscript of 'The Snows of Kilimanjaro.' " *Texas Quarterly* 9 (1966): 66–101.

Moddelmog, Debra. "Re-Placing Africa in 'The Snows of Kilimanjaro': The Intersecting Economies of Capitalist-Imperialism and Hemingway Biography." *New Essays on Hemingway's Short Fiction.* Ed. Paul Smith. Cambridge, England: Cambridge University Press, 1998. 111–36.

Santangelo, Gennaro. "The Dark Snows of Kilimanjaro." *The Short Stories of Ernest Hemingway: Critical Essays*. Ed. Jackson J. Benson. Durham, NC: Duke University Press, 1975. 251–61.

"THE SHORT HAPPY LIFE OF FRANCIS MACOMBER"

Blythe, Hal, and Charlie Sweet. "Wilson: Architect of the Macomber Conspiracy." *Studies in Short Fiction* 28.3 (Summer 1991): 305–9.

Cameron, Kenneth M. "Patterson and the Blyths: The Originals of Hemingway's 'Macomber' Triangle." *Hemingway Review* XI.2 (Spring 1992): 52–55.

Cheatham, George. "The Unhappy Life of Robert Wilson." *Studies in Short Fiction* 26.3 (Summer 1989): 341–45.

Galliard, Theodore L., Jr. "Hemingway's 'The Short Happy Life of Francis Macomber.' " *Explicator* 47.3 (Spring 1989): 44–47.

Greco, Anne. "Margot Macomber: 'Bitch Goddess' Exonerated." *Fitzgerald/Hemingway Annual* (1972): 273–80.

Johnston, K.G. "In Defense of the Unhappy Margot Macomber." *Hemingway Review* II.2 (Spring 1983): 44–47.

Kozikowski, S., S. Adriaansen, D. Moruzzi, and C. Prokop. "Hemingway's 'The Short Happy Life of Francis Macomber.' " *Explicator* 51 (1993): 239–41.

Kravitz, Bennett. " 'She Loves Me, She Loves Me Not': The Short Happy Symbiotic Marriage of Margot and Francis Macomber." *Journal of American Culture* 21.3 (Fall 1998): 83–87.

Morgan, Kathleen, and Luis A. Losada. "Tracking the Wounded Buffalo: Authorial Knowledge and the Shooting of Francis Macomber." *Hemingway Review* XI.1 (Fall 1991): 25–30.

Morton, Bruce. "Hemingway's 'The Short Happy Life of Francis Macomber.' " *Explicator* 41 (Fall 1982): 48–49.

O'Meara, Lauraleigh. "Shooting Cowards, Critics, and Failed Writers: F. Scott Fitzgerald and Hemingway's Francis Macomber." *Hemingway Review* 16.2 (Spring 1997): 27–34.

Spilka, Mark. "Nina Baym's Benevolent Reading of the Macomber Story: An Epistolary Response." *Hemingway: Up in Michigan Perspectives*. Ed. Frederic J. Svoboda and Joseph J. Waldmeir. East Lansing: Michigan State University Press, 1995. 189–201.

Sugiyama, Michelle Scalise. "What's Love Got to Do With It? An Evolutionary Analysis of 'The Short Happy Life of Francis Macomber.' " *Hemingway Review* 15.2 (Spring 1996): 15–32.

TRUE AT FIRST LIGHT

Reviews

Adams, Phoebe-Lou. Review of *True at First Light*. *Atlantic* Aug. 1999: 93.

Didion, Joan. "Last Words." *New Yorker* 9 Nov. 1998: 74–80.

Gray, Paul. "Where's Papa?" *Time* 5 July 1999: 76–77.

Jenks, Tom. "The Old Man and the Manuscript: Hemingway, in His Last Book, Writes His Own Sad Epitaph." *Harper's* 298.1788 (May 1999): 53–60.

Klepp, L.S. "Missing the Mark." *Entertainment Weekly* 9 July 1999: 67–69.

Lynn, Kenneth S. "Hemingway Ltd." *National Review* 28 June 1999: 50, 52.

Reynolds, Michael. Review of *True at First Light. North Dakota Quarterly* 66.2 (1999): 205–07.

Wineapple, Brenda. "The Sun Also Sets." *Nation* 14 June 1999: 24–28.

Wood, James. "The Lion King." *New York Times Book Review* 11 July 1999: 15–16.

Criticism

Beegel, Susan, ed. "*True at First Light* Special Section." *Hemingway Review* 19.1 (Fall 1999): 7–63.

FOR WHOM THE BELL TOLLS

REVIEWS

Adams, J. Donald. "The New Novel by Hemingway: 'For Whom the Bell Tolls' Is the Best Book He Has Written." *New York Times Book Review* 20 Oct. 1940: 1.

Barea, Arturo. "Not Spain but Hemingway." Trans. Ilsa Barea. *Horizon* 3 (May 1941): 350–61. Rpt. in *Hemingway and His Critics: An International Anthology.* Ed. Carlos Baker. New York: Hill and Wang, 1961. 202–12.

"Death in Spain." *Time* 21 Oct. 1940: 94–95.

"Hemingway's Spanish War." *Newsweek* 21 Oct. 1940: 50.

Littell, Robert. Review of *For Whom the Bell Tolls. Yale Review* 30 (Winter 1941): vi, viii.

Marshall, Margaret. Review of *For Whom the Bell Tolls. Nation* 26 Oct. 1940: 395–96.

Schorer, Mark. "The Background of a Style." *Kenyon Review* 3 (Winter 1941): 101–05.

Sherwood, Robert E. Review of *For Whom the Bell Tolls. Atlantic* Nov. 1940: front section.

Vaughan, J.N. Review of *For Whom the Bell Tolls. Commonweal* 13 Dec. 1940: 210.

Wilson, Edmund. "Return of Ernest Hemingway." *New Republic* 28 Oct. 1940: 591–92.

CRITICISM

Adair, William "Hemingway's Debt to *Seven Pillars of Wisdom* in *For Whom the Bell Tolls*." *Notes on Contemporary Literature* 17.3 (May 1987): 11–12.

Buckley, Ramón. "Revolution in Ronda: The Facts in Hemingway's *For Whom the Bell Tolls*." *Hemingway Review* 17.1 (Fall 1997): 49–57.

Cheney, Patrick. "Hemingway and Christian Epic: The Bible in *For Whom the Bell Tolls*." *Papers on Language and Literature* 21 (Spring 1985): 170–91.

Crozier, Robert D., S.J. "For Thine is the Power and the Glory: Love in *For Whom the Bell Tolls*." *Papers on Language and Literature* 10 (1974): 76–97.

Eby, Carl P. "Rabbit Stew and Blowing Dorothy's Bridges: Love, Aggression, and Fetishism in *For Whom the Bell Tolls*." *Twentieth Century Literature* 44.2 (1998): 204–18.

Gajdusek, Robert E. "Is He Building a Bridge or Blowing One?": The Repossession of Text by the Author in *For Whom the Bell Tolls*." *Hemingway Review* XI.2 (Spring 1992): 45–51.

Gould, Thomas E. " 'A Tiny Operation with Great Effect': Authorial Revision and Editorial Emasculation in the Manuscript of Hemingway's *For Whom the Bell Tolls*." *Blowing the Bridge: Essays on Hemingway and* For Whom the Bell Tolls. Ed. Rena Sanderson. New York: Greenwood Press, 1992. 67–81.

Grebstein, Sheldon Norman, ed. *The Merrill Studies in* For Whom the Bell Tolls. Columbus, OH: Merrill, 1971.

Hodson, Joel. "Robert Jordan Revisited: Hemingway's Debt to T.E. Lawrence." *Hemingway Review* 10.2 (Spring 1991): 2–16.

Josephs, Allen. For Whom the Bell Tolls: *Ernest Hemingway's Undiscovered Country*. New York: Twayne, 1994.

Martin, Robert A. "Robert Jordan and the Spanish Country: Learning to Live in It 'Truly and Well.' " *Hemingway Review* 16.1 (Fall 1996): 56–64.

Michalczyk, John J., and Sergo Villani, guest editors. *Malraux, Hemingway, and Embattled Spain. North Dakota Quarterly* 60.2 (Spring 1992): 1–284.

Plath, James. "Shadow Rider: The American Hero as Western Archetype." *Hemingway and the Natural World*. Ed. Robert Fleming. Moscow: University of Idaho Press, 1999. 69–86.

Price, Alan. " 'I'm Not an Old Fogey and You're Not a Young Ass': Owen Wister and Ernest Hemingway." *Hemingway Review* IX.1 (Fall 1989): 82–90.

Reynolds, Michael. "Ringing the Changes: Hemingway's *Bell* Tolls Fifty." *Virginia Quarterly Review* 67.1 (1991): 1–18.

Rudat, Wolfgang E.H. "Hemingway's Rabbit: Slips of the Tongue and Other Linguistic Games in *For Whom the Bell Tolls*." *The Hemingway Review* 10 (Fall 1990): 34–51.

Sabatelli, Arnold E. "Nowhere, Nothing Now: The Awkward Beauty of Language in *For Whom the Bell Tolls*." *North Dakota Quarterly* 66.2 (Centennial Issue, 1999): 147–58.

Sanderson, Rena, ed. *Blowing the Bridge: Essays on Hemingway and* For Whom the Bell Tolls. Westport, CT: Greenwood Press, 1992.

Stanton, Edward F. *Hemingway and Spain: A Pursuit*. Seattle: University of Washington Press, 1989.

Tyler, Lisa. "Dead Rabbits, Bad Milk, and Lost Eggs: Women, Nature, and Myth in *For Whom the Bell Tolls*." *Hemingway and the Natural World*. Ed. Robert E. Fleming. Moscow: University of Idaho Press, 1999. 125–137.

Waldmeir, Joseph. "Chapter Numbering and Meaning in *For Whom the Bell Tolls*." *The Hemingway Review* 8 (Spring 1989): 43–45.

Watson, William Brasch. "Investigating Hemingway: The Story." *North Dakota Quarterly* 59.1 (Winter 1991): 38–68.

———. "Investigating Hemingway: The Trip." *North Dakota Quarterly* 59.3 (Summer 1991): 79–95.

———. "Investigating Hemingway: The Novel." *North Dakota Quarterly* 60.1 (Winter 1992): 1–27.

THE OLD MAN AND THE SEA

REVIEWS

Adams, J. Donald. Review of *The Old Man and the Sea*. *New York Times Book Review* 21 Sept. 1952: 2.

Aldridge, John W. Review of *The Old Man and the Sea*. *Virginia Quarterly Review* 29 (Spring 1953): 311–20.

Breit, Harvey. Review of *The Old Man and the Sea*. *Nation* 6 Sept. 1952: 194.

"Clean and Straight." *Time* 60 (8 Sept. 1952): 114.

Davis, Robert Gorham. "Hemingway's Tragic Fisherman." *New York Times Book Review* 7 Sept. 1952: 1, 20.

Dupee, F. W. "Hemingway Revealed." *Kenyon Review* 15 (Winter 1953): 150–55.

Pickrel, Paul. Review of *The Old Man and the Sea*. *Yale Review* 42 (Autumn 1952): viii.

Weeks, Edward. Review of *The Old Man and the Sea*. *Atlantic* Sept. 1952: 72.

CRITICISM

Bloom, Harold, ed. *Modern Critical Interpretations: Ernest Hemingway's* The Old Man and the Sea. Philadelphia: Chelsea House Press, 1999.

Brenner, Gerry. The Old Man and the Sea: *Story of a Common Man*. Boston: Twayne, 1991.

Hurley, C. Harold. *Hemingway's Debt to Baseball in* The Old Man and the Sea: *A Collection of Critical Readings*. Lewiston, NY: Edwin Mellen, 1992.

Jobes, Katharine T. *Twentieth-Century Interpretations of* The Old Man and the Sea: *A Collection of Critical Essays*. Englewood Cliffs, NJ: Prentice-Hall, 1968.

Morgan, Kathleen and Luis Losada. "Santiago in *The Old Man and the Sea*: A Homeric Hero." *Hemingway Review* 12.1 (Fall 1992): 35–51.

Plath, James. "Santiago at the Plate: Baseball in *The Old Man and the Sea*." *Hemingway Review* 16.1 (Fall 1996): 65–82.

THE POSTHUMOUS WORKS

Burwell, Rose Marie. *Hemingway: The Postwar Years and the Posthumous Novels.* New York: Cambridge University Press, 1996.

A MOVEABLE FEAST

Reviews

Galantiere, Lewis. Review of *A Moveable Feast. New York Times Book Review* 11 May 1964: 1.

Kauffman, Stanley. Review of *A Moveable Feast. New Republic* 9 May 1964: 17–18, 20–21, 23–24.

Kazin, Alfred. "Ernest Hemingway as His Own Fable." *Atlantic* June 1964: 54–57.

Kermode, Frank. Review of *A Moveable Feast. New York Review of Books* 11 June 1964: 4–6.

Criticism

Beegel, Susan F. "Hemingway's Gastronomique: A Guide to Food and Drink in *A Moveable Feast* (with Glossary)." *Hemingway Review* IV.1 (Fall 1984): 14–26.

Brenner, Gerry. "Are We Going to Hemingway's Feast?" *American Literature* 54.4 (December 1982): 528–44.

———. *A Comprehensive Companion to Hemingway's* A Moveable Feast. Lewiston, NY: Mellen, 2001.

Dolan, Marc. "Becoming an Artist: Modern(ist) Life and *A Moveable Feast.*" *Modern Lives: A Cultural Re-reading of the Lost Generation.* West Lafayette, IN: Purdue University Press, 1996. 49–86.

Tavernier-Courbin, Jacqueline. *Ernest Hemingway's* A Moveable Feast: *The Making of Myth.* Boston: Northeastern University Press, 1991.

ISLANDS IN THE STREAM

Reviews

Howe, Irving. "Great Man Going Down." *Harper's* Oct. 1970: 120–25.

Long, Robert Emmet. Review of *Islands in the Stream. Commonweal* 23 Oct. 1970: 99–100.

Oldsey, Bernard. "The Novel in the Drawer." *Nation* 19 Oct. 1970: 376, 378.

Review of *Islands in the Stream. Virginia Quarterly Review* 47 (Winter 1971): viii.

Updike, John. "Papa's Sad Testament." *New Statesman* 16 Oct. 1970: 489.

Wilson, Edmund. "An Effort at Self-Revelation." *New Yorker* 2 Jan. 1971: 59–62.

Wolff, Geoffrey. "Out of the Desk." *Newsweek* 12 Oct. 1970: 118–20.

Yardley, Jonathan. "How Papa Grew." *New Republic* 10 Oct. 1970: 25–26, 30.

Criticism

Bier, Jesse. "Don't Nobody Move—This Is a Stichomythia (Or: An Unfinal Word on Typography in Hemingway)." *Hemingway Review* III.1 (Fall 1983): 61–63.

Fleming, Robert E. "Roger Davis of *Islands*: What the Manuscript Adds." *Hemingway: Essays of Reassessment*. Ed. Frank Scafella. New York: Oxford University Press, 1991. 53–60.

Hinz, Evelyn J. and John Teunissen. "*Islands in the Stream* as Hemingway's *Laocoon*." *Contemporary Literature* 29 (1988): 26–48.

Mathewson, Stephen. "Against the Stream: Thomas Hudson and Painting." *North Dakota Quarterly* 57.4 (1989): 140–45.

Murphy, Charlene M. "Hemingway, Winslow Homer, and *Islands in the Stream*: Influence and Tribute." *Hemingway Review* 13.1 (Fall 1993): 76–85.

Sabatelli, Arnold E. "The Re-forming of Word and Meaning in *Islands in the Stream*." *North Dakota Quarterly* 64.3 (1997): 177–83.

THE GARDEN OF EDEN

Reviews

Doctorow, E.L. "Braver Than We Thought." *New York Times Book Review* 18 May 1986: 1, 44–45.

Meyers, Jeffrey. Review of *The Garden of Eden*. *National Review* 23 May 1986: 44.

Prescott, Peter S. Review of *The Garden of Eden*. *Newsweek* 19 May 1986: 71.

Sheed, Wilfrid. Review of *The Garden of Eden*. *New York Review of Books* 12 June 1986: 5.

Sheppard, R.Z. Review of *The Garden of Eden*. *Time* 26 May 1986: 77.

Updike, John. Review of *The Garden of Eden*. *New Yorker* 30 June 1986: 85.

Criticism

Cackett, Kathy. "*The Garden of Eden*: Challenging Faulkner's Family Romance." *Hemingway Review* 9.2 (Spring 1990): 155–68.

Gajdusek, Robert E. "Elephant Hunt in Eden: A Study of New and Old Myths and Other Strange Beasts in Hemingway's Garden." *Hemingway Review* 7.1 (1987): 14–19.

———. "The Cost of Sin in the Garden: A Study of an Amended Theme in *The Garden of Eden*." *Resources for American Literary Study* 19.1 (1993): 1–21.

Jackson, Timothy P. "Back to the Garden or into the Night: Hemingway and Fitzgerald on Fall and Redemption." *Christianity and Literature* 39.4 (Summer 1990): 423–41.

Jenks, Tom. "Editing Hemingway: *The Garden of Eden*." *Hemingway Review* 7.1 (1987): 30–33.

Peters, K.J. "The Thematic Integrity of *The Garden of Eden.*" *Hemingway Review* 10.2 (Spring 1991): 17–29.

Powell, Tamara M. "Lilith Started It!: Catherine as Lilith in *The Garden of Eden.*" *Hemingway Review* 15.2 (Spring 1996): 79–88.

Stoneback, H.R. "Memorable Eggs 'in Danger of Getting Cold' and Mackerel 'Perilous with Edge-level Juice': Eating in Hemingway's Garden." *Hemingway Review* 8.2 (1989): 22–29.

OTHER SOURCES

Borden, Mary. *The Forbidden Zone*. Garden City, NY: Doubleday, 1930.

Britain, Vera. *Testament of Youth: An Autobiographical Study of the Years 1900–1925*. London: Virago, 1978.

Brontë, Emily. *Wuthering Heights*. 1847. Ed. William M. Sale, Jr. New York: Norton, 1963.

Donnelly, Honoria Murphy, and Richard N. Billings. *Sara & Gerald: Villa America and After*. New York: Times Books, 1982.

Fussell, Paul. *The Great War and Modern Memory*. New York: Oxford University Press, 1975.

Gellhorn, Martha. "On Apocryphism." *Paris Review* 79 (1981): 280–301.

Milford, Nancy. *Zelda*. New York: Harper & Row, 1970.

Ouditt, Sharon. *Fighting Forces, Writing Women: Identity and Ideology in the First World War*. New York: Routledge, 1994.

Stein, Gertrude. *The Autobiography of Alice B. Toklas*. New York: Quality Paperback Book Club, 1993.

Viertel, Peter. *Dangerous Friends: At Large with Hemingway and Huston in the Fifties*. New York: Doubleday, 1992.

Woolf, Virginia. *A Room of One's Own*. San Diego: Harcourt Brace, 1981.

———. "Mr. Bennett and Mrs. Brown." *The Essays of Virginia Woolf*. 6 vols. Ed. Andrew McNeillie. New York: Harcourt, Brace, Jovanovich, 1992. 3: 384–89.

WEBSITE

The International Hemingway Society. Ed. Bill Newmiller and Lisa Tyler. www.hemingwaysociety.org.

Index

About the Author

LISA TYLER is Associate Professor of English at Sinclair Community College in Dayton, Ohio. She has published essays on Doris Lessing, Margaret Atwood, Marsha Norman, and Virginia Woolf. In addition to her work on Ernest Hemingway, her current research interests include the writings of Anne Beattie and Joyce Carol Oates, crisis communication, and the healing power of writing about traumatic events.